MY
RIVAL
THE
KING

Jubilee Lipsey

Copyright © 2021 by Jubilee Lipsey.

All rights reserved. This book or any portion thereof may not be reproduced or used in any manner whatsoever without the express written permission of the publisher except for the use of brief quotations in a book review.

This is a work of biblical fiction. The characterizations are either from the authors imagination or are presented fictitiously. Any resemblance to similar works is purely coincidental.

Author Photo: Lyndsey Ashmore Photography.

Publishing Services provided by Paper Raven Books
Printed in the United States of America
First Printing, 2021

Hardcover ISBN= 978-1-7373447-3-5
Paperback ISBN= 978-1-7373447-2-8

To the broken kings

A NOTE FROM THE AUTHOR

Calling. Purpose. Destiny.

These glorious themes of our faith beckon us with persistent hope, drawing us further than we planned to go. As believers, we understand that we were made for a purpose, and our growth in God only deepens our yearning for it as His Spirit highlights the gifts He's put inside us. Scripture tells us God has lined up great works for us to walk in, and we're encouraged to dream big with Him, reveling in the evidence of our anointings.

But before too long, we find a thorn waiting just beneath the surface, usually about the time we realize that our callings are best fulfilled in the context of community. Therein lies the struggle.

People disappoint us. They don't recognize us. They're offended by us. We end up betrayed, wounded, rejected. Misunderstood. People who should have empowered us end up trying to control us. Lifelong friends are ripped out from under us. We're overlooked in favor of someone younger or smarter. In the midst of the pain, we find ourselves saying and doing things we never dreamed we'd say or do…to *them*. Confused and dismayed, we often withdraw or give up. Yet the longing still remains. We want to make a difference alongside others on the same journey. We want to grow in our faith and share it with others. Isn't that why we're here?

Whether we choose to acknowledge it or not, we know we've been commissioned to participate in the greater expression and advancement of God's Kingdom, and we know fellowship is a key element to walking out this destiny. After all, we're the Body of Christ, designed to build each other up in love (Ephesians 4). But we're living hurt, afraid to reach out and risk being trampled on. We toss around words like "honor," and "covenant," and "fellowship," but we're not really sure where to find the real thing. And every media portrayal seems to indicate that everyone else gets it but us.

In the wake of this jaded reality, we tend to regard stories like David and Jonathan's with a mixture of awe and suspicion. Was their friendship really that powerful? Does such a kinship even exist beyond the pages of Scripture? If so, when is it going to happen for us?

But David and Jonathan's timeless friendship has so much more to share with us than mere brotherhood. At its core, it's a poignant story of two men following God with passionate faith—not merely tolerating or accepting His plan, but joyfully embracing their part in it. Both were willing to keep after the Lord, even if the path became painful. Because they trusted in the Lord's resources over their own and humbly chose to place their futures in God's hands, they were able to remain bonded in unity as brothers.

The treasures enclosed in their unique story have the potential to change our lives, introducing us afresh to a God who is worthy of wholehearted devotion, even in the toughest of circumstances. Even in the valley of the shadow of death (Psalm 23). People change, but God remains, and the only solid place to stand is in Him.

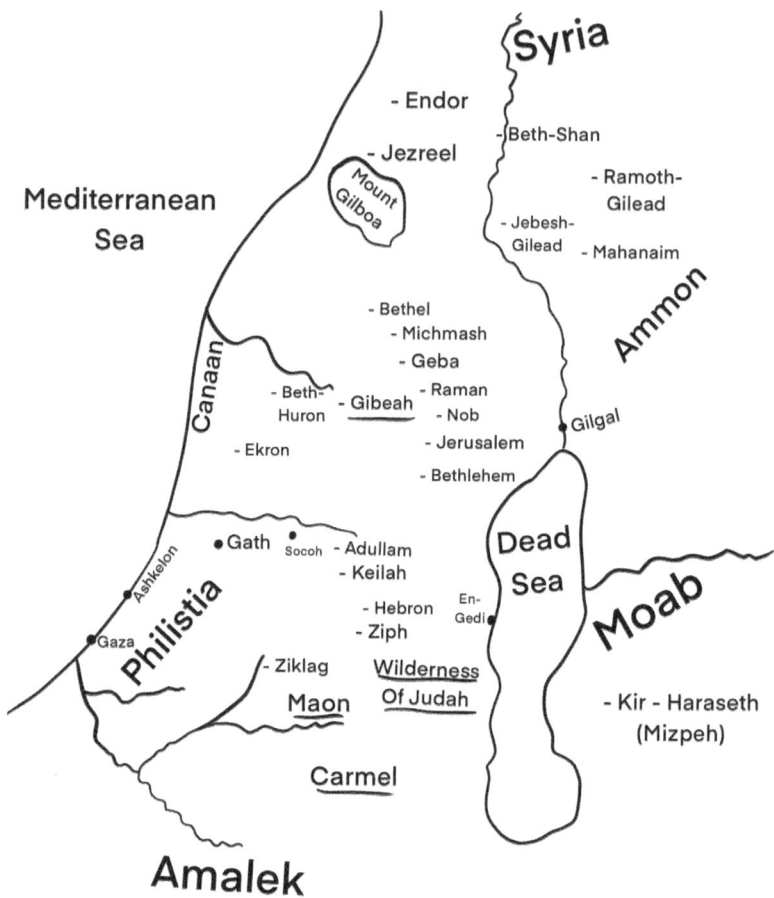

CHARACTER LIST

Aaron—*David's mentor as a shepherd*

Abiathar—*Ahimelech's son who survives Saul's massacre*

Abigail—*David's childhood friend and third wife*

Abinadab—*David's second brother*

Abishai—*Joab's second brother*

Abner—*Saul's general and cousin*

Achish—*Philistine king*

Agag—*Amalekite king, deceased*

Ahijah—*priest of Israel*

Ahimaaz—*Jonathan's maternal grandfather*

Ahimelech—*priest murdered by Saul*

Ahinoam—*Saul's wife*

Ahinoam of Jezreel—*David's second wife*

Ahithophel—*one of David's advisors*

Ammiel—*Saul's physician*

Asahel (Asa)—*Joab's youngest brother*

Asaph—*scribe who joins David*

Atarah—*Jesse's wife, David's adopted mother*

Ish-Bosheth—*Saul's youngest son*

David—*anointed second king of Israel*

Eliab—*David's oldest brother*

Eliam—*Ahithophel's son, one of David's soldiers*

Ezra—*Jonathan's armorbearer*

Gera—*Saul's armorbearer*

Goliath—*Philistine giant, deceased*

Heman—*Korah's son, one of David's spies*

Ishvi—*Saul's second son*

Ittai—*soldier from Gath who supports David*

Jehosheva—*Jonathan's wife*

Jesse—*David's father*

Joab—*David's older nephew*

Jonathan—*the crown prince of Israel, Saul's firstborn*

Korah—*an outlaw who follows David*

Machir—*Ammiel's son, a physician*

Malchishua (Malchi)—*Saul's third son*

Maoch—*Achish's father, deceased*

Merab—*Saul's oldest daughter*

Mephibosheth (Mephi)—*Jonathan's son*

Michal—*Saul's youngest daughter*

Naamah—*Jonathan's childhood friend, Michal's servant*

Nabal—*Abigail's abusive first husband*

Nadab—*Jonathan's new armorbearer*

Nahash—*Ammonite king, deceased*

Palti—*man Michal leaves David for*

Samuel—*Israel's chief prophet*

Saul—*first king of Israel*
Shammah—*David's third oldest brother*
Zeruiah—*Joab's mother*
Ziba—*Naamah's brother, Saul's servant*

GLOSSARY OF HEBREW WORDS

Abba—*father*

Adonai—*the Lord God*

Chesed—*mercy or lovingkindness, favor*

Eema—*mother*

El-Shaddai—*the All-Sufficient One; Yahweh's Name before Moses' time*

El-Jireh—*the God who provides*

El-Roi—*the God who sees*

Ephod—*ancient priest's garment used to inquire of God*

Hakkodesh—*Presence of God*

Hassar—*crown prince, a king's oldest son and heir*

Melek—*king*

Nephilim—*offspring of the giants mentioned in Genesis 6; Goliath was one*

Yahweh—*God's covenant Name given to Israel*

Roeh—*seer or prophet, messenger of God*

Ruach—*Spirit of God*

Saba—*grandfather*

Sar—*prince*

Sarrah—*princess*

Shekel—*Hebrew currency*

Sheol—*ancient Hebrew term for the grave*

My Rival, the King

Teraphim—*ancient household idols*
Torah—*Law of Moses, sacred Jewish writings*
Yeshu-hah—*salvation or deliverer*

PROLOGUE

David's fourteenth year

The sharp whistle pierces the hills, scattering my song against the rocks. I'm on my feet before the notes fade, tossing my harp against my bedroll. My sling is unwound, a stone already sliding into place while my eyes crawl the landscape to the east, searching.

The threat emerges from the forest skirting the tops of the sheepcotes. Ten or twelve armed men leave the cover of the brush, navigating the steep descent with practiced ease. Flinging themselves from their mounts, they swarm the sheep, trying to separate half a dozen or so from the flock.

I grab my shepherd's staff, every muscle tightening. Deep inside me, the praises I was singing before shift into prayers for strength.

Thieves are some of the worst threats a shepherd can face. Lions or wolves you can run off with a stone or a blade, but renegades almost always stay and fight. Especially the hill-dwellers who call themselves *the mighty*. On the run from the king, they tend to harass the southern farmers the most, hiding out where Saul's men don't spend much time.

I wipe sweat from my upper lip, my eyes grabbing whatever information I can before I show myself. They're not Amalekite raiders. No brands or Canaanite jewelry. The Judean pattern of their clothing gives them away. They're a band of Israelite outlaws, a father with sons and nephews. But they don't belong here.

I jump down from the ledge where I was encamped, up against the shearing caves outside Bethlehem. Several miles from town, we're not close enough to attract the watchmen. And my father won't start expecting me for another few days. But I'm not alone.

Sudden warmth spreads through me, and I breathe deeply, settling into the sensation. My mother says my songs bring our God close, and with Yahweh's praises still filling the air around me, how can I be afraid? After singing about His might in battle, why shouldn't I trust Him to defend me? He always does.

Singling out the oldest intruder, I jog into the midst of the sheep and shove my staff into the renegade's chest. "Leave them. This is not your property."

Prologue

The leather-skinned man is bigger up close. When I see who it is, my stomach drops. Everyone's heard of Korah. He's a noteworthy brigand, one Saul personally wants to capture. The rumors describe him as a lion-faced fighter and a brazen thief. He elbows past me, gesturing to one of his sons with a riding whip. "Drive that half toward the hills. I'll deal with the boy."

He kicks one of the ewes, herding her toward his mules while the rest of the flock scatters, confused.

Fresh anger flings the stone from my hand. It slams into Korah's son's shoulder, and the man whips around, cursing.

"Keep going!" Korah bellows at him. "I'll handle this."

He studies me over his shoulder with a sneer. "What's the matter, little one? Afraid you'll get a beating when your master counts the sheep?"

"These are my father's flocks. And you have no claim on them." Offense stings my tongue, making my voice warble more than it already does. "My father is Jesse of Bethlehem, son of Obed, son of Boaz."

Everyone around here has heard of my great-grandfather Boaz who left behind the sprawling legacy my father lives off of now. But people still have a hard time associating me with it. The son of a servant, I'm usually left with the sheep.

Korah chortles, already walking away. "Well then, your father should choose bigger sons to guard what he doesn't want stolen." He aims a derisive glance at the lyre leaning against the upper rocks. "Does he think you'll charm us away with your sweet singing?"

Indignation humming in my head, I pull my knife and throw it, pinning Korah's sleeve against the side of the sheepfold. I spring to his side and thrust my staff at his neck, the way Joab's shown me. Even as I do it though, I'm hearing my older nephew's scorn in my head. *You let go of your knife, stupid.*

Korah's surprise only lasts a moment. Every hint of mockery gone, he pulls himself free and rams my own staff into my chest. I stagger backwards, and he smacks my face, barely waiting for me to fall before bracing his foot against my side, holding me down.

I try to scramble away, my cheeks stinging. "You know the king already takes sheep from us. You hide in the hills to escape that, but we can't."

"Enough!" he snarls, releasing me. "I have no quarrel with you, boy. Saul collects his taxes, we take ours. For survival. Simple as that."

Prologue

Pushing to my feet, I retrieve my knife. Flames dart back and forth in my chest as I watch Korah's sons shoving sheep toward the edges of the pastures. I haven't saved these animals from lions and wolves just to lose this many to thieves. I can't return to my father and explain this. I won't.

I shout after Korah. "Our ancestors trusted Yahweh for provision in the wilderness. They didn't bleed their brothers."

My words bounce off the brigand's huge shoulders, and Korah whips around, his hand ready to free the sword at his belt. "Would you preach at me, shepherd boy?"

He advances, threatening, and when his sword appears, I use my weapon, slicing his forearm open when he gets too close.

Korah jerks back, sucking in through his teeth. Immediately, his sons' attention leaves the flock and snaps onto us. They spring into action, two of them seizing my arms and dragging me aside.

I try to twist away, but their grip only tightens, holding me against the stone wall I built around the sheepfold. One of them digs his thumb into my wrist, forcing the knife from my grasp. He tosses it to his father, who's still wiping blood from his arm.

Korah angles my own blade under my chin. "Do you think your father would rather lose a few sheep or a son?"

"He has seven others," I say through gritted teeth, hoping to end his bluff. But my throat pinches, insecurity surging up. I have no idea what Abba would say or feel if something happened to me.

Korah's heavy brows lift, revealing something inconsistent in his bloodshot eyes. With the conflict of harshness and respect in his weathered face, I can't decide what he'll do. I've seen the hill-dwellers from a distance, but I've never fought them before, and I have no way of knowing if they'd actually kill a fellow Israelite.

He's trying to read me too, moving the knife so the tip is positioned just above my breastbone. Fog pushes into my eyes, but I don't break his gaze. Something awakened in me years ago, around the time I started singing to Yahweh, and over the years, His presence has settled over me, like armor firmly set in place. I can hear the *hakkodesh* in the trees when I sing. And I'm no longer afraid.

"Adonai sees what you do," I gasp, regaining a measure of breath.

A puff of air escapes Korah's set teeth, and the hardness shifts in his face. "You're a brave one, for a boy without a beard. I'm tempted to take you instead of the sheep. How old are you, thirteen?"

"Fourteen." I try not to flinch, but every muscle is squirming under his sons' grip.

One of them glances to the hills. "If we take him with us, he won't be able to report that we were here."

"Hold it!"

The shout turns Korah's head, and my oldest nephew Joab rides into view, flanked by his brothers. Abishai and Asahel shrug their bows from their shoulders, aiming arrows in our direction. "Take your hands off him, Korah," Joab demands, pulling his sword from its sheath.

Korah lowers the knife, scowling at my nephew. "You're outnumbered, son of Zeruiah."

Joab kicks his mule, forcing his way between Korah and his sons. Dispersed, the sheep crowd aimlessly back toward the fold, looking for me.

"Don't be a fool," Joab bellows. "We have a deal. You keep your hands off what's ours, and we ensure your safety in Judah. Would you like to know how many times we've helped you avoid Saul's men? Not sure? Dozens." Joab bares his teeth, his eyes blazing dangerously. "But I have no problem breaking our agreement if you choose. The tax collectors will be here in another fortnight, and I'm sure they'd welcome the information I have."

Korah's countenance drops. "You wouldn't betray us to the king."

Joab's sunburned face turns even darker, his eyes hooded. "Touch my uncle again, and you'll see."

My relief battles with the sting of embarrassment. I can sense what's coming. Korah drags his puzzled gaze from me back to Joab. "Your…nephew, you mean?"

Joab rolls his eyes. "I mean my uncle. He's my grandfather's youngest. Call him an afterthought, a nuisance, a family embarrassment…"

"David," I snap, hoping to end the list.

Joab's lips tighten around a smile. "That too."

Korah laughs, looking back at me. "For the runt of the litter, he has a strong spirit. You're sure he wouldn't be of better use to us? With some sharpening, he could become a fierce weapon."

Joab shrugs, grimacing. "He's already spent his life in these hills. He dreams of bigger things."

Korah scowls at me, all the light leaving his expression. "Saul's kingdom is no place for dreamers. You'll see."

He flips my knife around, offering me the handle.

Joab nods toward the hills. "On your way. You'll receive word the next time Saul's soldiers come through here. I would avoid the roads until the end of the shearing."

Korah bows his head while his sons return to their mules. I retrieve my staff and whistle for the sheep, guiding the dazed animals back up the embankment to join the rest of the flock. They're pressed up against the side of the cave, bleating like they've seen a lion.

Joab rides up behind me. "You hurt?"

"No," I mumble without turning around. I don't need to see the grin on his face. Not until I've calmed the adrenaline crashing through me.

Joab nudges my shoulder with his sword. "Don't be like that. I won't say anything to your father. I'll take a thank you, though. If it's not too much trouble."

I wrestle my smile out of sight before facing him. "I chased off an Amalekite when he came to your fields two months ago. We're even."

Joab's laugh lifts his chest and shoulders. He looks back at his brothers. "I hope I'm there to hear him negotiate with Saul the way he does with me."

"A singing warrior," Abishai chuckles. "What will the king make of that?"

I flex my jaw, cleaning the blood off my knife. "Convince my father to let me go, and we can find out."

Korah pulls himself onto his mule, still watching me. His gaze deepens again, pushing beneath the surface.

"Keep an eye on this one, Joab. He might become one of us yet. If Saul doesn't sink his teeth in first."

* * * * *

Joab banks the fire, arranging the branches into a tent shape to help the flames climb. They're too hot on my face, and I move back into the cool of the cave.

The orphaned lamb I've been raising nestles up against me, and I rub my thumb up and down on his head. For two years I've pastured the flocks without supervision, and I'm not sure how I feel about having my solitude invaded.

Joab flings himself down next to me. "Don't sulk. I did you a favor."

I twirl my sling, the leather hot between my fingers. "I'm not sulking."

Joab snorts. "Yes, you are. No one sulks like David ben Jesse. It's the only time you're quiet, unless you're composing a song."

"Shut up." I pull away before he can tousle my hair. "You know how little separates you from men like Korah? How long have you been spying for him?"

"Long enough."

He pulls unleavened bread from his pack and breaks it, handing half to me. Chewing, he reaches for a wineskin behind him. "Don't look so shocked. Your father owns one of the biggest pieces of land in Bethlehem, and Saul's protection doesn't reach down here. We have enough to deal with from Amalekite raiders. The Mighty are not our enemies, even if Saul treats them like they are. It's our duty to remind them."

I lift my brows, watching the sheep through the flames. We don't talk much about the resistance in Ephrath. The elders view them as nothing more than raiders. Saul treats them like every other roving Canaanite band. He's killed a few, captured some for information. But mostly, they keep on the run, foraging and surviving, too disorganized to actually rebel.

I still wonder why they do it. Some are evading taxes or escaping servitude. But there are plenty of others these days—worthless men, my father calls them, who are ruled only by their hatred for the king. Many Judeans didn't want a son of Benjamin crowned. But who would choose to cut themselves off from the brotherhood of Israel simply to avoid serving Saul?

Joab's silence reaches over, pulling at the loose thread in my mind. "You could do it, you know," he finally says, edging closer.

"What?"

The fire turns his eyes golden. "Run away. Live up here. The resistance would train you. Many of them have become fierce warriors; they'd teach you anything you wanted to know."

I stare at him, transfixed. I should be more shocked by the suggestion, but Joab's not the first person to bring it up lately. I sigh. "Abigail said that too."

Joab leans back onto his elbow. "Your little friend is back?"

I look away, the fire stinging my cheek. "I saw her before she left. Her father wants her betrothed by the end of the year. She asked me if…"

Joab's hearty cackle cuts me off. Sitting up, he slaps my shoulder. "She asked you to run away with her?" He wipes his eyes, shaking with laughter. "I suppose you're a more exciting option than some old stranger who's the age of her father."

I glare at him. "If you tell anyone, I'll..."

"What? What are you going to do?" He waves me off, shaking his head. "Relax. It's not a bad idea. Abigail's bold for a girl."

I take refuge in remembering while Joab adds more sticks to the fire. Abigail is so different from every other girl. When her family would visit Bethlehem, she'd sneak out every night and race me to the edge of my father's pastures. Watching the same stars appear every season with Abigail next to me was the most natural thing in the world. I don't know when it happened, but it's still true.

"I love her." I say it out loud by accident and then brace myself for mockery.

"But her parents want status, and you know what you are," Joab mutters, watching the fire. He's no longer laughing.

I grimace. I hadn't planned to talk to him about this.

"What would they find so offensive? The fact that I'm the youngest? A shepherd?" Or is it the fact that my own father uses me as a servant because I was born one?

I dig my fingers into the dirt, collecting a handful of pebbles. Joab was there when Jesse officially claimed me as his own. I'd thought more would change after that.

A wolf howls in the distance, and I sit forward, grabbing my staff off the cave wall. The sheep bleat nervously, stirred by the sound, and the orphaned lamb nuzzles closer to me, burrowing its head into my side.

Joab slides his sword closer, and answering howls echo over the rocks. Maybe a mile off. Abigail and I used to howl back at them from the fenced edge of my father's property, where we could still scamper back to safety. She was the first person I told once I'd actually killed one.

I watch the edges of our camp while Joab studies me. "Everyone in the clan knows you're more of a warrior than a shepherd. But you're not going to find much use for battle skills in Bethlehem." He places his sword across his lap. "So, what's your plan? Stay here until your father dies and then live under Eliab's thumb once he inherits everything?"

Prologue

I shudder, my skin crawling at the idea. "No. Saul's soldiers make plenty of money on plunder. And if they're honored by the king, even better." Setting my staff aside, I fold my arms around my knees. "I can make my own way, build a house, and then afford a bride price. For someone."

Just not Abigail.

Joab sighs heavily, rubbing the hilt of his sword. "You won't like it. Saul isn't what he was. He's still a fierce warrior, but he doesn't follow Yahweh as he did before. He likes soldiers who put their heads down and follow orders. Men who have incredible skill but little ambition."

"Jonathan isn't like that." I've heard so many stories. The crown prince's best battles have been fought without the king's permission.

Joab rolls his eyes. "You don't *know* Jonathan. He almost lost his life because of his insubordination. And he's the king's son!"

The moment Joab's eyes grab hold of mine, I know he's about to get serious.

"You're different, David. You think your father avoids you because he's ashamed? Maybe he used to be, but now, he has no idea what to do with you, and he's afraid of what that might mean. He's afraid of you the way he's afraid of me. We're troublemakers, you and I."

Joab says it like a compliment. Sliding onto his side, he props his head in his hand.

"I'm not a rebel," I remind him. I'm affronted by the idea.

I don't see myself like Joab at all. He resents authority, bucking against it since his father died. And he's said more than once he'd rather fight against Saul than for him. I just want to fight for Israel. My dreams follow the path of our ancient stories—the judges and prophets who heard God's voice and went on to save our people from our enemies. How does that make me a troublemaker?

Joab's eyes hold me captive, waiting for something I can't name.

"You're a man of war. Everyone feels it when you walk into a room. But it's not just about fighting or advancement for you. You want what Yahweh wants. You've chased after Him since you were a child. And your songs…" His attention shifts over to my wooden lyre, propped against my bedroll. Joab rubs his chin, searching for words. "You see too deeply. You want too much."

I can hear my heart's rhythm in my throat, in my head. Joab's rarely shown so much interest in me. But it's more than that now. He's concerned, afraid even. And it looks completely foreign on him.

He pulls at his beard, thinking hard. "Believe me, David. You're exactly the kind of warrior Saul would hate."

ONE

David

Five years later

Thunder crackles through my mind, scattering my thoughts and burying them in the depths of the cave. Shards of jagged lightning break across the rock ceiling over my head, piercing the dark and allowing me a clear view of the southern countryside. The cave-scarred hills clump together in the rain like abandoned sheep, providing the only variation in the rocky landscape.

The sky breaks open again, and light spears the cavern, illuminating the sleeping bodies sprawled inside. Over fifty men have crowded into this cave alone, with more encamped on the lower rock shelf beneath us. They're all renegades, disgruntled defectors from King Saul's Israel, and every one of them is shrouded in sleep as thin as their tempers. I've sat awake for hours, waiting for one of them to interpret the tempest as an alarm and rouse the others.

They rest fitfully, their disquiet smoldering behind closed eyelids while their commingled snoring rumbles through the cavern. But discomfort crawls my skin, keeping me awake. I'm in the midst of lions. Just a different kind than I faced in the pastures tending my father's sheep a lifetime ago. These predators sharing my cave are men of war who've adjusted to the yoke I'm still fighting.

When they'd arrived in Adullam, filling the sheepcotes I've been hiding in, my older nephew Joab had pointed them out with authority, revealing just how far his influence has reached over the years.

"You remember Korah and his sons," he'd reminded me, pulling back the memory of how they'd prowl the southern hills, stealing from Ephrathites like my family. Joab had continued to list the men as they'd filed past me.

"Elhanan is originally from Bethlehem. Saul killed his uncles for raising questions about the Amalek battle years ago. There's Igal, Zelek, and Heleb. Their father would have had to sell all of them in order to repay the debt they were in. Zalmon and Eleazar are brothers. They've taken out half of the Amalekite remnant single-handedly with no help from Saul. There are a couple of Hittites who've fled the king's service. And Asaph over there is a scribe. You'll like him; he sings."

One

I had taken it all in without a word, wondering how Saul has discounted their strength for so long. Over the years, the resistance has grown from a handful of stragglers to the start of an army. They're skilled but unruly, fueled by the sufferings exile has forced on them. They've all heard of me, following the trail of my military successes and Joab's leaked reports about my anointing. I can see the way some of them look at me, like they've stumbled onto water in the desert.

Up till now, they haven't had definitive leadership, a direct plan to unite them. Now, they have both, and if I don't take charge, they might try to rise up against Gibeah or kill Saul themselves. Of course, once Saul hears that I'm leading "the mighty," he'll feel justified in calling me a rebel. He'll spread it all over Israel, telling everyone I've forsaken my country like a common raider.

Chilled to the core, I edge into the boulder behind me, keeping out of the cold strokes of rain. Meeting these men, listening to their discontented railing against the king has made it clearer than ever. I'm not like them. Even after dodging a few of Saul's spears, I'm still not a rebel. I'm just a shepherd, only I'm leading a very different kind of flock now.

Taking refuge in the wilderness should be natural to me. I used to relish my times in the hills, when I would drive my father's flock to Bethlehem's higher pastures to feed before shearing. I would gather the sheep in the caves at the back of the plateau and bank them in with stones. Then, I would lie at the entrance of the rocky hovel and listen until their contented bleating and the songs of the stars would put me to sleep.

No one questioned my worth or my status out there. Even the bears and lions I had to fight off were more excitement than hardship. And everything was begun and finished with a song to Yahweh.

The presence of our God had poured into my soul like an overflowing cup, too great for me to contain. But I'd never imagined the *Ruach* would come closer still, near enough to rest on my shoulders and breathe in my praises.

The Roeh Samuel had changed everything with his kingly declaration over me. The commission to be Melek Israel had opened my spirit wider than I'd thought possible. But the paths I'd always longed to follow, chasing after Yahweh, have been more like ruts, carved deep into my being with weapons forged by family.

I'd thought Saul would see me as an asset because of the favor following me. After getting close to his son and daughter, I'd even hoped the king would see me as a son. But my anointing had burned through all that, driving Saul into madness, and me into a cave.

Exile still nags at me, every ounce of my courage battling with the unfairness that's put me here. I never sought the king's life or attempted to steal the throne. Yet, here I am, driven out like a traitor.

The rain has slackened, and the wind drives it over the ridge, bringing with it a breath of desolation. I fill my lungs with it, fixing my eyes on a colorless sky inching towards dawn. Bent over, I release my breath in a silent groan that only Adonai will hear. The God of Israel is still listening.

Why, Yahweh? Why does it have to be this way?

Saul has taken so much from me, without cause. After years of fighting for honor among my people, I could only watch—and run—as the king of Israel took my home, my wife, and my reputation, all in a matter of days. Desperate, I ran right into the Philistines' arms, barely escaping a slow death at our enemies' hands.

But I'm alive. Safe. Surrounded.

Joab's hunting and Asa's foraging provides us with enough food. The caves shelter us from the windstorms and the freezing rain that almost killed me a month ago. I'm armed again, though not with Goliath's sword, which I lost in Gath. I should have known better than to carry the fallen giant's sword into his hometown. But I escaped with my life. My aging parents are safe in Moab, the land of my great-grandmother. I have my harp back, thanks to Jonathan.

A small flame of gratitude works its way through the coldness in my heart. Jonathan was the reason I made it out of Gibeah alive after Saul's attempts on my life. But what will stop the prince from turning to his father's cause now? After all, it would have been his throne. Will he really give it all up, even if we're covenant brothers before Yahweh?

My new companions don't seem to think so. They're certain he'll side with Saul and end up hunting me right alongside the king. It had angered me to hear them suggest it, but now the darkness is chilling my certainty.

Maybe I had just imagined the anointing, and Jonathan will really be king of Israel when Saul dies. And I'll just be David. The same humble servant of Yahweh. At least as king, Jonathan might be trusted to bring me out of exile.

The wind picks up again, and I shiver, chilled by a sense of disapproval. I have no right to question Adonai's Word. But why is it so much harder to believe out here? Why does the prophecy rest on the back of my neck like the cold flat of a sword, waiting to cut into me? *Melek Israel.*

"How, Adonai? How am I fulfilling that here?" I say it into the rain.

There are many steps to fulfillment.

I rake my fingers back through my hair. These days, I can't tell if it's God speaking or my own mind rambling, searching for a reason to hope.

Maybe if I sang more. I glance back into the recesses of the cave, thinking of all the songs I've written. Do I really believe them? I haven't touched my harp in weeks, haven't composed anything except a few verses of desperation fueled by my brief interlude as a Philistine captive.

Hunched over on my knees, I cover my face and let my heart bleed. "Why are you silent, Adonai? Why don't you rescue me from these people who hate me without cause? They devise despicable words of deceit and the king listens to them!"

The rumors surfacing from Aijalon are galling. Saul's captains report that I stole from Jonathan, tried to kill Michal, plotted with the priests. The songs praising my battle exploits have turned into ribald slander sung by drunkards in the gates. And after what Saul did to the families in the city of Nob, I don't know who will be willing to help me. All they'd done was give me bread and inquire of the Lord for me. And now they're dead.

I shove my knuckles into my eyes. "Don't leave me, Adonai! Rouse yourself for my vindication. My cause is your cause!"

"My lord?"

My face leaves my hands. Someone's moved up beside me, and I flinch when I see who it is.

I haven't been able to look Abiathar in the eyes since he arrived here two days ago. Fleeing Saul's rampage against the priests, he'd run south to Nob with barely enough time to hide in the hills. No one thought Saul would harm the priests' families.

After Nob burned, Abiathar had contacted members of the resistance, who'd promised to help him find me. Once he'd made it to us, the young priest had collapsed, too exhausted for tears, but I could clearly read the grief carved into his face. When he could finally speak, he'd explained how he'd escaped.

"Saul told his general to kill us, but Abner refused. So, the king gave his sword to Doeg the Edomite. Up until the last second, I didn't think it would happen. I thought with Jonathan begging at his feet, Saul would relent. But once Doeg cut my father down…" He'd breathed heavily for several moments before finishing. "I don't know what got me out of there. I jumped through a side window while the guards were busy with Jonathan. Part of me feels like I should've stayed."

Abiathar's story had enraged the others, igniting their ranks like a flame consuming brush.

"It's clear now. Saul has turned against Yahweh."

"Killing his own people? The families of priests! No such king deserves mercy."

"Saul has brought destruction upon himself. Every man in his household must die!"

"And the women! We'll do to them what he did to Nob's weakest."

Abiathar had said little in response, his anguished expression pleading with me to react differently. The Law of Moses demands recompense for blood, but vengeance ultimately belongs to Yahweh. I've felt the stirrings of rage against Saul, but I know a foundation of bitter violence won't support anything of value. My anointing has not given me license to take revenge.

Not that anyone in this cave will care. Joab and Abishai had barely contained the chaos erupting between the men over what was to be done. Now they're all finally asleep, and Abiathar is calling me *lord* as though I'm already king. Joab's brother Asa used to call me that when I was still living in Saul's shadow, invisible.

I don't move. Everything I want to say to Abiathar struggles beneath my skin without voice. It should have been me. Not his father and his family. Their blood is on my head.

Abiathar breaks the silence before I can figure out how. "You're anointed, aren't you? That's why Saul hates you." He speaks without moving any other muscles. "My father heard about Samuel's visit to Bethlehem. He wondered about you for years."

Heat surges into my face, but I don't know why I'm shocked. Of course a priest would discern my anointing before anyone else. But I'm too weary to react beyond shaking my head. "I should have warned Ahimelech. I should have told him I was on the run before expecting him to help me."

"He wouldn't have turned you away."

Abiathar's quiet sincerity stuns me. I should be comforting *him*. He'd escaped death, but now he carries the memory of his father and brothers dying under Saul's sword. Unruly emotion tosses in my throat, mangling every word on my tongue.

"Your father was the last person to inquire of the Lord for me. I can't stop hearing his voice."

"Neither can I," Abiathar whispers.

I wince at the raw pain in his voice. But it's still not the animosity I keep waiting for.

"Do you still believe what my father said?" he asks me.

Good question. Ahimelech's words have been running through my mind since I heard about his death. But have I been listening?

"You have nothing to fear," he'd told me, his gentle grip on my arm quieting the tremors in my body. "God is with you. Do you believe, David?"

I inhale sharply, swallowing down a surge of rebellious anger. I believe. I just didn't want this. I didn't want to leave Gibeah as a fugitive and join men who hate Saul. I didn't want to lose my family. I didn't want to break with the king.

I pinch the skin between my eyes. "The king believes them. He believes all these men who say I'm a traitor."

"You don't have to change Saul, you know," Abiathar murmurs. "You can't."

The statement startles me, and I wonder if Abiathar said it or if I heard the voice of God. Few people can uncover something so deep inside me.

Either way, it's true. And it shames me. I've acted like Yahweh's promise was contingent on Saul's acceptance. But it isn't. I'd hoped Saul would respond to my anointing the way Jonathan had, with bold acceptance. But regardless, Adonai always planned to look after His Word and perform it. It's up to me to obey my Shepherd. And teach others to do the same.

Forcing a slow breath over everything, I glance back at the sleeping forms in the cave. I still have to confront their anger, explain that I don't intend to seize the throne.

"All they want is to demand Saul's respect, make him pay for their suffering. He's killed some of their families, destroyed their homes. How will they understand?"

"If they want the blessing that follows you, they'll fall in line, whether they understand or not," Abiathar says firmly, folding his arms. "Your success has never been dependent on the size of your army."

One

Drawn by the way his strength is feeding mine, I finally look up at him. His loyalty would be touching if it hadn't cost him so much. I reach up and touch his shoulder briefly.

"At least you'll have a place here, Abiathar. Even if you despise me."

He shakes his head, tensing against tears. "I don't. If Yahweh has anointed you king and you intend to stay faithful to Him, then my father's blood will not be wasted."

TWO

Jonathan

"Do you have to leave?"

I lift my head and turn from the window, my prayers folding up inside me.

My wife's voice is still a sweet surprise every morning, drifting toward me across the room. One look in her direction, and I know I don't want to leave her side. Since I was a boy, my life has been consumed with fighting. Rest isn't something I do well. I would never have guessed that a reprieve would have filled my heart the way it has these few months.

For weeks since our wedding, I could slide back into bed beside Jehosheva and hold her while the sun came up over Gibeah's fields where I've spent decades training. I've heard the rumors for years, saying I'm too scarred, too battle-roughened to really open my heart to a woman. But they haven't met my wife.

I stare at her, taking her in. Still trying to believe that she's mine. I'm hers. Even before our hasty marriage at the king's command, Jehosheva was quietly, carefully picking up the pieces of my life and setting them back into place, reminding me it could be done. Showing me I could breathe around the breaks that have happened.

She was there the night of the New Moon feast, when my father threw the spear at me. The night my best friend had to flee for his life.

She listened with quiet humility when I told her I might not rule, because our God has chosen another to be king.

She understood how strange it was for me to prepare for a celebration after the chaos of the previous months. We had to watch my father shower her family with gifts as if he hadn't just killed an entire city of priests. I had to meet with him to discuss wedding plans and act grateful for his generosity with his curses still ringing in my ears.

But the day after our wedding feast, I'd wept before Yahweh in relief and thanksgiving.

After being forced to break with my sister's servant Naamah years ago, I'd put away thoughts of marriage, dreading the day when my father would force someone on me who would see only my position as the Hassar, the king's heir. Instead, I've found sanctuary with the woman who's become my wife.

It's been miraculous to see what Sheva's untainted sincerity has done for my heart. For four months, I haven't left her side, and it's been enough for me to listen to her, dream with her, rejoice over our coming child.

But today, I'm already dressed in riding clothes, and Ezra's waiting outside with enough armor to convince the king I'm ready for whatever he has in mind. Whether I am or not. I sigh, soaking up the sight of Sheva's shape under the coverlet. There's already evidence of the child inside her, and I could spend a lifetime marveling over that alone.

"You know I don't have a choice." I fumble with the jeweled clasp on my heavy cloak, and Sheva laughs, holding out her hands.

"Let me."

I go to her, and she fastens the cloak in place, centering the medallion bearing my father's seal over my chest. "The hero of Michmash has no choice," she smiles wryly, her fingers folding into mine.

I rub my thumbs over her hands and allow myself to think about it. For one moment. What would it be like to be free of all this, to take her away? Men have been living on the run for years in order to escape Saul's reach, with far less reason than a spear launched at their chest. Why shouldn't I do the same?

Tucking Sheva's hands against my heart, I touch my forehead to hers. "I'll do it if you want me to. Just say the word."

Sheva tilts her head back to see my eyes clearly. "You mean, leave?"

I make a low sound in response, still not willing to say the words. I would never have considered it before. But the only thing that frightens me more than breaking with my father is dragging this woman into the danger Saul's inviting by targeting David.

My friend is anointed by Yahweh, and the *Ruach* of our God breathes in his war and his worship. He will be the next king of Israel. And my father is determined to fight it, willing to take down anyone blocking his path to David.

Understanding gleams in Sheva's eyes. She held me after I saw Nob's ruins. After helping the men of a neighboring city to bury the bodies, I shook for days, knowing the images wouldn't leave my mind because I couldn't go after the one who ordered the carnage.

Two

I don't know who or what else my father will destroy in his pursuit of the Lord's anointed one. I haven't voiced my concerns to any priest, haven't heard directly that I should leave. To break with my father would be a serious offense. It would cut me off from him forever. Whatever I choose, someone will be hurt. I've prayed for wisdom, but I'm not convinced of either path.

And yet, my wife wears an undisturbed calm on her brow.

She breathes deeply. "If you joined David, would it not anger your father more? Wouldn't everyone blame your friend for inciting you against the king?"

"Of course." The words feel like nails in my throat. The lies being told about David are bad enough without adding my own insurrection to them. "But David carries the presence of the Lord with him. How wise is it for me to keep you here with a king who's determined to fight Yahweh?"

"I'm here with a husband who works *with* Yahweh," Sheva whispers, her grip tightening around my hands. "You're the only one who isn't afraid to speak reason and wisdom in the king's ear. You're one of the few who still can. He needs that."

I nod, exhaling with my teeth set. Sheva touches my face, her other hand drawing mine to her stomach. "We'll be fine.

Yahweh will protect us, and if you seek Him, He will not hide from you what you should do."

My heart full, I fold her in my arms, setting my chin atop her head. "Oh, if Abba knew how wise you are, he might not have given you to me. We're a dangerous pair, you and I."

"I hope our son is like you," Sheva says softly, something vulnerable surfacing in her tone. "I could never be brave enough to face what you do."

"You're already facing it with more grace than I've ever seen on any woman," I declare, refusing to consider Naamah. I study Sheva's gorgeous brown eyes instead. "What makes you think it's a son? You haven't…"

"Oh no." Sheva shakes her head, grimacing. Some of our friends still keep *teraphim* and other idols in their houses for various uses. But we agreed early on to keep our home free from any kind of divination. Sheva tilts her shoulder. "I don't know. It's just a feeling I have."

I return her smile, nervous energy battling with my excitement. If our child is a boy, Saul will pounce on the evidence that our dynasty will continue. I don't want my son drawn into some kind of battle among the tribes of Israel while men fight to see me crowned. I bend over to tighten the laces on my leather riding boots.

Yahweh, please scatter the clouds of insanity hanging around my father. Help him see the light.

Ezra's voice follows the knock at the door, and Sheva throws a thin blue robe over her shoulders. I kiss her, and she grabs my wrist, asking, "Do you know where you're going? When you'll be back?"

"I'm not sure," I admit. The familiar weight is already settling back over my chest like a breastplate I haven't worn in a while. "I'll send word as soon as I know."

Most likely, my father has a list of enemies he wants me to deal with while he continues to search for David. The Ammonites have been causing trouble to the east, crossing border lines and claiming land. But there's something else I have to answer first. "Pray for me," I tell Sheva before leaving the room.

Ezra's arms are full, carrying my breastplate and leg greaves after me with a strained look on his face. "My lord, I don't think you'll have time to see Michal. The king has already summoned Abner to the antechamber, and the commanders are on their way now."

I glance back at my armorbearer. Ezra has been at my side since we were fourteen. The last time I went anywhere without him, I almost bled to death in the forest outside Geba. He helped me train David, showing no animosity while the shepherd boy soared through the king's ranks like an eagle. He's also the only reason I know about Saul's latest command.

"Ezra, did the king meet with Palti of Laish as he planned?" I take the armor from him piece by piece, waiting for his answer.

Ezra nods, avoiding my eyes while he buckles the leather straps around my ribcage. "He did."

I tilt my head over my shoulder to look at him. "And? Is he still going through with this?"

Ezra sighs, spreading my cloak over the metal greaves. "It looks like it."

I lift my brows. "Then tell the king I'll get there when I get there."

Ezra hands me my quiver without answering. He knows that before Sheva or even Naamah, there was another woman I would always fight for, even if it meant taking Abba's wrath myself.

I haven't seen my youngest sister since David fled. When Michal married him, my father's jealousy was already clouding

Two

the air between himself and his most famous warrior, and Saul wasn't opposed to using my sister as bait to harm him. I didn't realize it at the time, too busy hoping for something else. But now I have to act quickly, otherwise my sister could be in the worst trouble of her life.

My mule is waiting outside amidst an unsteady quiet. The gentle birdsong and spring sunlight make my fields seem like a safe haven waiting to be invaded. As I leave the courtyard and ride out into the street, several men call out appreciative greetings. I haven't been seen in public since my wedding, but they've all heard about my child. And they all expect me to ride into the heart of Gibeah, to join my father in the palace.

I see the way people's faces drop when I angle my mule west. The men of Benjamin have been afraid to even look in the direction of David's house since he left. But my sister is there. Alone. And my father won't leave her in peace for much longer. According to the rumors filling Gibeah, he intends to marry her off to a nobleman named Palti, thus securing an alliance with his wealthy family.

No one comes to greet me when I ride into David's courtyard. Things have been in disarray since he fled. Saul dismissed many of the servants, leaving only a few to keep the house for my sister. For the first time, I'm glad Michal hasn't borne a child yet. I'm fairly certain any son of David's wouldn't be safe in Gibeah now. Not if Michal isn't.

I rein in my mount and head for the side door, berating myself for not thinking through this much sooner. Of course, my father would try to separate Michal and David. He wishes they hadn't married in the first place. Turbulent memories push into view, staining the outer walls over the garden.

A little over a year ago, my sister had to let her husband down through a window to escape my father's men. They'd brought Michal to the king instead, forcing her to lie to cover up David's absence. Michal had been shocked to discover his anointing soon afterwards. I can only imagine what she's thinking now. The last she heard about David was that he was in Gath with the Philistines. But she has to be horrified at Saul's latest suggestion.

The door opens before I can knock, and my stomach tightens. I really didn't think this through.

Naamah's mouth drops open, but she had to know I would come.

"My sister..." I begin, but Naamah just steps aside. She leads me upstairs in silence, letting me absorb how David's absence shadows every corner.

Ezra had tried to shield me from it at first, stepping in between me and every possible responsibility until my wedding. It was his way of sharing my grief. He'd even quipped that David might show up in disguise at the feast. As much as I hoped he would, I knew he wouldn't risk it. Not if my father's rage had forced him to take refuge with our enemies.

A few brave soldiers had commented on how strange it was not to see David by my side when I got married. But as it turned out, David wasn't the only one missing that night.

My sister has remained in seclusion since David left, so I'm prepared to find her desolate, perhaps in mourning. But the doors on the upper floor are open, and servants are moving quickly between them, carrying fresh linens, bright fabrics, and expensive oils. The hallway is heavily scented with some kind of perfume.

"We've been expecting someone else." Naamah explains softly, but I don't have time to adjust before Michal steps out in front of me, calling for her maid.

"Naamah—" My sister stops when she sees me, planting her hands on either side of the doorway. "What are you doing here?"

Not the response I was looking for. But seeing her draped in a multicolored robe and gold sash scatters me enough to keep me quiet for a moment. Heavy makeup circles her eyes. The hallway around her is lined with heavy cedar chests and trunks.

Michal angles her disapproval over at Naamah. "I told you to let me know when *Abba* showed up. Or Palti." My sister rolls her eyes, heading back through the door.

Alarm plucks the pit of my stomach. She's waiting for Palti? I follow her into her room, amazed at how the space has been stripped of all the old ornamentation, leaving nothing but her bed and a table. Both are covered with fine cosmetics, gold jewelry, and rich Syrian embroidery. Michal flounces over to the table and picks up a small bronze mirror.

"If you're coming to gloat, I've already heard about your wife and her pregnancy." She says it like it's a disgusting word. "And it only took four months. The king must be overjoyed."

I fold my arms, feeling attacked. "You make it sound like I planned this. I should be back with Sheva right now. But since she's pregnant, our father wants me back in court." Michal has to know that's all the king wanted out of my marriage. Another heir.

My sister's eyes shift in the looking glass. "We're tools, you and I. Part of being royal," she purrs, rubbing her finger around her lips to accentuate the color.

Two

I stiffen. "There are some things even a king cannot command. That's why I've come."

Her forehead slants into a frown, and concern worms its way into my urgency. I know I have very little time to say this. "Will you look at me, Michal?"

She sighs, purposely distracted. "No. Whatever you have to say, just say it. I have things to do."

My breath stuck in my throat, I study my sister. Everyone says we favor each other, and I've always been the image of our father, only an inch or two shorter, with matching hair and similar mannerisms. But I never really noticed Abba's resemblance on Michal. Now, it's unmistakable. It's not just the firm set of her shoulders and jaw, but the way her eyes open me up, deciding what to believe before I've said a word.

The false smile painted on with her cosmetics is starting to hurt me. She hasn't had it easy. But I'm tired of seeing her try to hide it.

"You know my maid is listening," Michal says, picking through the gemstones on her table. "That doesn't worry you?"

I refuse to look over my shoulder. "Naamah has seen more than you have, little sister."

Michal slams her hand down, turning. "Don't talk to me like I'm a child, all right? I'm a grown woman, and my husband has abandoned me without giving me a son. How dare you come in here to lecture me?"

"David has not abandoned you!" I cross the room in two steps, looking down at her. "He was driven out by the king. Our father would have killed him!"

"Like he almost killed you." She stares into my chest, too short to look me in the eyes.

I hold my breath, waiting. She hadn't been at the New Moon feast when our father threw a spear at me, screaming for David's death. "You heard about that?"

"Of course." Michal swallows. "Eema was frantic. When Abba came to see her after the feast, she screamed at him so much, I thought he was going to send her away." She sniffs, folding her arms. "It's always all about you."

I clear my throat, offended. "It's always all about Abba and what will benefit him. That's why he's pushing for this…this insanity with the man from Laish."

Michal's head comes up. "Palti? He's a good man."

I step back, astonished. "He's willing to defy the Law and steal you away from your husband just to keep favor with the king! How is that good?"

Michal juts her chin at me like a child. "How can you talk about the Law? Did you wait a full year to marry? Did you stay with her for the allotted time? No. And why? Because of the king."

"It's not the same, Michal. I'm not leaving my wife!" I raise my voice, my hands grasping at something invisible between us. "What Abba is forcing on you is a hideous betrayal of everything we value before God. You can't be serious about this."

Michal's face doesn't move. Her eyes are blank, like she's in a dream. "I wasn't before, but now I am." She blinks, straightening up. "I'm marrying Palti."

I drop my arms, dumbfounded. I had never expected her to go through with this willingly. "What about David?"

The way my friend grieved on his way out of Gibeah will be nothing compared to what he'll suffer when he hears about this. The night we'd said goodbye, he'd wept bitterly, believing he had seen his wife for the last time. Still, I'd been convinced my sister would stand by her husband.

"You can't betray him like this, Michal," I say, forcing my tone to soften. "He loves you."

"Don't be ridiculous!" Michal covers her rising emotion with a harsh laugh. "He thought marrying me would get him closer to the throne. Don't you care that he was using us both? Probably planning an assassination as soon as his radical nephews were ready to strike. If Abba had waited much longer, I probably would have ended up dead right along with him."

"That's a lie!" A dagger of light pierces my head as I shout at her. "How can you believe such a thing? Do you even hear what's coming out of your mouth?"

I'm furious at how easily these lies have taken root in her heart. I never would have imagined it after how close she and David were. Mist covers my vision when I think of how they embraced in the throne room after Abba acknowledged their betrothal.

Michal's eyes are stabbing me. "Abba was right about you. All this time, he knew you would end up turning against him. You just wouldn't do it openly."

I gasp, amazed I can breathe through the inferno filling my chest. "Do you want to keep talking, Michal, or do you care what I have to say to these accusations?"

Two

She bites the inside of her mouth, hugging herself tighter.

I clench my fists at my sides. "I have been your closest brother. I've shown you more attention than our father ever did. I would not lie to you, and I tell you now that David plotted nothing with me or anyone else. Doesn't my word mean anything to you? Don't you trust me?"

Her shrugged silence cuts me open, tossing a dozen broken memories back in my face. I keep talking, my heartbeat like a knife. "When Abba was sick and unstable, the council wanted me to seize power. But I didn't. And when David left, I didn't leave with him, even though Abba had threatened my life. Again."

"I know what he did to you." Her tone discounts it.

"No. You don't." She was still a little child when the darkness first came on Abba and he started hitting me. I hid it from Michal the way I hid it from everyone except Eema. Our mother couldn't be fooled. "You don't know the cost of all this. By design. I protected you from everything I could, and I'm here to protect you now."

I move closer and take her shoulders. "Stand with me against these lies, Michal. You're a strong daughter of Benjamin. You can get through this. Let me help you find David. I'll figure out where he is, and I'll help you get to him. You can be together…"

"You're insane! You've gone insane!" Michal pushes back from me until I let her go. "You expect me to leave here and wander the country like an Amalekite woman! You expect me to bear children in a cave and have Abba place a price on their heads because they're David's?" She slaps the idea away with her hand. "That shepherd is cursed, and I want no part of him."

"Michal!" My voice breaks. "David was chosen by Yahweh. Samuel anointed him in Bethlehem years ago."

"So, they're both the reason our father went mad," Michal's voice unravels and her eyes overflow. "But David's the one who stole Yahweh's heart away from the king."

"That's absurd, Michal. Men cannot command Yahweh. He *chose* David for his heart. Our father had already forsaken Him."

"And you think siding with David will make Yahweh change His mind about us?" Michal wipes her face with the edge of her robe. "Even if what you say is true, David won't win against our father. Abba's too stubborn to give up, and David's too weak to take the kingdom by force."

I steady my tone. "Who says it'll be by force?"

"What does that mean?" Michal loses control again, her voice cracking around a higher pitch. "David wants me to sit in a cave and wait this out? Like our people waited forty years in the wilderness before crossing into this land?"

"Disobedience kept them out!" I nearly shout. I was so certain Abba would be a better leader than some of our ancestors. Why do we fall into the same traps over and over again?

Michal laughs through a sob. "Well, I'm not going to wait four decades while David hides out expecting Yahweh to hand him the throne. Those Judean ruffians wouldn't accept a Benjaminite woman among them anyway." She fumbles with a cloth, dabbing the disturbed kohl around her eyes.

My shoulders drop. "Michal, don't do this."

Her voice hardens again. "I'm not going to waste my life on some misbegotten shepherd who betrayed us. I refuse to bear the curse you've brought on your wife and child by aligning them with David."

My mouth falls open, my chest turning cold. "How can you say that to me?"

If this were Ishvi or Malchi, I would be shaking them, trying to beat some sense into them. But she's my sister. She's poisoned. And I can't break her out of it any more than I could change Abba's mind in the grip of darkness.

I stare at Michal, feeling the grip of isolation clenching my limbs. My brothers refuse to speak out against either side, choosing to follow Abba's orders blindly without regard for David's past loyalty. Merab has been confined since her last child was born, and Eema has been sick for a year. Michal was all I had left, the only one of my family who I expected would understand. But instead, she's willing to sell her birthright as a daughter of Israel for temporary solace from a man who isn't her legal husband.

"Just leave," Michal says tightly. Her voice is hollow, drained of everything but anger.

I hear my tattered exhale in the silent room. "Sister…"

"Now. I don't want to see your face again." She looks at me one more time, then turns her back, moving to the other side of the room.

My fists open and close at my sides. No. I won't let her do this.

She doesn't know what she's dancing with by turning her back on Yahweh. She thinks she's just trying to do what's advisable, what's right in her own eyes. Like our father. She doesn't see the rebellion in her choice.

Two

The slippery slope for our people has always been subtle—consistent grumbling against Yahweh for what He hasn't done, what He hasn't provided. What isn't easy. Bereft, we search for something to give us meaning in the place of the One who chose us as His people. The ensuing emptiness makes us grasp at what will destroy us.

How can I watch that happen to my sister?

"You don't have to leave Gibeah if you're not ready," I appeal to her back. "I will speak to the king on your behalf. He won't force you if we tell him you don't want this…"

"Who says I don't? Now, go. And take this with you."

Michal yanks a thin cord over her head and tosses it on the floor in my direction. I bend to pick it up, remembrance turning it cold in my hand. It's a blue gem David brought back from Philistia after one of his battles. I'd been there to watch him put it around Michal's neck, blushing the whole time.

My heart like a stone, I turn and leave the room. Everything in me wants to rage. I want to destroy those gifts Palti's tempting her with, cleanse her house of this insanity. I picture myself in David's place, watching the woman I love taken by force while I had to run for my life. I came close to it when the king forbade my connection with Naamah. But she had never been poisoned against me. She never broke any vows.

Michal is David's wife, and she's going to another man of her own free will. It blinds me, like an ember trapped behind my eyes. What will happen to my sister when David becomes king?

Light footsteps chase mine down the stairs. "My lord…"

I turn back and Naamah stops on the step, her expression strained. "Give it time," she says helplessly.

Time for what? Time for the judgment Saul is heaping at our doors to come for all of us? I storm downstairs and slap the door open with my hand. This is the worst possible way for me to face my father, but maybe I can persuade the king myself. I'm already exasperated, anticipating the result. He won't listen.

"My lord prince!"

Someone calls to me from the gate, dismounting a black Philistine stallion in the courtyard. The man's garish clothing and the heavy gold hanging over his chest tells me he's come from the king, probably rewarded for providing information about David. But I don't know him.

Handing the horse off to a servant, the man spreads his hands, calling out again, "Hassar Jonathan!"

"Who are you?" I ask him, resenting how his expressive countenance sparkles at me, stinging what Michal left raw.

He bows deeply. "Palti of Laish, my lord," he gushes as though I should know. He clasps my arms, flashing an aggressive smile at me. "Or should I say, my brother?"

My stomach turns, my vision blurring red. It's bad enough I had to hear the news from my own sister. But to see the man who's casually planning to take David's place at her side, in her bed…

I glance past him to the gate, then over my shoulder at the house. But Naamah's the only one standing in the doorway, watching. She knows what's coursing through me. Besides, in a few days, I'll be long gone anyway, fighting some other battle. One I'll actually win.

Barely controlling a grim smile, I twist my seal ring off my right hand and slam my fist into Palti's jaw.

THREE

David

At dawn, Joab gathers the men of the resistance to hear what I have to say. They're an unruly bunch—bandits, criminals, tax evaders, runaways. They're scarred from battling predators, both human and animal, but most of their wounds aren't physical.

Each pair of eyes burns with unhealed pain, embittered pride. For years, they've been trampled on, ridiculed, forced away from the life every Israelite has fought for—peace in our own land, a home close to the presence of God. But Saul's predations have transformed every one of them into a fighter.

I've heard what they've done over the years, driving Ammonites and Edomites from our borders, pushing deeper into enemy territory than Saul's men would dare. Every man sits or stands with a hand on his weapon, anticipating a violent directive. And I will give them one, just as soon as we inquire of Yahweh. We're meant to fight. Just not Saul.

Once everyone is assembled and silent, Joab stalks between them like a wolf on the hunt, his commanding voice filling the cave.

"Many of you have heard of David from his years leading Saul's armies. He was the most valiant of the king's commanders, the only one who stepped forward against Goliath years ago. And yet, the king pursues his life to destroy him, which we all knew he would once he discovered what we've known for years." He plants his feet and faces the men. "David will be the next king of Israel."

Feverish murmuring rumbles toward him, but Joab doesn't move. His steely expression is an invisible wall, and his hawk eyes dare each man to cross over it.

"He was anointed by the prophet Samuel when he was still a shepherd in Bethlehem, not even in Saul's service yet. The favor of God has followed him since then, and that is what our apostate king fears the most. Many in Israel may side with Saul, fearing the repercussions of helping David. But we are able to see more clearly."

His eyes move over to his brothers. "A king that has forsaken Yahweh's instruction is destined to fail. Those of us Israel has cast out will be the ones to save her from his misguidance."

Three

Now the voices in the cave are swelling like a tide, bold and approving, and the fierce pride on their iron brows lights alarm in my chest. They'd rather save Israel now, help me take the throne by causing Saul's downfall. They've suffered for years as outcasts and criminals, exposed one moment and hiding the next, harassed by Philistines and Israelites alike. They're ready for an end to it all.

But they haven't seen what has opened my mind since the *Ruach* rushed into it. What we hold in our hands is the future of Israel, Yahweh's beloved. And we cannot sacrifice our inheritance on the altar of personal revenge. My heartbeat grows wild, anticipating the battle to explain this.

Adonai, give me wisdom.

On the heels of my prayer, my father's words enter my mind. *You are strong enough for this. And where you aren't, Yahweh is.*

The reminder is just as bitter as it is sweet. How many of these men have lost fathers because of Saul? That suffering joins us. But whatever we become cannot be built on hatred. Yahweh is the only guarantee of sustainable freedom that will grow beyond us and benefit Israel for generations. I had seen the dream in Jonathan's eyes the night we'd camped outside Aijalon when I was only a servant.

Building Israel. With Yahweh as the foundation.

It's an overwhelming task, only possible with God. But it's Yahweh's heart. And the certainty of it surges in every beat of my own. If these men choose to join me in pursuit of Him, then we'll have something to talk about.

Korah's voice breaks into my thoughts. "What do you say, anointed one?"

My eyes find him braced against a jutting shelf of rock, staring at me through the tangled darkness of his hair. The old outlaw still carries the intensity of a lion in his bearded face. I finally understand the way he'd looked at me before, when I'd met him as a thief in Abba's pastures. Of course, he's no prophet. But something in me then had sparked his interest and kindled his respect. Somehow, he'd known I would end up here.

Maybe I knew too. I just hoped for something different.

But here we are now. A cast-off shepherd and his band of mighty men. And only Yahweh knows the way forward.

I rise to my feet, moving up beside Joab.

"Brothers, I can't begin to know every battle that's brought each one of you here, but you all know mine. King Saul has ordered my death, and anyone who follows me risks the same. I don't know how long the king's hatred will burn or what it will consume in its wake. It may be some time before I can move about freely in Israel."

Low grumblings sweep through the men like thunder building on a ridge. I clench my fists, swallowing convulsively. They've already seen me cry once.

"I've seen Saul's hatred face-to-face, and I grieve knowing that it's broken out against others. I would gladly have taken a spear myself to save Nob." I glance at Abiathar, and he lowers his head. "Like every man here, I've had my home and family stripped from me." Stepping forward into their midst, I lock eyes with each man in turn.

"But I am no victim. I am Yahweh's weapon, and I gladly fought for Him before I ever commanded Saul's thousands. He spun His praises into my music, building His own strength into me before I even knew what He was preparing me for. He is the only One I am willing to follow to the ends of the earth. He has proven His faithfulness to me, and I will honor Him, whether I rise or fall. That is the only way to secure a good future for Israel."

I stop for breath, sensing an undercurrent of peace in my passion.

"If you are willing to trust Yahweh's promises to me, then my heart will be joined to you, and I will gladly spend my strength on your welfare. But God is my witness, I have never sought the king's life, nor will I plot against him now. If any of you desire to betray me to Saul, then may the God of our fathers see your plans and rebuke you Himself."

I see the glow in their eyes, the hard-bitten pride exile has burned into them. They have the muscle for this. But their hearts—Yahweh will have to take care of that.

My fingers pick at the sling wound around my wrist. "I'm not offering you anything easy, but every one of you understands what it means to fight for something. If you want to fight for me, you will submit to Yahweh's direction." I lift my chin, allowing a smile to break through the sorrow on my face. "And we will win."

I expect the silence to stretch on past my declaration, but Korah is on his feet almost before my voice dies. His hearty response and exuberant step decry his age.

"Yes, we will win!" He turns to face his sons. "Our ancestors Joshua and Caleb were held back from the Promised Land because of others' disobedience, and yet Yahweh kept His promise to them. If we show similar valiance in His service, Adonai will honor us for standing with His anointed."

Three

"And Israel will know what it is to have a truly great king." Abiathar speaks into the shuffling sound of men standing to their feet. Folding the priestly garments in his arms, he places his hand against his side in the gesture of a warrior. "We are with you, son of Jesse. All of us."

Gratitude swelling in my chest, I clasp his hand and go down the line of men against the wall, gripping arms and squeezing shoulders until I reach Korah. The aging outlaw's grip is every bit as fierce as a young man's, and a playful smile lightens the lines on his face.

"I knew there was a reason I didn't kill you that day in your father's pastures."

"You displayed a wisdom we haven't seen since," one of his sons jibes.

Korah waves him off. "I know a warrior when I see one. But I had no idea I was sparing a giant-killer. Or Yahweh's anointed." His eyes glisten. "What our God will do with you will rival the exploits of the judges of old."

"That reminds me." I raise my voice over the men's murmured agreement. "When I was in Gath, I overheard the Philistines' plan to attack Keilah, and last night you said they've been raiding the threshing floors."

Korah inclines his head. "Yes. Their elders have complained to the king, but he has not responded. Every month, Achish sends more troops and there's talk of a garrison being established."

It's the way of our enemies. Strike the sheep when the shepherd isn't watching. I feel a deep smile surfacing, old zeal building inside. "We'll have to see what Adonai thinks about that."

Several of the men exchange glances, and Korah's son Heman voices what's in their eyes. "My lord, we're afraid here in Judah. What makes you think we should take on the Philistines?"

I place my hand on his arm, just under the scar that circles his bicep like a rope. "We have nothing to fear if Yahweh is with us. Abiathar, bring the *ephod* here."

The others step back as the surviving priest brings the articles forward, spreading the linen across a flat rock and straightening the gemstones. I'm still stunned at Abiathar's wherewithal to escape with the elements used to inquire of the Lord. It's rudimentary, but Yahweh will answer. We need His wisdom.

A heavy hush falls over us, and I speak into it. "Adonai, my sword is yours. As always. And now, I have a hundred others. Should we save Keilah from the Philistines?"

Three

Loose rock crumbles in the back of the cave. No one breathes until Abiathar looks up with a broad smile. "He's with us. If we fight, we will succeed."

Gratified, I face my new army, hope awakened with our first directive. "We're going to Keilah."

FOUR

Jonathan

"Jonathan!"

I sit forward, catching myself awake. Ezra's shaking me, fresh vigor filling his tired face. I don't think he's ever called me Jonathan without my title before.

"Wake up," he urges me, but I barely have time to draw breath before the wild cry of an infant reaches my ears. I grab hold of Ezra's armor vest, and he helps me stand up on numb legs. After twelve hours of waiting, I'd finally fallen asleep against the wall in my armory.

"It's over, my lord." Ezra waits for me to focus, then clasps my arms, smiling into my eyes. "You have a son."

I embrace him hastily and run, nearly falling on my face on the narrow steps. I'm really too old to sleep on the floor. But in the moment, I feel like an eagle, fresh youth springing up under my feet.

Sheva is in our bedchamber, her hair falling raggedly around her shoulders. Her mother and the three beaming midwives melt into the background as soon as I enter. It takes two labored steps to reach my wife before I go to my knees, all the strength dropping from my body. I've never felt weaker in my life, but one look at the child's face, and I know I could stay this way forever.

"Meet your son," Sheva whispers through joyful tears, pulling the blanket down.

The wrinkled face with a tiny fist curled against his cheek mirrors me, my wife, and my brothers all in one. When I touch the blanket and see my huge calloused hand up against the infant's fingers, something unwinds in my chest, unlocking a deep need to sob.

Sheva reaches over, her free hand combing through my hair, but I can't take my eyes off the tiny boy. Every prayer, every praise concerning children rolls through me like a gracious tide, but David's words stand out in my mind. Something he wrote once.

Children are a heritage from the Lord. Blessed is the man whose quiver is full of them.

A tear drips down my face when the baby opens his mouth in a huge yawn. My little arrow. I kiss Sheva's hand, cradling it against my face. "Thank you, my love."

Four

Sweat pools in her throat, but her eyes are bright and overflowing. "What have you decided to name him?"

I'm quiet for a moment, sorting through everything I've considered over the past few weeks. I know what the king expects. Jonathan or Saul. But I'm not going to replicate either one of us. Bosheth is a family name, different variants showing up throughout our line. But it denotes shame, requiring something else to complete the meaning.

I let my vision pull out of focus, following the pattern of my thoughts. I've battled my share of shame during my father's kingship, something I never thought would happen to me. And yet, it has. As Samuel warned us, places of honor have turned into shame because our hearts were drawn after idols. Not just the idols of other nations, but the ones of our own making. Our own plans, our own ways. Status, position, a personal empire.

Fresh tears sting my eyes. *No more, Yahweh. Please! Burn in my son's heart. May our people go after you alone!*

"Mephibosheth," I say aloud to my wife. "One who destroys the shame of idol worship in Israel. Mephi," I amend, smiling crookedly when I realize what a heavy name it is for the infant right now.

Sheva grins. "Mephi. I love it."

There's a disturbance outside the room, and I turn to see every servant edging back against the wall or going to their knees. A huge shadow drops ahead of my father, who barely stops in the doorway, both hands on the lintel.

I'm frozen for a moment. I was expecting to bring the baby to him in the palace in ten days, after the official naming and circumcision. I get to my feet, blocking my wife.

"My lord." I take a few steps toward him and lower my voice. "Abba, we're still unclean."

Offense rears up armed behind his smile. "You think I don't know that? I've welcomed seven children of my own."

I hide a wince, realizing he's counting the children of his concubine Rizpah, two half-brothers I've never met.

He looks around me. "Let me see him."

I step back until I've reached Sheva, and she holds the baby out. I lift my son into my arms, resisting a surge of panic when my father takes him from me. Saul bends over and kisses Mephi, the edge of his beard dusting the infant's head.

Four

"Meet your king," he murmurs over the boy, the light barely reaching his eyes.

A tempest wakes up inside me, crashing over the peace of before. I lift my chin, settling myself. "His name will be Mephibosheth."

"Mmm," Saul doesn't lift his eyes. "That's the name of one of Rizpah's sons."

Of course. I resist the urge to fold my arms. "We're calling him Mephi."

Saul nods, studying the baby closely. "He's strong and healthy? Nothing wrong with him?"

I hesitate before answering. Would my father act differently if he wasn't? I look at my son, and my heart breaks open again. "He's perfect."

"How else?" Saul looks up, grinning. "He's a son of Benjamin after all." He looks past me to Sheva. "You've done well, my daughter. One day, your son will be king, once I've driven every imposter from the land."

I tense up, resenting the darkness in my father's praise, the yoke he's already trying to put on my infant son. Has he forgotten

Samuel's prophecy, Yahweh's words? Mephi won't be king. And I don't want him to be.

I gently take my son back, holding him against me. "Abba," is all I say.

Saul looks into me, reading everything in my mind. He touches my son, his seal ring standing out on his index finger. "He will be king. It's his burden, just like it's yours."

No. I step back, affronted. My son will not carry any burden Yahweh hasn't given him. He will not walk in rebellion if I have anything to say about it. God is my witness, he will know the freedom that comes from walking with Adonai, the way David does.

Mephi squirms, feeling the tremors stroking my arms. His dark eyes open, studying me with complete trust. Looking down at him, I've never felt so adamant. I shake my head at the king.

"The throne of Israel is not his burden, Abba. It's not mine. It's not even yours."

FIVE

David

Keilah isn't far. Once every man and his weapons are accounted for, we emerge from Adullam's caves and march three miles southeast into Judah's foothills, crossing the valley where I'd killed Goliath almost five years ago.

The wet smell of the ground pulls the memory back, plucking a wild chord in my head. My muscles squeeze and jump, and I have to swirl my sling to keep my fingers busy. All the springtime battles I fought for Saul dance back into view, but it's been years since I felt this much freedom riding out to fight.

I used to carry the weight of Saul's expectations into every battle. The shroud of his dark hopes for me to die fighting had weighed me down before I even realized it was there. Now, there's just my anointing, the promise of Yahweh's presence following us into Judah's territory. It's a welcome change.

Anticipation pulls beneath my skin, weaving melodies through my mind. I pluck at the reins, chewing on the phrases piecing together without me trying. I have to sing. Later. It's been too long.

For the first time since walking away from Jonathan, I can see a horizon through all the fog. I may have fled alone, but Yahweh sent me an army. Because He chose me. I look back at the hills dropping away behind us.

"You're the Maker of heaven and earth and every one of those hills. And you have always been my help. I sing for joy in the shadow of your wings."

I barely notice the way my tone slips into a melody until one of the men rides up closer and interrupts. "What did you say?"

Joab canters past on his mule, shaking his head. "He's singing. Ignore him. We'll all hear it later."

Refocusing, I recognize the other man. "Asaph, wasn't it? You're the scribe."

He nods, hiding a smile. "How long have you been making songs?"

"Since I was a child," I respond, refusing to feel sheepish. "You?"

Five

I've seen the small lyre he carries, along with a leather pack of parchments, animal skins, and crude ink pens.

Asaph pulls up on the reins, guiding his mule down a steep embankment. "The same. I lived near the school of the prophets in Ramah, and I would often see them go out into the hills, singing. It always made me think of the days of Moses, when our brothers and sisters would follow Miriam and Joshua to the mountain of the Lord to worship."

His breath catches around the words, and I grin. Joab was right. There's kinship here. It's rare to find someone with the glint of personal awe in his eye, the shake of adoration for Yahweh in his voice. What's stirred inside me since my youth rests on this man too, and I'm grateful to recognize it. It's like finding a brother.

Asaph pats the leather pack at his side. "I can help you write some of your songs down. Make some extra room up there," he quips, tapping his temple.

I chuckle, relieved to have something to laugh about. Just with their presence, the mighty men are feeding my resolve, building me back up in the places Saul left plundered.

Ahead of us, Joab swings his mule around, calling back to me. "What do you think, Songbird? We're within a mile now."

I assess the landscape, getting my bearings. Keilah is nestled against the foothills above Socoh, and the forests of Hereth lie just beyond. With the fresh green thickening the trees, there's more than enough cover for us to approach unnoticed. The Philistines don't have any reason to believe anyone's coming, an advantage we won't have once we strike.

I wave my hand to the right. "Tell the men to drop back into the woods. Assemble in the sheepcotes against the hill."

Concealed in the forest, we drink from the brook circling the city and decide who will ride down from the hills and who will charge on foot. I make sure I have the eyes of every man I've singled out as a commander.

"The foot soldiers will hit the city from the east. I'll go up the ridge with the bowmen and locate the stronghold. Remember, only Philistines are to be harmed. You can grab weapons and any livestock they've brought into the garrison, but take nothing from Keilah itself."

Asahel speaks up, twirling an arrow in his fingers. "Are you sure you should be risking this? You were just in Gath. If any of the commanders recognize you, they'll be even more eager to kill you."

Five

Several men murmur agreement, beginning to tell me I should stay back with the reserves who will wait in the forest.

Smirking, I shake my head, consumed with certainty. "I'm here to take ground, not guard supplies. Does a king send his men out to fight without joining them?"

"Some do," Abishai infers, speaking into every memory I have of Saul using me.

I straighten, looking past them. "This is where Yahweh wants me. He sent me an army, and I'll fight any battle he sends our way."

Asahel shrugs. "Then, I'm going with you up the ridge."

"I'll go too," Joab says. "Abishai can take the foot soldiers through the forest."

We clasp arms in agreement, petitioning Yahweh for protection I know He's already provided us with. I can sense His covering as we skirt the city undetected by the few Philistines guarding the watchtower.

They've barricaded the eastern wall near the threshing floors, blocking the gates, impeding trade. And so far, Saul has done nothing. He's grown too accustomed to sending me into battle amongst the people. Now that I've been removed from his presence, Israel is waiting for him to come up with a new strategy.

But they've forgotten about me.

Nearly on my stomach, I crawl down the embankment and crouch in the dirt several feet from the gate. Six Philistines stroll past the stronghold armed with bows. The flash of red on their armor vests ignites what's been smoldering in my veins since I ran from Gath.

I find a stone at my feet and slide it into the hollow of my sling, anticipation crackling behind my smile. Across from me along the gate, Joab rolls his eyes, pointing angrily at his bow.

"Relax," I mouth back, grinning. All that angry practice in the caves had to count for something. I breathe slowly, taking aim before skipping the stone into the midst of the soldiers. It hits one breastplate, and every eye snaps onto the trees, every bow aimed in the wrong direction.

Asahel's bowmen come up from behind and send a dozen arrows into the Philistines' unprotected backs, while Joab blows the trumpet and the roar of my men explodes from the trees.

I pull my knife and throw it into an enemy's side before he can lift his own horn. At the same moment, the sun comes up,

Five

a giant point of light sliding over the hills, hitting the town like a finger. I draw my sword, lifting it into the light. "For the Lord and for Israel!"

The rush of the fight makes me feel alive again. It's exhilarating to see us moving as one, driving the Philistines from the town's wheat stores and destroying their camp at the outskirts. Achish had sent only half a battalion, anticipating little resistance, so my new army completely overwhelms them, killing more than half and forcing the rest into the hills.

The ones who'd moved into the garrison had brought horses and goats, and we grab the livestock, along with swords and spears off the dead, spoils which will mean the difference between life and death for our band.

Unprepared, the townspeople barricade themselves in their homes. Some flee for the northern hill ahead of the Philistines who are caught in the streets, prevented from doing the same.

My men press hard until no one is left. Every Philistine who tries to escape is blocked in and cut down. They'd trapped themselves by building the garrison. Once the last Philistine falls, my men look at each other and fling an exuberant shout at the sky. The mighty sound should be enough to shake what's left of the garrison walls.

The men of Keilah emerge first while their families hold back, peering through doorways and out of windows. They don't know who we are or what to think. A few of them raise their voices, their nervous exclamations of relief joining the shouts of my men until one of the elders steps forward and barks directly at me, "Who are you?"

Caught in the heady swirl of adrenaline and concentrated rage, I'm not seeing clearly. It takes me far too long to bring the man's face into focus.

"I'm David, the son of Jesse."

Whispers ignite the crowd, sharpening the elder's expression. Everyone is openmouthed and horrified, staring at the blood-spattered streets littered with Philistine bodies. The elders gape at me as though I'm one of the *Nephilim* giants from Gath, and their eyes shift beyond me, trying to count my men.

I lift my hand at the others. "Stand down."

Joab repeats my order before it's echoed by my commanders, but the tight concern doesn't leave the elder's face. He gestures to his guards. "Bring him to me."

Joab and Abishai step up beside me, but I stop them before they can grab their swords. "It's all right."

Five

I push past them and cross the courtyard, stepping over several bodies before lowering myself to one knee. "I am David ben Jesse of Judah. I am the servant of Yahweh," I affirm, but the introduction doesn't seem to move the men.

They're still watching my army over my head, listening to the murmurs of the crowd. Still studying the Philistine bodies, the people are slowly reacting with suspicion and guarded gratitude.

The chief elder locks eyes with my nephews and pushes his guard's shoulder. "Take these four to the guardhouse. Keep the others here by the gate."

I stand up before the guards can lay hands on me, praying my men won't react to being treated like prisoners. "Wait for me here," I direct them over my shoulder. "Put your weapons on the ground. Do it!"

I wait for them to obey before I allow the guards to lead me away. Our short journey across the marketplace gives me time to consider the elder's reaction. I'm well known to his people, but Saul has told them I'm a condemned traitor. To find me leading a daunting number of mixed warriors outside of Saul's jurisdiction can't be sitting well. On the surface, there's nothing to shield us from the accusation of rebellion. All anyone can see is a group of ambitious men trying to make a name for themselves.

In the center of town, more men of Keilah join the elders in the guardhouse, concealing their relief under invisible armor while I explain what we've done.

"We heard your requests for aid had gone unanswered, so we inquired of the Lord and came down to drive the Philistines out before they gained a foothold in the area."

The chief elder keeps his distance, assessing me with caution. "How did you know the Philistines were down here? Were you not in Gath, joining Achish there?"

My throat closes. Of course, Saul would have painted me as a deserter when my location became known. "I was in Gath, but I had no interest in joining Achish. I fled to him for shelter, but when my life was threatened, I had to escape."

The elder stares me down, his sour expression letting me know exactly what he thinks of my choice of hiding place. One glance at the others reveals the same. They still see rebellion in my actions. They don't know how desperate I was.

"Saul did not sanction this battle," the elder says tightly, keeping considerable distance between us. "We know you no longer fight for him. What did you hope to gain from this?"

Five

I lift my chin, praying Joab stays silent. "Yahweh sanctioned this battle. And an Israelite city is free from enemy hands. That's enough for me."

Besides a tiny twitch around his eye, the elder's face barely changes. His attention moves over my shoulder. "And these others...?"

"These men are my nephews, the sons of Zeruiah, and the others came to me. They're under my command."

"Under *your* command?" The elder's stare turns colder. He glances at his kinsmen, suspicion passing back and forth between them.

I swallow. It might take a while for Israel to believe that the resistance will not operate the way it did before. Our movements will be coordinated by Adonai. But one battle won't be enough to convince everyone.

The elder studies me again as though I might have something hidden in my robes. "And am I to understand your men saved Keilah with no thought of personal gain?"

"Food and shelter will be more than enough."

The words taste bitter. It isn't hard to notice the disdain leaking into the elder's expression. But this is how we'll have to survive. Staying one step ahead of Saul, fighting the battles he ignores in exchange for sanctuary. We don't have much choice. Maybe once Saul sees what we're doing, he'll understand that I don't mean him personal harm. God, I hope.

The elder stares at his guards for a long moment, and then abruptly lifts his chin at me. "You can stay as long as you swear that no one in my city will be harmed. No one will be stolen from."

"You have my word. Thank you, my lord."

I bow my head, but the moment I do, a strange feeling leaps onto me. Something cold and sharply clawed. I study the elder's face, finding nothing to interpret. But the sensation has followed me into a dozen forests, a hundred different raids over the years. It's lurked in Saul's own chambers. It's the deep, sharp thrust of danger stabbing my middle right before an ambush.

* * * * *

We stay in Keilah longer than we planned. Too long. We all know it's not safe. Saul will probably hear about our victory and come down to investigate. But he hasn't so far. And the respite is too difficult to resist.

Five

Relieved of the Philistine threat to their borders, the town celebrates, spreading a feast for my men, making sure we eat and drink our fill. Several of the women mend our clothes, even offering us better garments. The town merchants trade some of the plunder for supplies we'll take with us. Their leaders keep aloof, observing us from a distance, but they don't interfere when we take up temporary residence in the guardhouse.

It should be a relief to have roofs over our heads again. After so long looking over our shoulders, it's gratifying to walk freely through a town with walls and gates and a place of worship. It's not a struggle to keep warm, and we can enjoy fresh food without having to hunt or forage. But the pleasure of the reprieve is weighted. Uneasy.

I haven't felt well since our second day here. The general sense of discomfort has been building like a cloud in my chest since then, joining the edge of the old cough that's still hanging on from winter. One of the elders keeps bringing me an herbal concoction for it, but I still don't sleep well at night, tossing through recurring dreams of Saul hunting me in a cave while I stay hidden, cutting through his robe behind his back.

I wake up one morning and find my own robe cut at the lower right edge, but none of my guards remember seeing anyone up on the roof where I've been sleeping.

I'm not the only one who feels shut in. Joab and his brothers prowl the hills and watch the roads during the day, sleeping out on the battlements on either side of me. We're not saying anything, but there's too much beneath the surface.

The elders clearly don't want us here, yet they could have thrown us out by now. Why didn't they? Why drag the celebrations out so long, with no discussion of our departure? Every night, it's another feast, and every day, Keilah's leaders regard us with closed silence.

By the tenth day, I'm done turning the possibilities over in my head. Once Joab leaves for the forest with his spies, I call for the priest's son. "Abiathar, we need to inquire of the Lord."

My friend knows where my concern lies. I wait at his shoulder while he places his hands over the *ephod* and breathes in prayer.

"Will Saul come down here?" I ask the heavy silence. "Will the men of Keilah hand us over?"

Panic grabs hold of me as soon as I ask. I don't want to know.

But Abiathar's face has no room for deceit. "Yes. And yes."

Five

His expression sinks into sorrow, but I barely have time to share his disappointment before Joab strikes the door open. He pushes into the room in fierce anger, dragging a man of the city by his arm. "I caught him leaving by the gate on the north side," he shouts, shoving the man down at my feet.

"Joab, you've overstepped your bounds!" I lash out at him, but he roars over me.

"He betrayed us! They all did." Joab slaps two parchments against my chest. "I found these on him. One is days old."

My defenses drop, sinking into coldness. The message on the first paper is glaringly clear, a brutal invitation for the king to send the full strength of his army out against us. No doubt they were hoping Saul would trap us while we were still confined by the walls and gates of the city.

But the second message bites deeper. It's Saul's own hand, writing to the leaders of Keilah, asking for a sure sign—proof of my presence in their city. Hence the other item Joab handed me, crumpled between the papers. It's the missing piece of my robe. Pain darts through my stomach.

"They cast lots to see who would carry it to Saul," Joab seethes, holding up a small bag of coins. "And these are from Gibeah. He was paid for this."

Joab's neck muscles are expressing all the anger simmering inside me. But the man of Keilah is calmer on his knees than my nephew is on his feet.

The messenger speaks to me in a dead tone, his unblinking expression lacking any remorse. "There were more riders sent out. The news will reach the king. He might not wait for proof." His brows tilt. "But why should you worry if God is with you? Go fly away to your cave, Songbird, and let Yahweh rescue you."

The barb slides under my skin like an infected dart. And just like that, my old nickname is poisoned.

Joab's fingers clench near the messenger's face. "Don't tarnish Adonai's name with your treachery, you miserable..."

"Stop." I push my fist into his chest, forcing him back a few steps. Bending down, I search the messenger's eyes while my pulse hammers in my head. "Why are you so eager to betray a fellow Israelite?"

For the first time, something shivers in the man's face. "Some of us don't want our towns devoted to destruction like Nob. No rebel is worth that."

"Shut up!" Joab rears over him, pulling his sword free, but a bold taunt surfaces in the man's eyes, clearly challenging me from the floor.

"Go ahead," he sneers quietly. "You run like cowards; why not kill me like one?"

Enough. I push Joab's wrist aside, spearing the man with my gaze instead. "Go home. On the way, decide how much your word means to you."

Once he's gone, I turn my back, shoving my distress deep down. I had hoped to avoid being chased across the countryside, forced to live on the run. But I highly doubt Saul will pass up the opportunity the messengers have handed him. Once he finds out I've returned from Gath, he'll search out every cave and hole in Judah looking for me.

Abiathar releases a long, slow sigh. "The Word of the Lord is clear. We should inform the others."

I nod, trying to settle the crashing in my chest. The scrap of my robe trembles in my hand, and I clench it tighter. Who knows what else the men of Keilah have stolen from us in order to tempt Saul? And after making us promise not to steal.

I turn around. "Those other messengers will take a few days to reach the king, but he could already be on his way. We need to be long gone by then. How far do you think we need to go to avoid him?"

Joab sets his jaw. "We can hug the river and push southeast around Socoh."

"Into the mountains," I finish. Once we hit the southern slopes, we should be safe for a while.

Joab nods. "The land of Ziph is good countryside. There's a stable water supply, and the hills will cover us. We'll have to set men at a perimeter so they can alert us if Saul is coming. I doubt he'll stop at Keilah."

I smile grimly, my throat like sandpaper. "He'll have to be faster next time."

* * * * *

My head pounds as we plunge into the wilderness, riding and running through the night. Even with darkness to cover us, it's unclear whether the men of Keilah will follow us and try to bring me back by force. But they've all seen my men in action. I'm not sure they're willing to risk a fight with a powerful rogue army just to snare me. By midnight, I'm sure we're not being pursued. But the slithering sense of betrayal still crawls my skin.

They cast lots for my clothing.

Five

The thought is like an infected wound leaching poison, and I can't rid myself of it.

The elders' faces linger in my mind, their taut expressions guarding treachery while they watched me settle into what I thought was safe. I'm furious that I was lured into complacency by a walled town and fresh provisions. I'm angry that our suspicions were confirmed. Are we to expect the same betrayal in every Israelite city?

I pull up on the reins, spinning my mule around to avoid a huge log in the path. I've lost all sense of direction in this fog, and I'm feeling worse than before. Strange pain lurks in my limbs, licking up my sides like flames. Heat rises in my veins only to be doused by a crashing wave of cold. My men catch up to me in the clearing, fanning out around me, but their outlines are murky in the early morning haze.

"My lord, we have to keep moving," someone says. "We can't stay in the open like this."

I know. But something's wrong. I'm gripping the reins too tightly, my nails chewing through my palms. My breathing is labored, and sweat paints my body like a second skin under my clothes. Voices grate on my ears, too loud.

"My lord? David?"

I pull my feet from the stirrups and slide to the ground, my hands and knees scraping into hard dirt. The landscape tilts when I try to get my bearings, and the truth hits me with another wave of chilled dizziness. It's not just the sting of betrayal.

It's actual poison.

The thought is like a pebble unleashing an avalanche of boulders heavy enough to crush me. It makes sense now. They kept us feasting long enough for the messengers to reach Saul. They gave me poison with my food, a little more every day so that when the king came for me, I'd be too weak and sick to fight back. They used my robe against me, the one Jonathan gave me as a gift, wagering on how quickly Saul would come down to capture me once he saw the evidence.

Another hot knife of pain tears my middle, cutting up too high. My heart bends like wax in my chest. I can't run. I have to rest.

"David." Asahel kneels in front of me. "David."

His face blurs, and I clench my fists, trying to hold onto the strength that's drying up, dropping away. "Why do they hate

Five

me so much?" My fists move to my eyes, smearing dirt into my face. "God, why have you forsaken me?"

As the hours inch toward morning, we fold away into the strip of woods west of Socoh, but the stormy, hazy dawn won't reveal much. My arms wrapped around my legs, I curl into the corner of an aging sheepfold at the edge of some man's field and shake fitfully while thunder rumbles the ground under me.

Pain climbs my chest, winding between my ribs like a snake. What did they give me? Some toxic herb lacing the tea they kept giving me, no doubt. I should never have accepted anything from the elders. But the reproach only worsens the pain. They're men of Israel. I should have been able to trust them.

Rain breaks the sky open, and I flinch away from the downpour, but I'm drenched in a few seconds, my shivers intensifying in the throes of fever. We should be moving. If we've miscalculated Saul's timing, he could be at Keilah's gates by nightfall. I watch the angry sky, rain slashing my face.

Come quickly, Adonai. You've never despised my affliction. I need you now.

The hint of a lion's growl joins the thunder, and I feel for my sling, even though I'm the lamb now, banked into a fold with stones while a turncoat shepherd hunts me for slaughter. The

103

rumbling sound mounts into a distinct roar, and I sit up sharply, gripped by different chills. I look out into empty, soggy fields, and my pulse beats out of time with understanding.

This is no lion on the hunt. Yahweh's here.

It's unmistakable the way the air thins, insinuating peace into the depth of many waters widening around me. The sound of the storm is deafening and myrrh tinges the breeze, riding the rain. I toss onto my other side, troubled. I usually sense Him in war and worship. Why now, in anguish? I shake my head. I might be dreaming.

My shoulder tingles, and I edge away from what feels like a hand, likely one of my men trying to rouse me. But the grip gets tougher, and chills erupt along my arms. "Leave me…" I mumble, but the words end in a gasp when I open my eyes.

The narrow space of the sheepfold expands, filling with a golden warmth, and a man steps through the opening toward me. My muscles pull, trying to back away, but I can't move. It's still raining, but the storm has no sound, no strength. I stop shaking, my senses drowned in fearful wonder. I don't see His face, but the Man is clearly looking at me.

He's robed in light, but He's bleeding from His hands, His feet, and His upper left side, where His heart should be. Agonized compassion pours out of Him, winding toward me like the fingers of a river as He breathes out, "They've rejected Me too."

The words open my side, cleaving my heart in two. I blink, and the Man disappears. Immediately, a lamb is there in His place, its side torn open, blood streaking the pure white wool. It's a lamb for slaughter. But I don't want to believe something so terrible. I don't understand it. Yahweh, rejected? I've pictured Him as a lion before, but a wounded man? A sacrificed lamb?

"David."

Yahweh's voice fills my body, shattering something. The pieces dig into my throat, threatening to leap out my mouth while joy and anguish battle for control. He's heard me. He hasn't turned His face from me. But His closeness is not what I expected, not what I've ever known. It's heavy and beautiful and terrifying. I can't contain it.

An old comment Joab once made shoves through my mind, heavy with meaning. *You see too deeply. You want too much.*

Here in Yahweh's presence, I know it more clearly than I ever have. There's too much. He's too much.

I bend over onto my knees, bury my face in Jonathan's robe, and wail.

SIX

Jonathan

Eight months later

"David must die!"

My father's epithet slashes through my mind, and I flinch, feeling the heat of his rage even in my dream. Torment distorts his face, making him unrecognizable. The tangled arms of a dark forest block my way on all sides, and the king cuts right and left, hacking into trees, screaming my name alongside David's like a possessed man.

"Where is he, Jonathan? I know you know!"

His spitting anger is lethal, but it can't reach cross the strange gulf between us, and I can't break through it to stop him.

A wide path opens to my right, promising safety, and I follow it into the hills. Relief rides my shoulders, releasing the strain in my muscles. I plunge into the thicket, moving faster than

I ever have on foot, and in less than a mile, the most beautiful mountain grove stretches in front of me.

Green-coated boulders spear the hillside, and a waterfall tumbles over them, creating a curtain with its spray. Its wild churning feeds the silence, blocking out the king's distant raging.

But something is wrong.

The lower boulders bleed, and the dark stains form a scattered trail to the side of a brook where I find David doubled over. His sword is stabbing the ground, and he's leaning into it, trying to stand, but he's bleeding deeply from a chest wound, and the rocks under him are glowing red.

I wait to feel alarmed, especially when I hear the king's sword cutting through the underbrush. This blood trail could lead any predator right to David's side. But my friend won't get up. His blank stare is more chilling than the sight of his wounds. He doesn't move, even when my father breaks through the edge of the woods. Panting, Saul staggers forward, gripping his sword, looking wildly in every direction.

His face is twisted, fixed on murder. "Move, Jonathan." He takes a step closer, but he's still glancing around aimlessly, even though nothing blocks his view of David lying on the ground.

Six

"Where is he?"

The question jolts my stunned heartbeat back into rhythm. The king can't see him. I'm certain of it. The Lord has covered his eyes. Turning back, I look down at David, certainty deepening inside me. "My father will never find you."

David looks up when I say it, but before our eyes connect, I'm sitting up in bed. Catching the sides to pull myself out of sleep, I snag back a shout before it leaves my lungs. I hold onto the bedpost, breathing hard, while the dream's images fade into the predawn darkness of my chamber.

As soon as my sight adjusts, I look for Jehosheva. My nightmares aren't helping her second pregnancy, which already has her up throughout the night. But this time, her eyes are still closed, her breathing steady. The silence from the little bed next to ours tells me I haven't awakened our infant son either. Growing in leaps and bounds, Mephi doesn't sleep well unless he's close to us.

I slide out of bed and escape to the balcony as quietly as I can, but in a few moments, my wife is at my shoulder.

"Another dream?" she murmurs, her voice distorted with sleep.

"I'm sorry." I comb one hand through my hair while Sheva's fingers thread through my other one. Maybe it's time I accepted the medicine Ammiel offered.

"Was it your father again?" Sheva asks.

Her soft face in the moonlight calms me, and I pull the feeling close to my heart. She and Mephi have been a sweeter comfort than I ever imagined, especially the past several months. In the better part of a year, everything's unraveled.

Eema is sick, shuttered away in her chambers. Michal is a changed creature, living with Palti after their blasphemous wedding ceremony. Only my father's closest supporters attended, and no one else speaks of it, least of all the remaining priests. They're understandably terrified of being killed for speaking a word against the king.

My nightmares started about a month ago, following the pattern of my father's continuing rampage. I had thought the advent of my first son would have given Abba pause. I had told myself once the king saw me married, with a child of my own, he would rest easier, even if little Mephi won't really be king.

But my father had barely missed a beat, picking up his hunt for David without even breathing hard. Hatred has become the air my father breathes, choking out every other pleasure,

Six

blinding his eyes to any other sight. Killing David has become Saul's obsession. It plagues our house with violence, haunting my dreams and distracting the king from the very real threats at our gates while he chases David all over the kingdom on a doomed mission. Cursed from the beginning.

Wrapping an arm around Sheva, I look out over the city, trying to soak in the illusion of calm that darkness brings. In daylight, Gibeah writhes, tense with conflicting rumors and concerns. The ones who sang David's praises in the streets are silent now, either hailing him as a courageous hero in private or joining in to slander him as a traitor.

The boldest council members asked my opinion at first, but the position I hold is too difficult to share. Abner sides with my father while knowing where I stand. Ezra quietly sides with me while fearing my father. No one knows what to believe.

After fighting Philistines at Keilah, David fled to the wilderness of Ziph, or so I've heard. Saul has left for Jeshimon with half the army, not even waiting to verify the reports I purposely manipulated to send him the long way around. With each failed attempt, Saul comes back angrier while David gains a larger company of followers. And dark dreams drag me through the nights. Though this one is different. And it's the clearest I've been able to think in a while. Maybe it's time to talk about it.

I glance at Sheva's face against my shoulder. She always understands, but her position hasn't been easy either.

She's been rejected by my sisters, ignored by the king, and she knows our son will not be what my father hoped. But she's handled the confusion graciously, remaining patient with my frequent absences and coaxing my heart toward strength again. She knows what David means to me, and I know she's offered frequent prayers for his safety, for my sake.

I tighten my fingers around hers. "I saw David this time. He was hurt. Or in trouble. I'm not sure." Now that I'm awake, my alarm has a sharp edge to it. Has he been wounded?

Sheva's eyes widen. "Do you think the king found him?"

"No."

For some reason, I'm certain he hasn't. And he won't. Because David is the Lord's anointed. It's only become more evident since he fled Gibeah. Everyone my father has alienated flocks to David like sheep in need of a shepherd. Abiathar, the sole survivor of Saul's rampage against the priests, now carries the holy *ephod* before David, giving him God's direct instructions. It's how he'd learned of Keilah's betrayal in time to escape it.

Six

When I'd heard how quickly their elders had summoned my father, offering to turn David over to him, I lost all respect for the men of Keilah. It grieves me to see David betrayed at every turn by the jealous and fearful in the land. Have they forgotten how bravely he led them into battle? Why should the warrior who defended all Israel against Goliath be hunted like a criminal, unsure of whom he can trust? He doesn't deserve this.

The gray emptiness on David's face in my dream uncovers all the old anger I'd felt at the New Moon feast. I've wasted too many years trying to make my father into something he doesn't want to be—a contented, faithful follower of Yahweh. But David is both. And he's in trouble. Why sit here and do nothing when I can help him? Do I dare find a priest and ask for counsel?

"I don't know what to do, Sheva," I murmur, half to myself. "I don't know the purpose of all this." I lean over the rail on my elbows, afraid to think of the weight of sin my father is heaping upon us. "It seems presumptuous to assume God would speak to me now."

Sheva's soft chuckle opens something in my chest. "He might just speak to whoever's listening."

I smile in spite of myself, feeling ridiculous for doubting. What do I have to lose?

Adonai, what would you have me do?

In the thin silence, a strange memory drifts through my mind—a battle where David dislocated his shoulder while fighting. Ezra covered us while I knelt next to David and made him brace against me before jerking his arm back into place. The sound he'd made was half-groan, half-laugh, and he'd punched me in the chest with his good hand. "You're welcome," I'd said, pulling him to his feet. He'd given me a crooked smile and kept fighting.

The memory feels heavy, weighted with fresh meaning. David is surrounded by plenty of mighty men now, perhaps hundreds. But they likely encourage him to end the struggle and kill Saul. Perhaps his courage is out of joint this time, and all he's lacking is a hand up from another warrior. One who isn't depending on him or planning to betray him.

I breathe deeply, my wife's head rising and falling with my chest. "Sheva, I think I have to go find him."

Her head lifts, but her manner remains quiet. "Where will you go? If your father hasn't found him, how will you?"

I shrug, strangely unconcerned. "If Yahweh is trying to show me where he is, all I need to do is follow. I have to try."

Six

As certain as I am, I still feel the edge of guilt. The Philistines have retaliated after Keilah, harassing nearby towns and taking advantage of Saul's preoccupation elsewhere. But my brothers and the king's forces have been on special alert. And Ezra knows to send for me if the danger pushes too close to Gibeah.

I pull Sheva as close as her expanding middle will allow and rest my chin on the top of her head. "I'll have Ezra send extra guards to stay here with you. And I will return as quickly as I can."

Sheva makes a gentle sound against my chest. Her contentment soothes me. "We'll be right here when you return."

After she returns to bed, I bow down and stretch out my hands toward the place of worship, the high point of the city.

"Adonai, you know I mean your servant no harm. I want to help him, but I can't do it alone. You guided Samuel to the next king of Israel when he didn't even know what he was looking for. Help me find him now."

I don't hear an answer in the silent glimmer of stars, but I know a heading when I see one. If I follow, Yahweh will order my steps.

Before dawn can bring any servants after me, I find Ezra in the armory restringing one of my bows.

"I need some of your clothes," I tell him.

He scoffs, confused. "I don't think they'll fit, my lord…"

"Just a cloak then. Something to cover my face and hide my armor. If the king returns, tell him I went to look into a Philistine threat. Our intelligence supports that. But only mention it if he asks. You are not to say a word to anyone else."

Ezra sets the bow aside, staring me down. "Why do I get the feeling…?"

I lift a finger. "Not a word. Trust me."

Retrieving my bow, I leave the room, resisting the urge to say more. I rarely hide things from Ezra, but it's safer this way. The less I tell him, the less he'll have to fabricate.

SEVEN

David

The city of Ziph is four miles south of Hebron in the mountains of Judah. The golden hills and scruffy mountain brush remind me of my younger days wandering with the sheep.

My men and I ride at a steady, practiced pace, more accustomed to the slanted, rocky terrain than the rolling meadows around Gibeah. With each step into Judah's territory, I pray we'll find a more permanent refuge, one that will last us more than a single season.

These southern mountains make my mind skip ahead toward Bethlehem, turning over every memory of those early years. Judah was my home for so long, but when I last lived here, I was completely distracted, my feet set on a different path. I was so eager to set off from here and join Saul.

We're not far from Socoh, where the king first rallied Judean troops against Philistia before we knew Goliath would emerge among their ranks—the year I was sent back to the sheep with a burning ember in my heart. I knew then my yearning for the battles of my God wouldn't be quenched, but I didn't guess it would lead me into a war against my own kinsmen, one that would scorch me from the inside.

My heart pulls toward the land of my childhood, but we're as close to my hometown as we can get without endangering the Ephrathites. My clansmen have already taken enough punishment for me.

The Philistines have taken advantage of Saul's preoccupation, freezing trade and travel with their posted raiding parties. Another garrison is being established outside Bethlehem, and like the threat at Keilah, Saul has yet to answer it, preferring to use our enemies to keep my tribe in check. My fingers itch to battle them, to open the way through our land again. But first we need to set our sights on survival.

These remote hill towns are providentially close to the abundant fields of Maon and Carmel, with plentiful stores of grain, wool, and oil pouring in from the surrounding farms. But Ziph is more isolated than the other Judean cities, nestled up against the jagged hundred-foot peak that wears the forest of Hereth like a garment of green.

We've cut our own trail between the rocks, hugging the mountain and keeping clear of the well-worn paths taken by the

Seven

Ziphite shepherds. A few trees have been marked, leading to the caves where they camp on their way to Maon's lower pastures.

We pitch tents within the hill Hachilah, as close to the spray of water as we can get. The crashing tumble over the rocks will provide us with plenty to drink and cover the sounds of our camp.

"How long before they know we're here?" Abishai asks me.

Every step into the forest, Joab's brother has kept a hawk eye on every cliff face, every hideout. I want our company to remain hidden for as long as possible. But it will be difficult. Ziph doesn't draw much attention, but it's on the way to everywhere important, and Saul has his eye on all the trade routes.

I let several other men ride past us before answering Abishai. "It won't be long."

Saul's rumors travel faster than we can. We've been riding in clutches, spreading out the women and children between us to appear like travelers whenever we came within a mile of a town.

I count the groups like sheep while the commanders of each company direct the families in their charge where to camp. The rough edges of the boulders provide natural shelters, with plenty of space underneath to pitch a tent.

Joab's wife, Deborah organizes the women near a pool carved out below us, and they start spreading dust-stained clothing out to be washed while their children play in the water, flinging their voices at the rocks without fear. They haven't laughed or yelled like this in weeks, sobered into silence during our travels.

My throat closes. The lies about my apparent treason have now been laid at the door of this company, these families. Because they follow me.

"The elders will be receiving plenty of news about us, and it won't be good," Abishai reminds me, his squinting eyes searching for his own wife in the group. "Saul will try to paint Keilah as an attempt by you to seize authority. We have to control the information as much as possible. What's your plan?"

I draw in a deep breath, the scents of every tree filling my lungs. "We have to let them see us. The men of Ziph. We need to let them see firsthand who we are and who we're not."

"And are we revealing your anointing?" Abishai ventures, watching for my reaction.

I have to think for a moment. "With great caution, only to those we can trust."

"And who would that be?" Joab rides up, overhearing.

Seven

My throat pinches. "We'll find out."

Joab points up toward the waterfall. "There's a natural cave up there in the cleft of the rock. It doesn't look like it's been used by any travelers recently. You're sleeping in there, with guards on the ridge outside. My men can handle anyone who gets close."

I nod, dismounting. "Send the commanders up there now. We need to work a plan."

Joab's mouth tightens. He knows what I mean. War maneuvers and long-term strategies are a battle for another day. Right now, we need food. Not just tonight, but tomorrow. And the next day.

I send half the men to hunt and forage under Asahel's direction. Joab's youngest brother still moves faster and with more stealth than any man I ever met in Saul's army, and he's become a skilled hunter. Hesitant to make fires, the women set about unpacking whatever bread we have left from Keilah. I hand over what's in my pack to Asa's young wife, trying to ignore the way my body aches with hunger.

My victory at Keilah has drawn more men to our cause—mostly disgruntled Judeans and a handful of Hittites. Already living on the fringes of Israel, the Hittite foreigners who fled to me were under such heavy debt that they feared losing their families to slavery. Their wives and children have swollen our ranks, and I'm feeling the strain of their support.

Hand over hand, I climb the slippery rocks to join my makeshift council in the upper cavern. Every step of the way, I'm shadowed by my nephews and the guards they've appointed to stay by my side.

I'm not used to being watched so closely, but the betrayal at Keilah upended all of us. Joab and Abishai haven't let me out of their sight since I recovered from being poisoned.

The rest of what happened in the wilderness outside the city was much harder to explain.

When I could speak without weeping, I tried to recount the vision I saw, but my men have convinced themselves it was only a hallucination. They're afraid to leave me alone, depriving themselves to keep me eating. But for a week, I've been taking only half of what I'm hungry for, sparing as much as I can.

"Provide for us, Adonai," I pray aloud, covering my face as my men gather. "You have always been a refuge for the needy, providing water in the desert and food in the wilderness for our ancestors. We place our trust in you," I finish, refusing to let my voice waver.

Seven

I push back my cloak and lean against the damp rock shelf behind me, studying the faces of my commanders. Keilah bound us closer. Their valiance in battle and their loyalty since then have convinced me we're much stronger standing together. But they've been used to a different kind of freedom. Their old roving ways kept them scattered across the countryside, desperate and hated. That can't continue.

I draw my sword and place it on the ground at my feet. The men circle around it.

"Things are different now," I remind them. "We are a formidable force, but we have become too many to move quickly like raiders. We need a way to sustain ourselves and the people who follow us without resorting to thievery." I look in Korah's direction.

His expression stays calm, but the heaviness in his eyes weighs on my shoulders.

"I took little pleasure in it," he mumbles. "After losing honor with the clans, it was the easiest way to get by. People expected it of us."

"We've tried to be accepted in the towns," his son Heman mutters. "It's not easy. Half the time, they'd drive us away with stones."

I stiffen my tone. "Maybe it's because you came down out of the hills like Amalekites and pounced on their flocks. To the average Israelite farmer trying to balance a living against Saul's taxes, our lifestyle isn't appreciated. We have to give them reason to trust us." Quickly. Before Saul's men teach them otherwise.

I stare down at my sword, another stolen Philistine blade. Adonai gave me favor in Saul's army, helping me rise through the ranks and prove myself when everyone thought I was just a crazy shepherd. God's power took me further than I could have gone on my own. I need nothing less if I'm to convince the people I'm not a brigand. That I follow Yahweh still.

But I won't repeat the previous winter. The wails of hungry families grabbed a desperate nerve inside me that I don't want touched again. I'm afraid of what it might do to us. We're not bandits. We won't play into the lies Saul's sending ahead of us.

Korah folds his arms. "Where do we start?"

I watch him, taking stock of what I know. He worked with iron ore before moving to the hills years ago. His skills will be valuable in a town with few blacksmiths. And he's not the only warrior here who can do more than fight.

I push off the wall. "Those of us with skills to sell can hire ourselves out in Ziph. We'll stay separate, not drawing attention.

Seven

We can divide our time between defense up here and work in the fields. Once we've proven ourselves with the shepherds and watchmen, we can become more open with the elders. Perhaps they'll help us when they see what we really are. But we can't expect support until we show them we can be trusted."

Insecurity teases my confidence, warring against the victories I've seen. Fighting for honor is nothing new for me.

Back in Bethlehem, the elders and townspeople hadn't known what to make of me, with my own father refusing to acknowledge the son of his maidservant. But years of faithful service in Abba's pastures had shown them different.

As soon as I'd mastered the slingshot, I'd joined other shepherds fighting off rogue bandits and packs of marauding wolves. I'd played my harp for the elder's son who'd been tormented by dreams after an Amalekite attack, and before long, my music became synonymous with my name. I found my place.

Now, I'll have to prove myself again, shepherding men.

"We can do it," one soldier murmurs, gripping my wrist. "Adonai is with you."

I touch his shoulder, grateful for the reminder.

Leaving half the men behind to guard the camps and mend the weapons we plundered in the Keilah battle, I ride into Ziph with several others, fanning out from them. We can't reveal our numbers yet. Joab's brother Abishai stays by my side. He'd fought to be here, preferring it over training the new recruits.

One is a Hittite youth named Uriah who'd escaped an abusive master. The boy was starving when he reached us, and his feet were bleeding from the journey from Socoh, but he hasn't shown much weakness. Since his arrival, he's followed me everywhere, embarrassing me with incessant questions until Joab agreed to take him under his wing and train him.

"How long do you think Uriah will last?" Abishai chortles. "A couple hours with my brother should send anyone running."

I smirk, remembering how harsh of a teacher my nephew can be. But he's fierce and experienced, an invaluable combination. Uriah can learn from no one better.

"Joab will be able to tell if there's a fighter in him. If the Hittite wants to be of use, he'll have to reckon with my general."

"This is a bad idea," Korah mutters, eyeing the Ziphite market with distrust. "I might be recognized. All of Israel knows me as a thief. And more."

Seven

I've always suspected that he's killed fellow Israelites, but the reality thrusts my stomach. "We're all starting again," I tell him, reaching over to grip his shoulder. "And when I'm king, we're going to restore everything your men stole. We're doing things differently now. If we honor Yahweh and trust Him for provision, He will honor us."

An enigmatic smile darts between the two men.

"You've never said *when* you're king," Abishai points out, appreciation splitting his hard face.

A flash of pleasure warms my neck, dousing the chill of shame. I've allowed far too much doubt to get under my skin, poisoning the promise Yahweh made to me. But if the God of Israel named me king, I have no business fearing otherwise.

Instinct darts through my fingers, an old spasm from when I twirl my sling. Every time I touch the weapon now, I remember Goliath and the awe that gripped Israel after he fell. I let myself smile at all the names Jonathan started calling me afterwards. *Where's your faith, Slingshot?*

If Yahweh shielded me from Goliath, He can help us now.

Abishai studies the men in finer robes clustered by the well. "Should we approach the elders?"

"I don't know," I pull the reins, considering.

Keilah still weighs heavily on me. I don't know how much word has spread or which story these people have heard. They're already glancing in our direction, and they had to notice that we came from the hills, not the gate.

"Follow me," I tell Abishai, riding up to the men. "Shalom," I greet them.

One elder squints up at me. "Shalom. Where have you traveled from?"

"From Keilah," I tell him, watching all the questions go back and forth in his eyes.

"The Philistines were just driven from Keilah," the oldest man says, stepping forward. "Reportedly by a band of soldiers who don't follow Saul."

I swallow. "It's true. They destroyed the enemy garrison outside the city."

The men study me, exchanging silent opinions. I'm a confusing sight with Jonathan's princely robe covering my dented armor vest and dusty clothing.

Seven

"Are you a Judean then?" the first man asks.

"I am," I try to lighten my tone. "My nephews and I are encamped in the mountains with our families. We are shepherds, and we've come to offer our services to the landowners here."

The elder's thick brows lift, betraying every one of the emotions trapped in his eyes. "You're armed heavily for shepherds," he comments, his gaze indicating my sword and battle axe.

"The roads aren't safe with so many fleeing Philistines around," Abishai answers over my silence.

"The mountains aren't much safer," the elder counters. "Our shepherds have their hands full with the remnant of Amalek. You'd be better off lodging in town."

I resist scanning the market beyond him for my other men. The layer of understanding unfolding on the elder's face stirs my defenses, but I refuse to touch my sword.

"With our families, we're too many to burden anyone in town. We'll be fine on the mountain," I assure him.

The man folds his arms. "How long do you intend to stay? Where are you headed?"

129

I hadn't anticipated so many questions. I lift my shoulders, feeling foolish. "Wherever Yahweh leads."

The elder glances at his brothers, then back at me. "You have no destination, do you? You're dodging Saul. We're not fools."

Alarm cuts through me, and I grip the reins. "We've done nothing against the king. We're just looking for work. Our families are hungry."

The man's face relaxes, the lines in his forehead smoothing out. Without unfolding his arms, he turns toward the market, nodding at a few well-dressed men with servants.

"Many of our brothers own fields in Carmel. They're always in need of more laborers." He studies me again. "I would suggest approaching them without the weapons."

I force a smile, patting my sword. "I'll gladly defend any man's sheep the same way I defend my…family," I finish weakly, realizing I have none. My parents and brothers are in Moab. Michal's been taken from me. The men in the mountains are all I have.

The elders step back to let us pass, and I release the breath that's stuck in my chest. Korah's right. This won't be easy. With

Seven

the disgusted way the nobles are looking at us, we might as well be the flea-ridden beggars on the side of the road.

I pause by the well, unsure if I should venture to draw water. Perhaps we should have approached the shepherds outside of town first.

"Would you like a drink?" A young woman pulls a dripping bucket from the well and tilts the contents into her jar. She fills a clay cup and holds it up to me.

"Thank you," I smile, grateful for the momentary refuge of a friendly face.

The woman looks about my age, but she's much smaller, with more delicate features than Michal. After I'm finished, she fills the cup again for Abishai, but once he's had a drink, her questions begin. "Are you soldiers?"

"Yes," I answer simply, but I'm no longer at ease. I told the elders we were shepherds.

Unwelcome stares creep over my skin. Under the shade of a nearby animal stall, a couple ragged men are slumped together on the street, obviously drunk. A few broken clay bottles litter the ground around a man with a bruised face. He laughs shortly, his glazed eyes snapping at me.

"He's a musician," he slurs at the girl, gesturing at the side of my mule with his wineskin. He heaves another laugh before I remember my harp. It goes everywhere with me.

Tossing the wineskin aside, the man slumps onto his hands and knees, his manner darkening. "Haven't you seen beggars before, fool? Sing us a song!"

His companions join in, ribbing me. In the haze of mockery, I don't notice the woman's face changing.

"He sings for the king," she says distinctly, staring through me. "Isn't that right? You're…you're the giant-killer."

The beggars hear her, and the drunkard's eyes turn narrow, searching me. "David," he drags out my name like a curse. He sits forward, his broken teeth flashing a grotesque smile. "Saul's bastard son-in-law. The traitor."

Ice slides into my veins while my mind races, trying to decide where I've seen him before. But what does it matter? Saul and his generals have cast out plenty of servants in my time. Some of them could be from Ziph.

The woman steps back, holding her jar closer. A few men in the streets turn to look at us as the beggars start flinging handfuls of dust, sharpened with taunts.

"Where's your God now?"

"You think you can hide from Saul here? Go back to the Philistines, worthless shepherd!"

When the drunkard throws his bottle in my direction, the girl screams, "Stop it!"

"It's all right." On impulse, I touch her arm, and the drunkard sneers at me.

"Why don't you kiss her? Saul's daughter isn't here to stop you."

I jerk my mule around, but Abishai grabs its halter. "Don't—"

The door of a nearby house opens, and sandals slap the stone steps before a finely dressed man yells into the street. "What do you think you're doing?" He waves an angry hand at the beggars. "You think you can dishonor my daughter right in front of my house? Get out of here, or I'll call my guard!"

Scowling, the beggars draw back against the market stall, but not before the first man spits in the dust in my direction.

The nobleman's eyes follow the gesture, and he beckons at me. "Come in here, boy. You too, Ahinoam," he tells the young woman. She ducks her head and slips inside behind him.

I leave my mule with Abishai at the door and follow the man through a stone hallway into an inner room. It's not as spacious as Saul's chambers, but it's likely one of the biggest homes in the area. He points at a bench near the fire in the corner, but I stay standing.

"Are you hurt?" he asks, peering at me.

Only inside. My heart is a stone in my chest. But I shake my head. "I've dealt with worse things than stones," I mumble, not trusting my full voice yet.

It's been a while since I've been called a bastard, but it's never stopped hurting. Hearing people talk about my marriage like it's been nullified makes me crazy to know what Saul has done with Michal.

The nobleman looks toward the window, gentle humor surfacing. "For the warrior who's killed tens of thousands, you really hesitate to fight."

So, it's obvious who I am. I look down, folding my arms over the ache. "I knew what I was defending then."

"Not now?"

"I don't know." Part of me worries I might be what they call me. I can bear the hatred of the Philistines, but how can I fight against lies the king has sown himself? I face the man, freshly agitated. "We don't want to cause you any trouble. We're only here to find work and lay low for a while."

The man's forehead lifts. "We? So, it's true, then? The resistance follows you?"

I stiffen, wounded pride unleashing what I hadn't planned to say. "They're mighty men of valor who have believed lies about themselves. They've been rejected by their brothers, but once they learn honor, they will be the greatest force Israel has ever seen."

I harden my jaw against the tremors building from my spirit like a bubbling brook. Why do I believe so strongly about these men? I never intended to join them, but once again, I'm filled with gratitude. Yahweh isn't making me wander this path alone. Their strength fuels mine.

Understanding softens the nobleman's face. "We heard what you did in Keilah. We weren't sure if it was just rumors."

I shake my head again, lowering myself onto the bench. "It's true. We saved Keilah from the Philistines, but the men of the city betrayed us to Saul. We had to leave."

The man lets me listen to the crackle of the fire for a few breaths before continuing. "We've also heard you are anointed, as Saul was. Is it true you carry Yahweh's power and blessing with you the way he used to?" He's standing in front of me, waiting.

My face flames, and I pause, considering my words. I have to set the record straight. Rumors already abound.

"I do not seek the throne, only the inheritance Yahweh has chosen for me. I will not strike Saul. We do not intend to march against Gibeah. Not now, not ever. Right now, we just need provision for our families."

The man nods as if he expected my answer. "What are your skills, besides fighting?"

I clear my throat. "Several of my men worked a trade before leaving their towns. They're carpenters, weavers, a few ironsmiths."

I see his eyes light up with interest. Iron work is still a rare skill in Israel.

"I was trained as a shepherd," I continue. "My men and I can be a wall around your city, holding back the Amalekites."

The man smiles. "My city is Jezreel. My estate isn't far from Gilboa in the north. This is my son-in-law's house. My daughter just had a son, so we've come to see the child. I have

Seven

five daughters," he explains, smirking. "And their marriages have connected me with several Judean elders. I can tell them you need assistance. We can do it without Saul knowing, make him think it's for our shepherds on the mountains."

I stare at him. "You're Judean?"

His face stiffens, and I wonder how I missed the lionlike pride all over him. "Purchasing land nearer the king doesn't make me any less a son of Judah. We take care of our own."

Gratitude clouds my vision. I start to stand, but he pushes me back down. "Stay for a moment. We'll wait until the street is clear."

He steps out through the door, looking up and down the street, and after a few minutes, I hear him speaking to Abishai.

Another step scuffs the floor, and I look up to see Ahinoam standing in the doorway with a platter of bread in her hands. She blushes, moving into the room without taking her eyes off me. It's been a while since a woman watched me this closely. But Michal was different. Her intentions were obvious. When I was home in Gibeah, her smile flashed around every corner, beckoning me.

My beautiful Sarrah. As much as I hated to leave her behind, she wouldn't have come willingly. What do I have for her now?

Ahinoam places the food down on a low table. "Will you eat something, my lord?"

"I'm just David," I say softly, getting up to reach for the bread. "You don't need to serve me."

Ahinoam's eyes widen, traveling down my arm. "Is that from the battle with Goliath?"

I glance down, startled. It's been years since anyone's been unfamiliar enough to notice my old scars. "No. I killed a lion when I used to watch my father's sheep. Goliath didn't touch me."

Everything changed after the battle with the giant. Girls all over Gibeah found excuses to talk to me in the street, dancing around me during celebrations. But after I knew Michal loved me, I hardly saw any of them.

Ahinoam laces her fingers together, inquisitive. "I heard one of Saul's soldiers got an arrow wound in his shoulder, and he touches it before battle."

"That's Jonathan," I inform her, my chest tightening. I still carry the threatening message I'd retrieved from the arrow that

Seven

struck the prince. I'd always imagined the Philistine king would come after me before Saul ever would. But again, I was wrong.

Ahinoam waits, pensive. She breathes twice before asking, "Where is the Sarrah? The daughter of Saul whom you married."

"She stayed in Gibeah," I answer, hoping the hardness in my tone will fill in what I can't explain. She hates me like her father does. Just another tool Saul used to humiliate me.

Ahinoam is silent for a few painful seconds. I'm not sure why she's still standing there. She reaches behind her neck and unfastens a long golden chain, revealing a pierced gold piece hidden by the neckline of her dress. She lets it hang in front of me a moment. "Here."

I smirk, shaking my head. Does she think I need charity? "No."

Gently taking my wrist, she drops the coin into my hand, coiling the chain on top before closing my fingers around it. A hint of sincerity deepens her tone. "My father might have had to fight Goliath if you hadn't. He was in Saul's forces then, before he was injured. Allow me to share what I will."

I let myself look at it, then at her, gratitude and awkwardness fighting for mastery in my throat. I'm about to thank her when her father steps through the doorway again. I shoot to my feet, backing away. "I should go."

Her father waves his hand, smiling tolerantly as Ahinoam leaves the room. "She's my youngest, the only one not married," he says, eyeing me, and my cheeks burst into flames again.

What is wrong with the fathers in Judah? None of them wanted me when I was a shepherd. Now, I'm Saul's cast-off champion, and they're all ready for me to abandon my wife.

I adjust my cloak, forcing my eyes up. "God bless you for your kindness, my lord. Your daughter gave me this." Showing him the gold piece, I place it back on the bench.

He picks it up and weighs it in his hand, watching me. "Your nephew told me who you are. What you've been anointed to do. And yet you wait for Yahweh, refusing to take anything by force."

He pauses, filling the room with his thoughts before continuing. "The Ziphite elders have been losing herds to wandering mountain lions. The Amalekites have driven the predators out into the hill pastures around Hachilah. If you'll bring some of your men to help them, I will make sure you get your wages."

Seven

"Thank you." I stretch out my hand to clasp his, breathing in hope for the first time today.

I step around him to the door, and he follows me through it, waiting on the outer steps. When he raises a hand, I see the gold piece clasped in his fingers.

"May Yahweh go with you," he says. "And when God has done for you all that He promised, remember us."

EIGHT

Jonathan

I've cleared the outer fields before anyone else is awake, following the streambed southeast until Gibeah's countryside gives way to wilderness. I'm riding Ezra's mule, and I've hidden every princely ornament out of sight so I won't be recognized from a distance. Still, I keep to the thicket, avoiding the towns. All of Benjamin knows me.

Once I have cover, the forest air settles me, concealing my progress into the southern mountains. I slow my pace, realizing how long it's been since I've ridden anywhere without an army behind me and armorbearers watching my every move. And I haven't left the city without the king's orders since after the Amalek battle. The one and only time I ever tried to run away.

Terrified and heartsick over my father's continual explosions of temper, I'd fled without a clear plan, only to be trapped by Philistine scouts. But Yahweh sent Abner after me, to save my life. The pine-scented solitude beckons into the trees, reminding me.

I breathe it in, grateful to have a clear heading. My father is taking the long way to Ziph, circling southwest around Adullam and Keilah. Meanwhile, I'm riding directly south through the wilds, where David will actually be. I smile, more than a little encouraged. I didn't even have to think it through. Yahweh's leading is apparent, readily available wherever I need it.

Alarm from my dream creeps after me in the thicket, trying to guide my movements, but I restrain myself, forcing a more relaxed pace. Yahweh brought me out here, but He didn't say I had to run. I twist the reins, remembering Abner in the early days of David's training, accusing me of trying to guard my little brother. But even then, I didn't need to. He always had a much better Shield.

My eyes sting. David's my brother, but I don't need to protect him. Not anymore. My father will never find him. He just needs reminding. Encouragement.

Twenty miles deeper into Judah's territory, I'm not surprised to find a collection of shepherds encamped in a clearing up ahead. Their sheep chatter nervously from within a makeshift sheepfold while the men prepare a small fire in front of it. Most of the shepherds are old, and judging by their weathered clothes and leathery skin, they've lived outside most of their lives.

Eight

There's a good chance they've never seen me up close. Still, I wrap Ezra's cloak tighter around my face and tuck my weapons behind a rock before I approach them.

The youngest shepherd smirks over his shoulder. "You can come closer. My father saw you coming."

Of course. They know the sounds of the forest. No one could sneak up on David either when he tended his father's flocks. I greet them, carefully matching their accent.

"Heading into Ziph?" The oldest man squints at me through the fire.

"I'm traveling to meet my brother there." I almost smile. There's no need to lie.

"Where are you from?" is the next question.

"I'm a servant in Gibeah," I say simply, and the men fall silent, content.

I retrieve my things from the mule and divide the food I've brought among the shepherds, casually examining my surroundings. I have to be in the fringes of Horesh. The reports put David in Ziph, near Jeshimon. But he wouldn't hide in the city after what happened with Keilah. He'll be in the forest in some sort of wilderness stronghold. Hachilah is the highest peak in the area. It should be easy to find.

Halfway through the evening, I check with the shepherds and they point me in the right direction. Their conversation shouldn't mean much, but I've learned how to listen between men's words. They pasture animals for rich men in town, and someone has been helping them. Men of the hills. Men of war. There's more of them every day. It's not hard to guess who's leading them.

I say very little, absorbing all I can, and the next day, I meet more laborers ten more miles into Horesh. It isn't long before one of them accidentally mentions David. Not everyone knows who he is, so I'm careful not to repeat anything. He's kept to the outskirts, rarely seen directly, but his presence has been felt, his armies shielding the town from the lions and raiders still plaguing the mountain roads.

"First he slew thousands, now he commands them," one old shepherd mutters, leaving me wondering how much has changed in almost two years.

David is a shepherd once again, but a different kind now. He can never fully go back to what he was. Yahweh's mantle cannot be hidden, and now everyone is starting to see it.

Eight

Confident that I can search him out, I leave the foothills behind and enter the wilderness. Riding upwards along a trampled path, I finally dismount to guide the mule as the climb steepens. Boulders jut out of the landscape, and the tangle of forest leaves few clear paths. The wind breathes loudly in the trees, making itself heard over my thoughts. But within a few more steps, a different feeling crowds closer.

I sense the blade at my neck an instant sooner than it appears. I pause only a moment, then straighten up, and shove my hood back.

The surprise on Joab's face instantly darkens. "What are you doing here, son of Saul?" he demands, tightening his stance.

I speak without moving. "I've come as David's brother."

Joab advances, resentment leaping to his eyes. "Don't speak to me of brotherhood! David's brothers are *here*, fighting to protect his life from people like you."

"And I've been fighting back in Gibeah for the same end." I edge away from the blade, resisting every urge to reach for my own. The calm spreading through me is proof enough that I won't die. Not here.

I rush to explain. "Joab, I would not have come if God hadn't sent me. How else would I have found you when my—when the king has been searching for months?"

"He won't find him." Joab nearly spits the words. "David is chosen of Yahweh. He will rule."

"I know that. And he trusts me."

"I didn't say he was smart." Joab's smile shows the edge of his teeth. I can feel his rage waiting to slide the weapon across my throat.

"Here." Unbuckling my sword, I place it on the ground next to my bow and lower myself to one knee. "I just want to speak to him. Please."

Joab angles his head, conflict evident in his face. "Abishai! Asahel!" He calls toward the trees, and his two younger brothers materialize so quickly and silently that I wonder how many more are concealed all around us.

"Take the weapons," he orders them. Joab advances toward me, keeping his sword aimed. "Get up."

Now there are three weapons trained in my direction.

Eight

Joab whistles to the trees, and more men emerge, their movements equally silent and precise. "Abishai, take half of the Thirty and go on ahead. I'll follow behind you."

The men move into position until I'm completely surrounded. They don't need to speak. I can feel their hostility turning the air sharp around me. I could take several of them at once, but not this many. Not without my weapons.

The men Joab called "the Thirty" tighten around me, and Joab shoves me from behind. My stomach tightens. I hadn't considered walking into David's camp as the son of Saul. But as we proceed up the ridge, I can see Joab's leading me around to a secluded spot, more men dropping back the farther we climb.

I tense, every instinct telling me I'm about to die. As much as I hate to admit it, Joab and I are fairly matched, but then there's his brothers and the rest of this band. I steal a glance at some of them, carrying old Philistine weapons and dressed in mismatched armor. Where did they all come from?

Once my ears catch the sound of rushing water, my heart picks up speed. Everything around us reminds me of my dream. The rocks are huge now, cutting the canopy overhead. The collection of them appears haphazard, as though a mountain broke into pieces over the hills. A sweep of water tumbles over the ridge just beyond, creating a narrow enclosure. We must be close because Joab stops and turns to me.

"I don't know why you're here, but if he won't see you, I'll drive you away myself."

I fold my fists at my sides, refusing to fiddle with a sword I don't have. "I just want to speak to him, Joab."

"To make sure he's well? So you can ease your conscience?" Bitterness stains Abishai's comment.

Joab's face spreads into a mirthless smile. "If you're looking for Saul's shepherd warrior, you're wasting your time. The king has crushed him into the dust, and we have to make do with what's left."

"Commander?" A much younger voice interrupts from a rock ledge just above us, and a Hittite steps around the boulders, his sword drawn. His huge dark eyes take immediate note of my lack of weapons and then dart over to Joab, who shrugs.

"He's unarmed, Uriah. I brought him here."

The boy's sword doesn't move. His stance is taut and experienced for someone who can't be older than sixteen. "You're Saul's son," he says in my direction.

Eight

Everyone here must know me that way. "Yes. Whose son are you?"

"He's dead." Without blinking an eye, he speaks past me. "He wanted to be alone, Joab."

"I know that!" Joab barks.

Abruptly, every soldier tightens his guard.

"Uriah, what's…?" David emerges from behind the rocks, his words breaking off. His hand on the boulder, he inhales once, his eyes locking onto me. "Joab, what is this?"

Joab gestures at me, his expression twisting. "We found him at the perimeter, wandering around at the base of the hill. If I hadn't brought him here, he would have started questioning in the town. He insisted—"

"Stand down," David commands, and the men fold away as he approaches. "That means lower your sword, Uriah." David's eyes hold mine, his voice strained. "Joab, you can go."

"David—" Abishai retorts.

"That's an order!" David cuts him off. "You too, Uriah."

The youth starts to protest, but Joab looks weary with experience. "Come on. We talked about this. If he wants to risk his life, that's his prerogative. He won't lose to a son of Saul."

They slowly descend the rocks and disappear into the thicket, probably still watching from a short distance. Once we're alone, David exhales tightly, a muscle jerking in his jaw. "Why did you come here?"

I can't decide if he's pleased or not. Too many other emotions war in his face. But I've waited long enough. I cross the space between us and embrace him. Something shudders in his chest, and I hold him tighter, memories crashing over me.

"Yahweh," I say against his ear.

"You mean, He sent you?" David asks.

"It feels like it. I had a dream about you…"

I pull back to study him. He doesn't look wounded. But he's changed. Layered sunburn gives his skin a tight, dark look, and constant sunlight has pulled more redness into the brown of his hair. Hard-bitten strength has clawed its way through his younger confidence. But his ribs are too sharp under my hands. His clothes look like he's slept in them a dozen times. And the heaviness in his face grieves me.

Eight

"Do the men of Ziph know you're here?" David scans the hills, looking hunted.

"No one does," I promise him. "My father is searching on the other side of the mountains, following some pointless lead that I may or may not have presented to him." I allow myself a slight smirk. But Saul can't be far off.

I look around, my gaze pulled to the spray of water smearing the hill's jagged edges like anointing oil. "It's another world up here. Hard to get to. Plenty of water."

To hide the sounds of the camp, no doubt. I squint at the dark, rocky space where David had been concealed. "What were you doing in there?"

An explanation struggles on David's face for a moment, but something else wrestles it aside. Giving up, he pushes a crumpled shred of parchment into my hand, and I recognize the seal of the Moabite king from Mizpeh. I catch the names of Jesse and Atarah, and the rest of the words dig into me.

David watches the waterfall. "They're gone. In their sleep, within a week of each other." He arches his back, folding his arms within one another. "The king of Moab uncovered a plot to kill them. Apparently, his decision to shelter them wasn't approved by everyone. But by the time the threat was uncovered, they'd already…"

His fingers tighten around his elbows. All the skin is scraped off his knuckles. "I knew they wouldn't last long," he mumbles. "They were very old."

Aching at the news, I watch the sorrow work its way through him. "I'm sorry."

When I touch his shoulder, he tenses, covering my hand with his own. A hundred different sentences begin on his lips before he chooses one.

"It's good to see you, brother." His face is firmly set, but his eyes are swimming.

"It's been too long." I pull a hearty smile through the weary sadness I feel. Losing David was like losing family, and there was no escaping the pain for either one of us. "At my wedding, I kept expecting to see you standing there beside Ezra."

David's brows lift. "Saul finally found a woman who can put up with you?"

"You could say that." I chuckle, glad he still has some humor in him.

"And?" David probes.

"Let's just say she's the one bright light in all the darkness," I smile, allowing myself to remember the moment when I realized she actually loved me.

"Good," David says. "You deserve that."

I can feel the invisible gate that imprisons him rattling, trying to unlock. But he can't seem to decide if he wants it to. He swallows hard, looking past me up at the water, anywhere but my eyes. He rubs the back of his neck.

"How is…?" He leaves off her name, his voice turning shaky.

I hesitate, struggling to force a calm expression through the pain in my face. I haven't decided how to talk about Michal yet. The blue stone is tucked away in my quiver, but there's no way I can give it to him now.

"She's…different," I say awkwardly. "I miss her."

I can't tell him the rest. As far as I can tell, my father's hatred has worked through her like an evil sickness. And my sister is gone.

David stands there and takes it, his jaw tight. "*I'm* different. I doubt she'd be able to stand the sight of me."

"My lord—" Joab calls out from below us, pointing my sword down the hill to the east. "Korah has returned."

David sighs quietly, stepping past me.

"Korah?" A dozen rumors dart through my mind. "The rogue warrior? The one everyone says has the face of a lion?"

David smirks. "Yes. That Korah. Not everyone knows he's with me now, so his sons keep a wider perimeter and spy out Saul's movements to see when he's getting close. Follow us back."

David walks ahead with several guards, but Joab hangs back, clearly aware of what we were saying long before he showed himself. He studies me, his arms folded tight.

"She's left him, hasn't she?" he demands. "The Sarrah he risked his life for. Saul's persuaded her to abandon the future king of Israel."

I lift my chin, hating the truth. Joab won't be interested in my efforts to change Michal's mind. Or the fact that it's cost me my sister.

Joab grinds his teeth. "Are you going to tell him, or should I? In just about every territory we've passed through, there are dozens of women willing to follow him. The sooner he can forget the past, the better."

Eight

The reality eats at me. As much as I hate seeing Michal with someone else, I'm not ready to think of David taking other wives. "Leave it for now. He has enough on him."

Joab's face hardens. "What did I tell you?"

As soon as he turns his back to me, I shrug my quiver off my shoulder and retrieve the blue stone. I'm not carrying it for Michal any longer. But I'm not going to shove it in my friend's face either. Coiling the chain around it, I leave it on a rock at my feet, half-hoping he won't find it. But it's David. He notices everything.

My heart drags as I follow the guards down the ridge and push deeper into the forest. But once we enter David's camp, my shock crowds out everything else.

For years, the resistance was just a handful of disgruntled rogues, a few thieves, some runaway slaves. But this camp is swollen with people. There has to be hundreds of men sharpening weapons and women polishing dented armor or stretching out threadbare clothes. A few children scamper between carefully banked fires, covered to prevent smoke from riding the wind.

I highly doubt all of these people are tax evaders. When I venture to ask David, he lowers his voice.

"Some were criminals. More of them are delinquents. No more land or livestock. Nothing to sustain them back home. Some of the children were infants when their parents brought them out here. They've known nothing but the wilderness."

I know I'm gaping, but I can't help it. "They're so many."

"Try feeding all of them," David mumbles.

At the camp's edge, a handful of little boys run toward us, shouting happily, and Uriah sheds three years, jogging ahead to meet the children. He catches one up under his arm and swings another onto his shoulder. They're all talking at once, comparing feats of strength and trying to unbuckle his sword.

Uriah bends down to talk to a boy with a sling. "Getting better with that?"

"I almost hit Abba today." The boy's response is both proud and sheepish. "But David couldn't shoot very well when he was my age."

His father limps up from behind and takes the boy's shoulders, his eyes never leaving David. "It's all he talks about, killing giants. I keep telling him to practice and wait for the chance to honor his king."

Eight

I can't tell who he's talking to, but I avert my gaze, hoping he won't recognize me. I don't recall his name, but I remember my father blaming him for an oversight in his fields. An oversight that left the laborer partially crippled, unable to work. This ragged outlaw represents any one of the dozens who have watched Saul take their fields bit by bit until there was nothing left.

I half-turn away, battling sorrow over what my father failed to cherish. But admiration wins out, watching the way the outlaw looks at David.

In less than two years, my friend has captured the heart of the nation, even more so than when he was lauded from afar. The most desperate people in Israel know he can be trusted to live and die beside them.

When the men move away, I lean over to David. "They admire you."

"Of course they admire me. Every lowlife in Israel admires me," David's response bites, but a moment later, a sigh rattles his chest. "Don't listen to him."

His voice dissolves into a strange shudder, and he turns his face to his shoulder, nearly bending over to try to repress it. An older man approaches from one of the fires and hands David a cup, which he drains quickly in between coughs. The scent of hot herbs drifts toward me.

I watch in silence, concern plucking my nerves. When I'd sent my father in a circle to Jeshimon, I hadn't pictured women and children hiding out on the other side of the ridge. No doubt, they're accustomed to packing up in a hurry, but this is the largest company I've ever seen outside of Gibeah, and they're all extremely vulnerable.

As soon as I have David's attention again, I turn my back to the camp, my voice lowered. "You shouldn't stay here. If my father went to Jeshimon, he's only a few miles north."

"I know. But we won't know for sure until Korah's sons return." David sounds older than his years.

Again, a flash of bitterness rushes through me at what we're being forced to endure—both of us. Saul will force David to another place, then return home raging that he wasn't able to trap him. And the pattern will continue, with me in the middle, watching the man my father used to be disappear with each day.

I could stay. Have Ezra bring my wife under cover of darkness. Leave everything behind. David would welcome me without hesitation. But as quickly as the thought arrives, it falls

Eight

flat. God sent me to help David, not betray Saul. But how long will this go on? Will I have to see my father die before David can rule? I have no right to beg otherwise, but I do anyway, my eyes briefly closed. *Please, Adonai. Not my Abba.*

His fist against a tent post, David drops his tone so only I can hear it. "They all think it's going to be over soon. They think I'll confront Saul and end our wandering. They have no idea how long it could be, what I'm asking them to endure. I have no idea. And yet I've allowed them to be here. I've led them to believe I can be..." He shakes his head, giving up. "What am I doing, Jonathan?"

My faith leaps up in answer, reminding me what I came here to do. "You're learning to lean on the One who anointed you."

David doesn't lift his head. "It's a battle. Every day. Just to survive, earn our bread. Hope Saul doesn't..."

"My father will never find you," I interrupt him with the conviction I'd felt in my dream.

David doesn't look convinced. "He's been so close..."

"No. Listen to me." I walk around in front of him. "He will not find you! The Lord is not a man that He should lie. You will be king of Israel. My father knows this."

David stares at me, unblinking. "And what about you?"

I shrug. "What about me? I'll be at your side, helping you lose some of the habits you've picked up out here."

David gives me the baffled look he used to, then we both laugh as he realizes I'm serious. How I've missed this.

"How can you have such faith in me?" David wonders aloud. Beneath his laugh, there's something shaky, a deep desire to know.

I refuse to take my eyes off him, even feeling the stares of others. "I have faith in the One who's with you. The Lord does not abandon His anointed. I've seen what happens when a man turns from God, but I've seen a different spirit on you. Yahweh isn't with Saul anymore, David. He's here in these caves with you."

David's eyes flush with tears, which he barely covers with a wry smile. "But you won't stay with me until I wear a crown?"

I smirk back and grip his shoulder, fighting how much I want to remain here.

"You don't need me, David. But God willing, one day, I'll be at your side, whether you like it or not."

NINE

David

Jonathan stays with me while I gather my commanders in the hillside cave for council. Every night, my brothers and nephews meet with the chiefs of the Thirty to address concerns and talk through the next week's survival.

We've been able to avoid having to plan an escape for several months, finally settling into a steady rhythm of hunting in the hills, selling our skills in Ziph, and guarding the town's unprotected edges from predators and scavengers.

But several of the men worry that we've revealed too much, and once Saul closes in, he'll find plenty in the town ready to betray us. And I should have known they wouldn't ignore the sight of Jonathan standing at my side.

The first few who enter the cave give an excellent impression of men turned to stone.

"My lord, what is this?" Eliam's tone betrays more disapproval than he's ever voiced in my presence. "Do you expect us to reveal anything in front of the son of Saul?"

As reasonable as his concern is, I'm instantly offended, readying every defense for battle. I never make it there, though. Jonathan touches my shoulder, then steps outside and melts out of sight before I can get a word past my throat.

"The Hassar is my brother and my guest," I finally manage, my chest still heaving. "You will all treat him as you would treat me."

I'm still shocked that he's here. However my men choose to see it, he's risking his life. And with a wife and child back in Gibeah. I've heard the rumors about the son his wife has given him. Though Saul doesn't seem very distracted by his new grandson, he has to be planning for him to rule after Jonathan.

I have mixed feelings at best. Seeing Jonathan by the waterfall was like being handed a gift from Adonai Himself. A reminder that I'm not alone. Darkness has been trying to swallow me for months, and the news of my parents' death pushed me deeper into its arms. My grief wakes me up in the night, and only Yahweh's closeness has kept me from drowning in it.

Nine

Having Jonathan here has steadied the tumult inside me. But it's also awakened a hundred other things I would rather not think about. Things I've been trying to forget. Now they're all in the way, pushing into the forefront while my men try to hold my attention. Weak firelight pulls at the conflict in their faces.

"The Ziphites suspect nothing," Ahithophel argues. But Eliam talks over him.

"You haven't been down there, Abba. In order to earn enough provisions, we've had to reveal too many of our numbers, and they'd be foolish not to keep track. They know about Keilah. They'll find out it was us."

"What do they have to fear from a handful of day laborers and their women?" Ahithophel demands. "Doesn't the Law command the wealthy to provide for those in need?"

Abishai's arm muscles tense around his sword. He and Joab rarely let their weapons go. "Their fear has nothing to do with us," my nephew explains. "Saul has destroyed towns before, with much less provocation than he has now."

Several men lower their eyes. Everyone remembers Nob. People hesitate to speak of it, but the massacre has changed how they see Saul. It becomes clearer the farther we wander.

Folding my fingers over my sword to steady my nerves, I glance at the door. If I were Jonathan, I wouldn't be able to resist listening. Part of me wants to urge him to get away from here. The rest of me is terrified to see him leave.

"We're not criminals. We are men of Israel. With families." Ahithophel folds his arms, but Abishai shoves off the cave wall, confronting him.

"It should be evident to you by now that Saul doesn't care. It only takes one of those half-dozen shepherds we've worked with to hint to the elders that we're a resistance army. Saul will run with any information they have."

Eliam shakes his head, hiding emotion. "It destroys me to think of my daughters growing up under the cloud of war, running for their lives."

"Calm yourself, Eliam." Joab appears in the doorway with Korah's oldest son. "You all took the same risk, you and your families, when you came to join David. But the God who anointed him will protect those who follow him. If you don't believe that, feel free to go."

"No one's going anywhere." I turn to Joab, disgusted. His loyalty is the mainstay of my army, but occasionally his fierceness goes too far. No amount of insubordination could make me turn away a man with three young daughters. I turn my attention to Heman. "You have news from the other side of the mountain?"

Korah's son nods once, his breathing tight and labored from the hike. "It's not good. Saul has been received by the men of Jeshimon with a full contingent of warriors."

I resist the thrust of anger in my chest. He could still miss us. We could remain concealed if the men of Ziph don't betray us. But I know how it feels to have honor be your only protection against Saul. And the people of Ziph don't have their own armory. With little else to guard them, I doubt their word will hold them for long.

"How long do we have?" I ask Heman.

He edges his hands upwards on his spear. "A few more days at least. There's no guarantee that Saul will stay. He's dealing with conflicting reports concerning Philistine raids outside Gibeah."

"You'd think real enemies at his own gates would keep him home. At least to protect his new grandson." Eliam glares. "Instead, he comes after us."

"We don't know that," I insist, suddenly too exhausted to argue further.

This persistent cough is wearing on me, battling with my strength every day it lingers. I can feel its sharp edge sliding against my chest, prodding its way up my throat again. I drop my tone, holding it back. "We will wait until the others return."

Korah's other sons have been scattered across the mountain pass, and once they come back with their reports, we'll know for certain if we stay or if we flee.

I leave the cave, resenting how my mind is jumping ahead, anticipating an organized escape. In the battles I fought for Saul, I had varying orders and strategies. Now, there's only one. Run. Survive. Repeat.

Maybe the men are right, and I'll have to face him. If he gets too close, I might not have a choice. The thought tightens my stomach. I can't kill Saul, but I'd confront him any number of times before letting him touch anyone here. Which leaves me at an impasse. It's why I'd rather run than fight.

Jonathan's waiting just up the hill, leaning against a tree, watching the camp. I fold my arms, hiding my discomfort.

It's troubling to see my life here through his eyes. I'm the one anointed king in Saul's place. In *his* place. And look at me. Leading a bickering band of malcontents from cave to cave, making them live on the fringes of Israel because I won't take what's mine by force.

"I don't want to cause you any trouble." Jonathan startles my train of thought.

"You won't. They're always like that."

Of course, he's thinking of anyone but himself. I still can't decide why he came here. I hate standing several feet away from him as though we're strangers. As though I can't get to the other side where I used to be his little brother.

Jonathan pushes off the tree and crosses the distance, searching my eyes. "Are you in danger?"

Heavy question. I arch my shoulders to shrug it off, scanning the distant ridgeline. "Not today."

* * * * *

I can't get through the evening meal fast enough. Everyone is completely unnerved by Jonathan's presence, especially as more people find out who he is. Uriah lurks with my other guards, refusing to leave my shoulder while the men's grumblings get louder. Jonathan ignores their contempt, but I can't. Few of them understand what he means to me. They only see the son of Saul.

When it's clear that the prince is staying the night, Joab glares at me and doubles the guards outside the upper cleft of rock where I sleep.

"You have a formidable force to guard you." Lounging up against the cave wall, Jonathan seems far too relaxed for where he is. "Did they all swear to you?"

"Didn't even hesitate." The weight on me intensifies just mentioning it. The mighty men swore to me hoping I would be their king and free Israel from Saul's grip. Which I haven't. I reach back into the darkness, searching for sheepskins to cushion the cave floor.

Jonathan nods toward the door. "Where did the Hittite come from?"

"Uriah?" I look up. "He's all that's left of his family. He was already in servitude for his father's debts, and once his mother died, he just walked away into the wilderness. Joined us five months ago."

"Does he remind you of anyone?"

"No, not really." I unbuckle my vest, pretending not to see the playful slant of Jonathan's smile.

Nine

I know what he's saying. Uriah swore allegiance to me without flinching, as if he hadn't even heard the evil rumors Saul has been feeding anyone who will listen. The boy hasn't left Joab's side since, staying close enough to learn my movements and anticipate my needs. Sometimes Uriah's humble courage makes me catch my breath. Was I ever that bold?

I'm no longer so trusting. No longer blindly willing to spend my energy on someone who will just betray me. "I've changed," I whisper, hating the truth of it.

"Not as much as you think." Jonathan's presence reaches out to me across the cave, opening the ache for my father that's been throbbing like a wound for two days. He crouches next to me, keeping his tone light. "Just wait until you're about to welcome a son of your own. You will see how fast your youth will return."

The thought should be welcome, but instead it stings. I'll need a wife first, and that's another wound I'd rather leave closed. Though Joab tries every day to open it.

I exhale slowly, try to bury the pain before looking up. No one will say it, but I know Michal isn't coming back to me. Not willingly. And I don't want to talk about it. I know Jonathan doesn't either. He had to be the one who left the blue stone on the rock outside my cave.

Aloud, I say, "What's his name? Your son."

"Mephibosheth. We call him Mephi."

I stare at Jonathan, catching something different in his face. His smile is bolder, lacking the restraint it used to have. Even with the chaos of recent years, his wife and son have changed him, softened him. The knowledge warms and chills me at the same time.

"And your wife is pregnant again?" I ask him.

Jonathan nods, a quiet awe filling his face. He nudges my arm. "One day, our sons might end up playing together in the very halls where you used to sing to my father."

I almost don't want to imagine it. Is there really a time of peace and stability coming again? I want to believe it, but the hope is always shadowed by the specter of the present. And no one has seen my deepest fear, the one I keep carefully buried.

What if I misunderstood? What if Samuel was wrong? If I'm leading all these people to ruin, it would be better for Saul to kill me.

I shouldn't have thought it. Jonathan lifts his chin, torchlight moving across his face.

Nine

"I told you, my father will not find you." He places a firm hand on my knee, bending to see into my eyes. "You will die an old man in your bed, surrounded by sons."

My heart swells with gratitude. He's not just encouraging me. It's the truth. I can see it in the steadiness of his eyes. In the surge of faith surrounding us.

"And what about you?" I press him. Surely, he's thought about Mephi's future. What does his wife think about me taking their son's place?

Jonathan's hesitation lasts only a second. "When I look at Mephi, it's hard for me to understand why Abba would persist in what he's doing. I've wondered if he realizes what he's choosing for us by choosing…this." He's silent for a few breaths, staring down an old invisible enemy. "But I placed my life in Yahweh's hands a long time ago. I can trust Him with the rest of it."

I try to respond, but the cough claws its way up my throat again, sealing off words until Jonathan moves over to slap my back.

"You all right?"

I just shake my head until I can breathe again. "This cough won't leave. It's been coming and going since I escaped Gath."

When I was drenched in winter rains on the hills before Joab found me.

"Over a year?" Jonathan frowns. "Can you still sing?"

"Some. I've been composing more since I've been out here. One of my men, Asaph, is a scribe. He's been writing everything down."

I nod behind Jonathan, indicating the leather pack. He reaches inside and pulls out layers of parchment. I watch him handle them, expecting to feel embarrassed. My men know my music, but few of them have seen what Jonathan is holding. Few of them would understand how sacred they are, the way my friend might.

In the uncertain light, Jonathan's face is unclear, but I keep seeing the ghost of a smile flickering past. His eyes lift over the paper. "Every time you have to leave a place, every time you're betrayed…you sing."

I pause, chewing my lip. It's been a while since I paid attention to the dates and headings Asaph adds to each psalm after I write them. But it's what gives order to my suffering.

"It's like an offering of my days," I explain. "When I pour everything out, God adds His vision to it all, and it seems

Nine

redeemed somehow. Not so broken. Singing it out to Him makes sense of what…doesn't."

I still haven't forgotten the look on my men's faces the last time I sang the song from Gath. They all view me with a mixture of awe and concern, amazed at what Yahweh has brought me through and yet unwilling to venture as deep as I go. I tremble just thinking about it. I never thought I could be this comfortable in the fear of the Lord. But the heavy presence from the prophet Samuel's upper room has followed me out here. And created a home for me in the wilderness.

I don't remember a clear moment of deciding to go deeper, to pursue Yahweh even in the dark, but desperation has forced me there. I'm convinced He draws close when I sing because He knows I'm nothing without Him. Because He knows *I* know.

I'd reveled in His majesty as a boy, imagining the heights I would scale with Him at my side. Now, I've learned that even the depths can be redeemed. The wild moments of leaping off a cliff into an abyss. It all means something. Even beyond me. Writing the songs down brings it all into reality. Otherwise, I would doubt my own mind.

"When did you write this one?" Jonathan holds up one piece of paper, and my face catches fire.

"That one is always following me." It's an account of the worst kind of pain I've experienced yet.

After escaping Keilah, the depth of my anguish had tugged me over some kind of dark edge I didn't know existed. The dream of the wounded man and the sacrificial lamb repeated itself for three nights until I put it into song, tangled up with the agony of the betrayals I've suffered. It could take me a lifetime to comprehend what emerged. I shouldn't have let Jonathan see it.

He reads it in silence, his brow pulling.

"What?" I finally ask him.

"I don't know," Jonathan picks at the edge of his robe. "It's chilling, but some of it...I can barely understand. The divided garments. The pierced hands and feet. What are you referencing there?"

"Yahweh knows." I pull in a long breath, remembering the jagged refrains.

"My God, My God, why have you forsaken me?

"I am poured out like water, all my bones out of joint.

"Evil ones encircle me like a pack of dogs,

Nine

"They pierce my hands and my feet,

"My garments are divided among them while my bones stare and gloat over me."

"It started like they all do. Everything was so heavy, and I was just pouring myself out, trying to release some of the burden, but then—I don't know, it was like He started talking. And it became…that."

Jonathan's eyes are trying to lift, but he can't tear them off the paper. "So…this is about Yahweh? Not just you?"

I fidget, restless to find an explanation for what has none. "Three nights before I wrote that, I had a dream about a perfect lamb, like the ones we keep for sacrifice. But then he turned to the side, and it looked like he had been slain already. Torn apart. I heard a lion in the distance, but I don't think he caused the wounds. It was more like they were the same. And then they became a man. A man who was both. He carried all my pain in Himself—and more. And I woke up weeping. Harder than I have in a long time. I couldn't explain it to the others. I still can't."

Imprisoned by the memory, I sigh, trying to break free. "You think I'm crazy, don't you?"

Jonathan's eyes are huge, but his face holds no judgment. He slides the parchment back in the leather case. "No. If having such insight into the thoughts of God is crazy, then Moses was too. He asked to see God's glory, and we can only imagine what he was shown. It just—reminds me of how much we have to learn. The vastness of what He's called us into."

I take the case back, setting it aside carefully. Exile has broken my life wide open, allowing more pain to rush in than I'd thought I could take. But I've also learned more about Yahweh than I'd thought I could possibly hold. The treasures are increasing in the darkness. Maybe one day I'll understand what I'm to do with them. If I can fight through to the end.

Jonathan watches me, pensive. A strange tremor winds through his voice. "Samuel was right. You are a gift to Israel, not just because you're a fighter, but because of…this. You hear Yahweh's heart. You speak it, even when you don't understand. That's why He's giving you the kingdom."

Pain bunches my jaw. "Do I want it?" After what power has done to Saul, I wonder if it wouldn't be better to spend my life as a shepherd, unknown, but able to seek Yahweh with no distractions.

Jonathan holds his wrists around his knees. "When Moses questioned Yahweh's commission to free our people from Egypt, what happened?"

I sigh slowly, pulling the story back. "God reminded him that He was the Maker of Moses' mouth, and he would give him the strength he needed. God didn't call him because he was perfect. When Yahweh speaks, we are to obey and leave the rest to Him."

My spirits lift with the words. This is why my people recite our stories like our lives depend on it. The power of belief is released when we speak the truth aloud. It puts us back together, like armor snapping into place.

"Joab was wrong, you know," Jonathan murmurs.

"About what?"

"He said there wasn't anything left of the warrior I used to know. He was wrong." Jonathan's confident smile warms me. "Thank God."

My heart groans behind my ribs, yearning to believe. "I thought I knew what it meant to be Yahweh's warrior. But it's buried so deep, sometimes I can't find it."

"That's the way of the harvest, isn't it?" Jonathan continues, "Only what's buried grows up to produce enough to feed a multitude. That's why you're crushed the way you are. Yahweh has a harvest to reap from your life. One that will sustain generations."

I stare at him like a child listening to a story. Emotion spears my jaw. "I wish I were more like you."

Jonathan smirks gently. "No, you don't. There's so much I don't understand, but I'm confident Yahweh will reveal what I need to know in time. You were a shepherd. You know about leading and following. Just show Him you believe. Listen for God's instruction and obey completely. And if you fail—" He inhales sharply, glancing to the mouth of the cave. The edge of Uriah's shoulder is visible from where he's standing guard.

Urgency pulls at Jonathan's voice. "*When* you fail, repent. Immediately. Cast yourself on Yahweh's mercy, and don't let go. Don't run from Him. Run closer. He's everything, and you can't survive without Him. He's the only One who makes this worth it."

I hold his gaze like it's a torch in a storm. "You're so certain I can do this?"

Nine

Jonathan straightens, facing me on his knees. "Only because I know who goes before you. I gave my word to Yahweh; now you give your word to me. Follow Him. Lead Israel. And remember our covenant. Take care of my family, even when Yahweh has wiped every enemy of yours from the face of the earth."

"I promise," I whisper, stirred by his fierceness.

I always knew he would end up teaching me, but he's done so much more. Jonathan's faith is heating mine, like bellows torching metal at a forge. Yahweh was wise to send him to encourage me. Wise and incredibly kind. My covenant brother is one of the few men I'll promise anything to.

* * * * *

Joab's war horn pulls me out of sleep only seconds before Jonathan is standing over me.

"David?"

"I heard," I mumble, struggling to my feet.

I'm already dressed and ready to move, with my sword attached to my side. In the five seconds it takes me to grab a flint and light a torch, I try to wrangle the conflicting thoughts that have been startled awake.

We don't sleep deeply anymore. We live ready for movement; we've discussed every sudden possibility we could think of, even practiced escape several times. But the reality is more deadly than the motions. If Joab has sounded the alarm, then Saul is close.

Jonathan's face is the first thing I see in the shadows, right before Joab appears at the cave's mouth. Torch in hand, my nephew is already tense with fury.

"Korah's sons are back. They've seen Saul at Jeshimon. He spent the night with the elders there, and they directed him to Ziph. He'd planned to leave before dawn, which would put him just on the other side of the ridge by now."

The shock darts my chest, shuddering into panic. We'd barely spent time in Jeshimon, keeping more to this side of the string of mountains. Saul must have been following preemptive messages.

"He can't be so close," Jonathan protests. "He sent word to Gibeah that he would return as soon as he'd spoken to the elders."

Joab turns to Jonathan, his stare heated. "And how many weeks ago was that?" he scoffs, dismissing him. "You shouldn't have come. You'll only cause us trouble. Unless you want to die for David, you'd better leave now."

Nine

"Has everyone been warned?" I don't really have to ask. The guards and watchmen know their duties. Abishai and Uriah appear on the heels of my question.

"The commanders have assembled the families in groups, with their elders accompanied by guards. They're moving to the other side of the ridge by way of the forest path. It's darker and more treacherous, but we'll be concealed." Abishai keeps to the facts, his expression trained in covered tension.

Uriah, on the other hand, is still too young to hide much. "They'll be too slow. Especially in the dark. We may have to hold some men back to fight—to block Saul's way," he amends, glancing at Jonathan.

Before anyone can respond, Jonathan steps out in front of me. "I'll ride and meet him. I'll go and tell him the Philistines are attacking and he must come home at once."

Joab scowls. "You'll be coming from the mountain, not Gibeah. If you can't convince him of your story, then you'll have no way to explain why you're out here."

"I'll go then," Uriah speaks up, and everyone looks at him. "I'll just be another messenger to him."

Joab groans. "Why should Saul believe you? He's never seen you before. Besides…a Hittite?"

Uriah doesn't back down. "He has Hittite servants. The Hassar can say he hired me in town and sent me after him because the news was urgent and he couldn't spare any men. That will give the prince time to get ahead of Saul to Gibeah."

Joab rubs his beard. "And when he returns home to find out his son lied?"

Jonathan fastens Ezra's cloak around his shoulders. "My brothers have been dealing with skirmishes for the past three months. I can control enough of the information to make the king think it's more recent. I've done it before." He's trying to sound casual, but I don't miss the hint of satisfaction in his eyes.

Saul's kinsmen would have been affronted by the idea of the Hassar undermining the king, but all I can feel is pride. And then disgust at myself for being so willing to accept Uriah's plan. I grab the front of the boy's armor vest.

"Are you sure about this? We can send other men after Saul, lure him away…"

Uriah shakes his head. "He's already suspicious. Better for him to think the conflict is in Gibeah, not here. Besides, I found my way to you. I can find my way back."

Nine

Amazement sweeps through me, and I place a hand on his shoulder. "God go with you."

"And with you, my king." He brushes past us, and I snap at Joab, trying to clear the thickness from my throat.

"Go get the prince's mule and weapons. We don't have time."

In the few moments Joab is out of sight, I grip Jonathan's arms, refusing to think about how long it could be before I see him again. "Thank you for coming. I—I was…"

My voice pulls dangerously, but Jonathan smiles over my discomfort. Placing his hand along my neck, he leans his forehead against mine. "You are the chosen of Yahweh, a man after God's own heart. You will be king of Israel, and I will be next to you." He pulls back, fierce certainty glowing in his eyes. "Don't doubt it again."

TEN

Jonathan

I've never been so grateful for Philistines. Reaching Gibeah ahead of my father, I'm confronted immediately by my youngest brother, frantic over the enemy units that have been pushing closer ever since I'd left.

"How close are they?" I demand breathlessly, fitting a battle axe onto my back. "Have they gotten past Aijalon?"

Flustered, Ish-Bosheth follows me to the armory. "If you knew they were coming, why didn't you send word back to me? Where've you been?" My brother fumbles with his robe while I yank weapon after weapon. "Ishvi has scouts dispersed around Aijalon, but the Philistines have been burning threshing floors to the west, always one step ahead. Malchi is in the south, and Abba has the best men with him."

I brush him off, shouldering my bow. "Abba's right behind me, Bosheth. He'll meet us in the valley."

And he'll find me beside my brothers, defending Israel. As though I'd never left. Things couldn't have worked out better.

"What should I do?" Bosheth's frustrated gesture frays my nerves. I'll never understand why Abba's shielded him from the fighting so much. If anything happens to me and my other brothers, it would be too late for Bosheth to learn what he should be comfortable with by now. His incompetence could end up harming him one day.

"I'll send a unit of archers up to the battlements in case the Philistines push into Gibeah. Get up there with them." At least there he'll be out of the way. "Now!" I yell, making him jump.

I wait for Bosheth to scramble off, shouting for his armorbearers. I don't need to search far for mine. Ezra's already at my side, fully armed, carrying my spear and two fresh quivers of arrows. His face is heavy with questions, but they'll keep.

"Ready, my lord?" he asks.

I nod. After the anxiety of staying ahead of my father all the way from Ziph without being seen, I'm eager to fling myself into battle and expend some of the energy buzzing in my veins.

I grab Ezra's shoulder. "When this is over, I want you to ride back to the city ahead of me. Inquire at the gate for a Hittite messenger named Uriah. He's about sixteen years old."

Ten

Alarm sparks in Ezra's face. "Is he a threat?"

"No. He alerted the king about the Philistines before I could get to him. I wanted to see him properly rewarded."

Ezra knows me too well. His eyes burrow deep, searching for more information. I slap his shoulder. "Let's go!"

Our horses and mules take wing outside the city gates, and it's so satisfying to feel their hooves eat up the ground beneath us, charging west after a real enemy. In the distance, I hear the collective shout of my father's troops, the ones who'd followed him after David. I raise my sword over my head and yell after them, even though they won't hear me.

It's so like the old battles that I keep expecting to find David charging with his thousands ahead of me. Or waiting in the trees around Gibeah with bows and arrows ready. Regret pierces my pride. My father was so close to attacking David's camp and terrorizing everyone in it. But now, thanks to Yahweh and Uriah, the king is back where he belongs, facing the Philistines.

And not a moment too soon. Less than a mile outside Gibeah, Achish's cohorts are swarming the valley like locusts. Searching the soldiers, I pin my gaze on the general who leads them.

This is our fight, and my veins are alive with it.

Flinging a war cry into the midday sun, I charge for the center while my commanders' units spread out, enclosing the Philistines in the valley where they'd been hoping to travel unnoticed.

Startled by our presence, our enemy's defense is sloppy and disorganized. After all they've heard about Saul's campaign to kill David, they hadn't expected to find us ready for them. *Refocus my father, Adonai. Refuel his passion for his true duties as king.*

The sunlight glints off the Philistine general's helmet, and he grabs for his horse, pulling himself up into my sword as I ride past. My weapon catches him under his arm, and I feel the blade digging through bone before I pull it free. Sliding my sword into its sheath, I reach out and catch my spear when Ezra tosses it.

While my arm's aloft, I barely miss the arrow that tears through my robe, glancing off my breastplate. I readjust my grip and fling the spear, pinning a Philistine to the ground against another.

"Duck!" Ezra's cry reaches my ears as my body is already obeying.

Ten

My chest touches my mule's neck, and Ezra's arrow splits another before it hits me. Grasping for the reins, I haul my mount to the side, remembering to breathe. Each time I fight, I forget how much can change. In half a second.

I ride uphill for a wider glimpse of the battle, and my eyes pull through the tumult until I find my father fighting from his horse beside Abner. The armorbearers keep close, killing anyone who pushes near them. A quick count of the bodies—the ones fighting and those stretched out on the ground, tells me we're advancing, driving the Philistines back.

Achish didn't send them out in full strength. He's testing us again. Counting on Saul being occupied elsewhere.

Ezra holds his sword aloft, ready to signal my archers who cluster behind him, their bows drawn at the handful of foot soldiers still standing. Our enemies edge toward the trees, hoping to make a break for Aijalon before we close the gap around them.

My father looks around, searching, and when his eyes find me, they jump over my head. A Philistine leaps from a tree to my right, and the flash of his upturned blade catches the corner of my eye before his body slams into me. Trying to fling him from my back, I slide out of the saddle, my left foot still caught in the stirrup.

My assailant is a comparable opponent; I can feel it as his strength battles mine on the ground. He's heavily muscled, matching my width and almost my height. Reaching back, I grab the leather strap of his armor, pulling his arm down so he can't raise the axe. His other arm locked around my neck, he strains for mastery of the weapon while the mule jerks to the side, dragging my leg with it.

Blood slides down my arm as the flailing edge of the axe cuts into my wrist. I hear the shouts downhill, the release of a hundred arrows, but I'm locked in my own narrow world, trying to survive.

My hand cramps around the Philistine's wrist, but when he regains his balance on the ground, he tears his arm back, breaking my grip. His blade hacks deep into my arm, but a second later, the man is facedown on top of me, Ezra's foot in his back.

I feel the spear pull from his body, and his hot blood spills over my breastplate, soaking the hollow of my throat. I thrust the man off of me, and my head spins, heat chewing through my wound.

Ezra offers me his left hand, since my right can't grasp anything. On my feet, I pull his shoulder into my chest. "Thank you," I mumble, pain crashing into me.

Ten

It would be impossible for me to count the number of times he's cut down Philistines ahead of me. Our lives are bound together with blood and battle, and for a moment, I wonder why I've never thought of him the way I think of David.

Ezra's been with me longer, and I've come to view him the way I do my Benjaminite cousins. A relative I command. It's different with David. I knew from the beginning I wasn't his superior. But instead of threatening me, that understanding drew me closer. It's still not something I could explain to anyone.

I shake my head, wondering if I'm losing too much blood. I'm just standing there, my good arm draped over Ezra while he binds up my shoulder. A strange pain digs through my head with each rough twist of his hands, and I study him, wondering at his manner. He's not sparing me, and his eyes are full of questions. He may have stepped in to save me, but his mind is far away.

"Thank you," I say again, not sure if I actually voiced it through the initial rush of pain.

Ezra's eyes lift once, his jaw bunching. "I know my place. But I can't occupy it if you're not in yours."

* * * * *

In another moment, the king and his men are crowding around me, forcing further discussion aside. But the hint of a larger conversation remains buried on Ezra's face in plain sight. Saul counts the fallen with his commanders while his physician checks my arm for breaks, sealing the deep slice with a thick oiled balm.

"You'll need to avoid swinging this arm over your head for a while so the wound doesn't rip back open," Ammiel advises, smiling wryly. He knows it will be a challenge for me to keep either of my arms immobile.

Over his shoulder, I make eye contact with my father. When he sees me looking, Saul ends his conversation with Abner and moves up behind Ammiel.

"You've been fighting how many years? And no one's ever taken you from above. You know better than to charge a hill alone without Ezra." He studies me before turning on his heel. "You're slipping, Hassar."

"Thank Adonai you returned when you did," I venture, stopping him. "I rode out to find you, but when the danger grew too great, I came back."

"Yes," Saul answers, weighing each word. "A Hittite boy rode into our midst; he said he had been hired by you to inform

Ten

me of the threat. I didn't realize your messengers were in such short supply."

I refuse to lower my eyes, but he's right. It's been years since I've had to hire a Canaanite servant from the city to do my bidding. I have plenty of more experienced riders to command—if I'd been in Gibeah at the time.

I speak before I can give any impression of guilt. My father knows every slant of my face. "Should I ride to Aijalon, my lord? See if there are more raiders hiding there in reserve?"

Saul watches me for several breaths before answering. "No. We left a few of the foot soldiers alive for questioning. They'll tell us where Achish is planning to strike next." He reaches over and I tense up, but his touch is easy. "Get some rest. Look in on your wife and your boy."

I try to thank him, but my words are all tangled up in the throb of my shoulder, in the strange forced tenderness on Saul's face. He's done this my whole life, always keeping me guessing about his intentions, even though I've left him in no doubt of mine. *Until now.*

I swallow, my thoughts correcting me. It's been a long time since I felt I could really trust him with everything I know. The growing distance between us used to hurt me; I'd felt it like a cut ripping open. But now, the sadness is much duller. Just like on the hill, I'm locked in my own world, fighting to survive.

And he's right. I'm slipping.

Ezra rides back into the city behind me, discouraging conversation with his distance, but once the king's men disappear through the gate, I angle my mule around toward the south field. Ezra follows without being told, and I lead him to the giant boulder Ezel, where David hid out on the day of his departure.

"Did anyone say anything about Uriah?" I ask without turning my head.

Ezra moves his mule up beside mine. "No one's heard of him. At least no one at the gate." He's careful to keep suspicion out of his tone, but his eyes are overturning every stone beneath the surface.

"I see." I dismount and lean against the boulder, but Ezra's gaze doesn't let mine go. He swings himself to the ground and comes to stand in front of me.

"My lord, I've earned the right to speak to you man-to-man, haven't I?" he asks.

"Yes." I can guess what's coming. I can see it surging in Ezra's throat.

"You're playing with fire. You're playing with your life, and mine, and everyone else's." His voice shudders. "You know I don't believe in coincidence. Not in battle. I know David was in Ziph, but he escaped. He made it to the other side of the mountain in the time it took Saul to return. Shortly after you did."

Ignoring the fire eating up my chest, I reach under my armor vest and adjust the bandage over my arm. "Who gave you that information?" I ask while Ezra fumes as calmly as he knows how. His split-second hesitation pushes into me, and I look up. He didn't...

Ezra tips his chin. "I heard it from a Ziphite. I went after you."

Pushing off the rock, I plant my feet hard, my vision blurring Ezra's face into something unrecognizable. "You...*what?*"

Ezra tightens his jaw, adjusting to my height as I advance on him. But he stands his ground, refusing to step back or bow his head. "I wanted to know where you would go without me. I wondered when you decided to stop trusting me."

"I did trust you!" I slap him in the chest, my shout making him flinch. "I trusted you to cover for my absence and not disobey my orders!"

Ezra's face jerks. "You didn't order me not to follow you. This is treason we're talking about, my lord. And I wish I could understand why you continue with it." He's trying to stay calm, but his chest is heaving, his breaths coming fast. "I liked David too; he was a gifted warrior. But are you aware of what his men will do to your family if he takes the throne?"

"You have nothing to fear from David, Ezra. We made a covenant before God. He doesn't plan to bring harm to any of us." My mind is pulling in a dozen directions, wondering how Ezra managed to follow me without crossing paths with the king.

Apprehension pulls Ezra's expression. He grits his teeth. "David may not want to harm you, but he'll be forced into it. How can you be sure he even remembers your vow?"

"I went to see him, as you know." But not only to solidify my future. David had been drowning under his own skin. God had led me there to remind him how to breathe. I had to set him back on his feet.

Ezra exhales, aghast. "And what happens if the king finds out? Your father may be mad, but he's not stupid."

"You didn't plan to tell him?" I fume, pacing.

Ezra's face whitens, his eyes wide. "I would never do that."

Ten

"Jonathan!" The king's bellow across the field buries Ezra's defense, too quickly for either of us to react.

Frantic interruptions have become commonplace over the years, but the moment I see my father's wild expression and driving pace, my heart stops. Riding over to us, the king dismounts with his sword unsheathed, barely stopping with the blade inches from my neck.

I hold out my hands, stepping back against the boulder, and Ezra leaps to my side, protesting, "My lord, he's done nothing—"

"Nothing?" Saul grinds the words, pressing closer. "You didn't come after me, did you, Jonathan? You went in search of my enemy. *Days ago!* And you said nothing."

My mouth goes dry. "Why would you think that?"

Saul smiles grimly. "Doeg told me. He knew if he followed Ezra, he would find you."

The face of the Edomite spy jumps into my mind, and heat scorches my neck. Doeg's spiteful lies had sent David into hiding the first time. He's my enemy. And he won't live to betray me again if I get out of this.

Adonai, give me strength.

Veins writhe in Saul's neck. "Where is David?"

My stomach drops. I won't lie to him. But my silence is an answer by itself. I fist my hands at my sides, moisture edging my eyes. As angry as he is, I doubt he has it in him to make my wife a widow and take Mephi's father.

"My king…" Ezra reaches out, averting Saul's attention but not his blade.

"Ezra, don't." I grab his wrist.

But Saul instantly sees the opportunity and angles closer to me, forcing my chin up with the blade. Gripping my arm with his other hand, he stares right into Ezra's lifelong loyalty and gets what he wants.

"I heard from the Ziphites, my lord," Ezra divulges. "David has fled to the Negeb. Everyone expects him to take refuge in the cliffs of En-Gedi."

Saul removes his sword, sheathing it sharply. "God bless you for showing concern for me." He touches the young man's shoulder before walking away toward his mule.

Ezra doesn't breathe until my father is riding back toward Gibeah. Once he's gone, I exhale, fierce anger surging up over the momentary threat of death.

Ten

"How could you do that?" I grasp Ezra's shoulders, pushing him into the tamarisk tree. "You already sent Doeg after me. You had no right to tell my father anything! You promised me loyalty!"

"And you have it!" Ezra shoves my chest, driving me back apace. "I've fought beside you my whole life, since we were children. I'm honor bound to you, not David. And by the way, which one of us saved you just now?"

I laugh, harshly. "You think that was the first time he's pointed a sword at me? He's angry, but he won't take my life. He will, however, take David's if he gets the chance. All he wanted was the information you gave to him. He knew one of us would weaken."

Horror winds through Ezra's face. His voice rises, turning hoarse. "I am the strongest ally you have, but nothing is secret from the king. I will not become a traitor like David."

Vehemence singeing my vision, I lunge at Ezra, knocking him flat. I don't want to hurt him, but he's gone too far. He's supposed to be an extension of me, not Doeg! I hook his breastplate and dig my knees into his shoulders, pinning him against the ground.

"You think David's a traitor?" I bellow in his face. "Then, let me hear you say what you think of me! Say it! I dare you to call me a traitor!"

After everything I've endured with my father, this is what I get? Betrayal from my closest servants? Ezra buries his fists in my chest, but it takes me far too long to realize he's being careful, refusing to claw at my bad arm. I fling my fist back and punch the ground next to his head. "Answer me!"

"Are you breaking with Saul?" Ezra heaves, his heartbeat wild under me.

"Of course not!" The shout rips through me, and a deep sting enters my arm. "Why do you think I'm still here, putting up with all of this?"

Ezra stiffens, his eyes moving to my shoulder. Fresh blood is smearing the edge of the bandage. I breathe heavily and relax my grip, sitting back against the boulder. Each time my chest lifts, pain radiates down my arm.

Ezra pulls away, rubbing sweat from his forehead, his eyes lowered. "We promised we'd never fight each other."

I press my hand against the axe wound, hurting deeply. "We've all promised a lot of things." When he reaches for my bandage, I pull myself out of his reach.

Ezra sits back on his heels. "I didn't know Doeg would follow us. If David dies, you can kill me."

Ten

I just might.

I'm angry enough to say it, but then I picture the battle at Michmash and the boy who'd carried my weapons into enemy territory without a word of complaint. The one who would bind my wounds in silence after my father beat me, pretending to believe my excuses to spare my pride.

Ezra chose me a long time ago, the way I chose David. I just didn't know it then. I was too busy fighting and grieving. Trying to spare myself more pain. David changed me. My friendship with the shepherd uncovered everything I was refusing to feel.

But I could never kill Ezra.

I know one man who deserves to die though. At least in my book. Sitting forward, I push onto my feet and grasp the hilt of my sword from its sheath on the mule's back. Ezra leaps up. "Woah…where are you going? You can't use that arm now."

I know. I'm already dizzy with the pain. But I'm tired of being followed, lied about.

I smirk. "I doubt Doeg will put up much of a fight."

Ezra's stance tightens. "Then I'm going with you."

We ride back to Gibeah in search of the Edomite, but when we reach the palace courtyard, two of my servants run out to meet us. "My lord, we were looking for you. Sarrah Jehosheva has sent for the midwives."

Instant apprehension takes over, winding cold fingers through my battle fury. I haven't been counting the weeks as carefully as my wife has, but even I know it's too early for the child to come. Ezra's voice barely pushes through my whirring thoughts.

"Go home, my lord. I'll send Ammiel after you to wrap your arm." Ezra removes the sword from my grip, looking me carefully in the eyes. "Save it for later."

He slaps my mule, sending me off toward my house, but something in his tone follows me as I ride home and head upstairs to my wife's chambers. Calm restraint, covering darker zeal. Like a greater storm is coming.

ELEVEN

David

When the news that Saul is no longer following us sweeps through our company, I go to my knees in the dirt while the men release shouts of hearty relief. The first full rays of morning sunlight are spearing the forest, and the women and children are about to fall from their mounts with weariness. Barely waiting for instruction, whole groups collapse, despite the commanders' protests.

"Let them rest for an hour or two," I tell Joab. "Saul has broken off pursuit." For now.

The stream we've followed through the darkness is visible now, threading the forest like a vein of silver. I head for its banks and stop to cup water, then change my mind.

Unbuckling my armor, I lay my weapons aside and wade into the current up to my waist. The sudden chill is invigorating, and yet the promise of peace sweeps in right behind it. Drained,

I let my knees touch the stream's silky floor, bending over so the water can close over my back.

Saul was too close this time. In the quiet gurgle of the water, I let the threat lift from my mind, hoping to leave it in the current. I'm sitting on the bank when Joab joins me.

"He came too close this time," my nephew intones, repeating what I was trying to forget.

I close my eyes. "And now he's gone. You were suspicious of both Uriah and Jonathan when they came, and yet they saved us all."

Joab's jaw squeezes. "We cannot risk the lives of this company on the good graces of Saul's son and a Hittite youth. We need trustworthy men of Israel who will conceal our whereabouts, men who won't betray us at the first bit of pressure from the king. We need allies."

Allies. The word darts my stomach. Joab has been pulling strings for weeks, insisting that if I were married to some town elder's daughter, they'd stand with us against Saul. Starting seven days ago, his plan has a name. Ahinoam of Jezreel. The woman who'd met us at the well on our first day in Ziph.

Eleven

I reach beside me for my cloak and dry my face with it. "I told you, I can't. Not like this."

Kings are known to take multiple wives, but I hadn't planned on starting so soon. Not before reaching some sort of understanding with Michal. But the weeks of anticipating Ziph's betrayal have worn down any sympathy Joab had left.

His expression darkens. "Did Jonathan tell you Michal spends her days pining for you, waiting for a chance to join us?"

I grimace. "Don't be an idiot. That wouldn't have been the truth." I hate talking about this.

"But he didn't tell you the truth either, did he?" Joab snarls. "His sister has betrayed you. My spies found out weeks ago. At the king's command, she's taken another husband, turning her back on the Law and every promise she's ever…"

Leaping to my feet, I grab my sword and aim it.

Joab is speechless for a second while I force angry breaths in and out. "I know what Saul's done. I heard you with your spies. I'm not deaf."

His face tightens around the slightest shiver of pity. "She'll always be your wife in God's eyes. But there's nothing to be done to get her back. Not now. Your only choice is to make the most of your freedom."

I squint at Joab, clenching my teeth against the burn in my face. "And what will Ahinoam think about the kind of freedom that keeps us on the run dodging a murderous king?"

Joab releases a long sigh, as though he's dealing with a stubborn child. "It hardly matters what she thinks. Kings form alliances. If you marry her, we'll have access to the provinces her father oversees. They'll be honor-bound to assist us."

"Until Saul finds out and removes the provinces from his control! Does this man even realize what he's sending his daughter into?"

"Of course," Joab chortles. "He's making her the future queen of Israel."

And I'll wager that's all she sees in me. "Saul is still king, Joab."

Joab's brows knit together. "And he does exactly what will benefit him without a thought for anyone else."

"That doesn't make it right."

Eleven

Joab picks up my other weapons, handing them back to me one by one. "We would simply be using her father's interest in you to protect us. It wouldn't mean anything."

"Every marriage means something, Joab." I focus on securing my sword, ignoring how my vision wavers.

"Then what if I told you she loved you?"

I can tell he's jesting, but I've had enough. I grab the front of his cloak, yanking his face close to mine. "Don't you *ever* speak to me of love."

Joab's shoulders settle, and he stares straight through my anger. "Do your duty, then. Put your past behind you, and put your fame to work."

* * * * *

Joab's spies make hasty arrangements, and I marry the girl from Jezreel under the cover of night before we plunge deeper into the wilderness.

Ahinoam says little, standing silent and moon-eyed while her father gushes about my future as king. But once we're on the move and the massive southern cliffs of En-Gedi build shadows over our heads, I can see the blushing veil of her politeness dropping away.

At first, her shock stays silent. But then she starts talking to the other women. I know the moment she realizes that our exile is fairly permanent.

"So, you won't kill him? Even if he keeps chasing us?" Her breathing shifts from her stomach to her chest, and her cheeks flush. She's barely concealing her fright and disgust.

I feel for her. She doesn't have much in common with the other men's wives, women who've lived for years this way. She's a rich man's daughter. Not a Sarrah, but she definitely expected more. She was thrown into this with very little understanding or preparation. We have that in common at least. But like Michal, she has little idea what my anointing means.

"Yahweh has not given me orders to kill Saul." I speak as gently as I can, wishing I could open my heart to her. But it's closed, with new locks on it. I can tell by the walled look in her eyes that the feeling is mutual.

"What if he kills you?" she asks, refusing to blink or breathe until I answer.

Eleven

I start to begin a longer explanation, but Jonathan's counsel stops me. Adonai has anointed me king, and He's kept me this far. It's time I start believing He'll continue. I cup my hands around Ahinoam's face, making her look deeply into me.

"Yahweh will not give Saul that chance."

TWELVE

Jonathan

Two grueling days later, I've buried my second child. A daughter who barely breathed two hours. I'm horrified by the empty look on Sheva's face. She's weak from grief and blood loss, and the midwives are worried about infection. But it kills me how she keeps her face turned to the wall, refusing to let me see her weep.

"Sheva." I try twice to get her to face me, but she won't until I send all the servants from the room. Then she buries herself in my chest and wails.

I hold her as tightly as I dare, but she feels so fragile in my arms.

She finally looks up, cupping her sobs in one hand while the other grips my robe. "Has Adonai forsaken us? Is that why this…?"

"No!" I assure her, pulling her face back into my chest. "No."

I'm offended by the suggestion, hoping none of the servants voiced something like that in her hearing. But I don't like the way it echoes inside me, over and over.

Only a few moments later, one of the maids tells me I have to leave. The king is demanding I join him in his armory. I have to force myself to comply without arguing. I can't imagine it's important enough to rival what's happened. I wash my face before heading to the fortress, but it won't hide anything.

In the outer courtyard, Abba's forces are lining up, preparing to ride to En-Gedi to pursue David. I don't need to count them to know there are more this time. They drop their heads when I pass. Most of them have heard by now.

Up in the armory, the king barely pauses when I force the words I already hate past my throat. Saul winces once, then takes his knife from his armorbearer. Inspecting the blade, he conceals it in the sheath along his leg.

"There will be other children," he says. "Your son will carry on our name. If indeed our name survives David's treachery."

A tempest builds in my chest, threatening to erupt, but Saul keeps talking. "You've understandably failed to notice that your armorbearer is gone. And if he returns, he's as good as dead." He lifts his eyes once, and the breath leaves my lungs.

Twelve

"What?"

Saul speaks to his weapons, his casual tone burning me from the inside. "He killed Doeg the Edomite with your sword. I'm afraid I cannot allow an unpredictable man of violence to serve you."

A harsh burst of air escapes me, and I turn to one side, then the other, pacing, trying to outrun my anger. How many brothers will this man take from me?

When I speak, I don't even recognize my own voice. It's lower and darker, like someone else's. "I did not know the life of one accusing Edomite was worth more than the man who has saved your son's life."

"He never saved your life," Saul snorts, his brow furrowed.

"You don't see everything."

He has the decency not to scoff again. The next time he looks at me, something makes him shudder. "If his loyalty to you meant more, he might still be here. But if I find him among David's renegades, I'll tell you."

My vision sparks as Saul brushes past me, followed by his guards. I shove my hands into my hair. Ferocity grinds my nerves, begging for release. But I won't give in. Not until the king leaves the fortress.

When I hear the collective shuffle of horses leaving the courtyard, I grab the nearest tapestry and tear it in half. My anguished shouts keep the servants at bay while I break anything I can get my hands on.

When my anger has shattered half the room at my feet, I stand there trembling, trying to regain a semblance of breath while my knuckles bleed down my wrists. But the rage won't lift. I can't go back to my wife like this. I can't risk a rash move that might cause my own death or banishment, leaving Sheva and Mephi vulnerable. I need to clear my head, release this iron grip.

Eema. My mother has always been able to settle me. And she'd wanted me to come as soon as I had news. Back at my house, I make sure Sheva is sleeping before heading to the separate palace quarters above my father's chambers.

My mother turns her head when I arrive. Nothing more. She's been sick for the better part of a year, and the nameless illness has drained her strength and withered her frame. Her hair is thin and white. Her smile is the only thing I recognize. Broken bravery reaching out to me through her own tears. She can't lift her hand much higher, so I kneel by her bed and lean over her.

"She's gone, Eema. The child."

Once I get the words out, my mother's fingers move to my hair and then drop. I fold my hand over them. Their coldness terrifies me.

"I'm sorry," Eema exhales, and my heart wrenches. Apparently, that was too much for my father to say. "How is Sheva?" she continues.

"She's broken," I whisper, wincing deeply. Broken and afraid. And it's my fault.

I say it aloud, and alarm whitens Eema's face. She pushes up onto an elbow. "How is it your fault?"

The touch of her hand is too much. My whole body quakes. "Everything is. David. Michal. Ezra."

My mother frowns and I realize she doesn't know about Ezra's exile.

"Everything Saul's doing," I summarize. "I can't stop him."

I rub my forehead, the ache too deep beneath the surface. I've noticed that I call him *Saul* when I talk to my mother about him. Not *Abba*. I don't even know when the change started. Eema looks confused, but I don't have the energy to explain. Seconds later, it's coming out of me anyway, disjointed and fractured.

"Everything is crumbling beneath me. I stay here and battle Philistines, and there's always more. The enemies of God continue to rage against us, and all Abba can think of is David. He won't adjust strategies. He's trampled on the Law. It's been a year since he's even spoken to a priest. He's dragging us down, and he doesn't see it. And I gave my word—I gave my service to Yahweh years ago at Michmash, and I don't know if I'm pleasing Him by staying here. I can't stop the king, and the more I fight, I just keep losing."

I shake, my wife's fear burrowing into me. I want to cling to Yahweh's faithfulness. But I can't deny what I see. I've lost my sister, and my mother is disappearing before my eyes. I've lost my two closest friends. And my second child. Is it because I stay with a king who's bent on destruction? Is Mephi in danger, doomed to carry some curse?

My next breath doesn't open my lungs, and my mind struggles to grip a clear thought. "I don't know what to do. I don't know what to do. Eema, please just tell me what I'm supposed to do."

"Jonathan." My name lifts my head.

Twelve

Sitting up in bed, my mother cradles my face, tears dripping from her cheeks. "I knew…what he was doing," she wheezes, each sentence a struggle. "For years, he thought you were his enemy. But I knew when he changed targets, when he started looking at David the way he used to look at you. And I knew you wouldn't be a part of it. You may be his son, but…you're different. Believe me. Yahweh…sees you…different."

Her face folds in half, and I know she's speaking the truth. She's always been honest with me, her openness providing a safe place for me to land when every other foundation felt fractured. My heart drinks in her counsel with shaky gratitude. But in the same moment, I know I won't hear her voice much longer. The reality shoves every other bit of pain aside for the moment.

Yahweh may not have forsaken me, but I'm going to lose her. The woman who silently fought for my life, building me back up every time Saul knocked me down. She was always there for me in ways my father wasn't. And now she's dying.

Eema.

Surrendering, I bury my head in her lap and shake with sobs.

THIRTEEN

David

"**H**e's here, David."

I'm sitting in the cleft of a rock, concealed between two heavy boulders, watching the road from above. The massive cliffs of En-Gedi provide a haven for wild goats and a handful of traveling shepherds who use the dusty, gated folds built into the lower hillsides.

My army is encamped within the heart of these mountains, waiting for Joab's spies to tell us it's safe to move. Our families are folded up within the town's stronghold several miles beyond, spreading out from us to avoid being followed. The only news in two days is that they're safe and concealed, for now.

But we knew Saul would track us here. The information he got from the Ziphites was too pointed for him to ignore.

Joab and Abishai have stationed men above every ridge and at the mouth of every cave, watching the lower paths winding up into the crags. And now they're standing in front of me, along with three of my own brothers. They're men of war, each of them older than I am. It's so strange to see the cloud of fear staining their brows.

Joab's report winds into my stomach, dragging every undefined anxiety to the surface. "Asa spotted him farther down the road, but he'll reach the cliffs by nightfall. He has three thousand men with him."

My heart drops. "Three thousand? What happened to three hundred? Your spies said…"

Joab waves off the figure. "I don't know who said that. He has three thousand this time, Israel's choicest warriors. Men who fought beside you against the Philistines. Thanks to the Ziphites and that fox Doeg, he'll know right where to find us, and he'll search out every cave in these hills until he does. This place will end up being a trap instead of a fortress." He shifts his weight, anxiety rising. "Is that your plan? To have us jumping from hole to hole like prairie dogs?"

"Of course not." I glance at my brothers, but they look away. Their hands are folded over their swords, but I can see the rigidity in their jaws. They don't think there will be an escape this time.

Thirteen

I breathe in slowly, pushing a hand through my hair. We've been here less than a month, and already the king is closing in. I let my hand drop over my face, listening for answers that don't come. *Why won't he let me go, Adonai? Why do you allow him to get closer and closer?*

Thus far, I've taken refuge in Yahweh's nearness, choosing to believe He'll help us stay concealed. But I'm tired of waiting for something undefined. I thought surely by now, Saul would have tired of the hunt and returned to the people who need him. Then, in the midst of his kingly duties, his wrath would be abated. But no.

My brother Eliab's hand wanders across his belt, fumbling with each weapon concealed there. "What do you want us to do, David?" His brows bunch together, folding his forehead. "It's not like you haven't tried to avoid him. But now, he's come to you. To us. And he won't hesitate to…do as he pleases."

I turn my back, walking several paces out onto the plateau. I can't wrap my mind around it. Why is it so hard for me to believe Saul would strike me now? He's tried before.

Shammah grasps my shoulder, turning me back. "David, you shouldn't be out here. He'll be able to see you from the lower paths." His voice tightens. "You've spent enough time meditating on this. He's gaining on us, and we have nowhere to go."

I look into my brother's face. His concern has been growing since the day I was anointed. When Saul's men came to Bethlehem to bring me to the court as a harpist, Shammah had warned me we could all die if the king discovered who I was. And yet, my brothers have remained at my side through it all. How can I fail to protect them, or at least defend what Yahweh has given me?

Abishai steps forward, reading my thoughts. "We all know how you wanted things. You were a faithful son to him. But is it right to insist on something Saul will not agree to? He doesn't want peace with you, David. He's made it very clear."

Shammah's face creases. "You said you've been having visions since Keilah. Hasn't Yahweh said anything more? Given you any further instructions? Anything at all?"

Alarm flickers in my chest. I'd been hesitant to tell them, but it seems unfair to hold it back now. Yahweh's Word is their sustenance too.

I pick at my sling. "I had a dream the night we fled Ziph. I saw Saul like a fruitful vine, spreading himself like a green laurel tree, his limbs reaching in every direction, but he had no root. I could see the darkness creeping up each branch, even though he didn't notice."

Shaken, I look into Shammah's eyes. "Yahweh's voice spoke over me then. He said I would be faced with my enemy, and he would be given into my hand to do with as I chose."

My men react exactly as I expected, gasping shocked laughter and clapping their hands.

"Praise be!" Joab exclaims, incredulous. "Why didn't you say so before?" He spreads his hands at Shammah. "You have to pry these things out of him."

My gaze sharpens on them. They have no idea what it feels like to carry the weight of such a dream.

"As I *chose*," I enunciate with my arms folded. "He didn't say what I should choose."

Eliab scoffs, looking out toward the sunset. "Maybe He assumed you could think for yourself."

My oldest brother has said little since he returned from Moab, keeping his opinions to himself and diligently working wherever he's needed. He's a courageous fighter, and his varied skills have benefited us greatly wherever we've stayed, but I know his pride has taken a beating these last few years. He's had to watch Saul make our family a byword in Israel, doing everything in his power to destroy us. He's lost his parents, and he's had to bring his wife and his children into exile. Like all of us.

Abishai weighs a stone in his hand. "We all knew this day would come. You knew it too, ever since you were anointed. You just couldn't comprehend it at the time. But now, Yahweh has prepared you to defend the people He's given you. To save Israel from the curse Saul has brought on her." He moves closer to me, speaking gently. "It wouldn't be the same as attacking Saul in his own fortress. He's come out here to find you and kill you. And all of us with you."

Joab unfolds his arms. "David, if Saul's men capture you, they will not show you mercy. They'll make an example of our whole company. Everyone will suffer. He'll burn En-Gedi and sell the Hittites into slavery. These are men who have followed you and put their families in your care. You owe more to them than to Saul. God knows you have never taken anything from him, but he has trampled his own honor underfoot. Yours is here with us."

He grips the front of my cloak where it's knotted over my chest. "Defend us, anointed one."

I lose my breath again, and Joab pulls me closer, dropping his tone to a tight whisper. "This isn't about personal revenge.

Thirteen

Think of the priests. All those families murdered in their own city. Do it for them."

The burn in his eyes ignites my stomach, and the war tremors start building inside me. Joab can feel it, and triumph slides into his face. I remove my robe from his grip, studying the lower paths through the brush.

"We can't get out of here easily without being seen, so we'll have to stay here another night. Then we'll go up to the stronghold and join the women." I look around Joab, commanding the others. "Eliab, Abishai, post more watchmen to the north and the south. They're not to sleep. I'll take men to the west cave, as far back as we can go. If Saul comes up here, no one is to touch him but me."

Joab nods curtly, the mask on his emotions firmly in place. "Of course. Just promise me you will."

The men disperse, and I follow the narrow path back toward the western cave. It's the largest one we've come across, a mammoth cavern within earshot of a splashing stream that spills over the boulders to collect in a lower pool. The rocky depths beyond will conceal my men and me for the night.

But what if Saul doesn't leave? What if he catches us trying to escape, or pushes through to the stronghold and finds our women and children? Against three thousand of the king's forces, my six hundred might not make it out alive.

I pause in the brush, glancing back through the gap in the cliffs. The Dead Sea is a blue jewel in the distance, the sky over it drowning in the smelted gold of the sunset.

In the beginning, I'd determined to think of my exile like a refining. Yahweh had seen fit to put me in the fire, as Jonathan said He would, and I was willing to submit to the flames and learn anything I would need to be king. But the test is changing. It's no longer just about endurance. What am I to do with a king who hunts me down until he's at the door of my cave? How many men am I willing to lose in order to avoid killing Saul?

None, Yahweh. I don't want one more man to give his life for me. I'm done running.

With tremors taking over my body, I stand there and let the walls come down. Everything I've built around Saul with love and loyalty, believing I could do this without harming him. Believing I had no right to. I let it all go, opening my ears to everything else that's been trying to reach me.

Saul hates me. He's not the same man he used to be when Yahweh anointed him. He has continually repaid me evil with

Thirteen

good. Though I never sought his hurt, he rejoices when I stumble and fall. He has knowingly multiplied those who hate me without cause. The words of his mouth are all trouble and deceit. He has ceased to do good and only plots evil on his bed, planning how to do me harm. He wants to tear me apart until there's nothing left. He has broken Yahweh's laws, and now my God has given him into my hand.

Deep in thought, I jump out of my skin, drawing my sword when two men jog around the corner. But it's only Abishai and the Hittite boy. I roll my eyes at Uriah while my nephew shoves him toward me.

"He wants to stay with you. Saul's men are spreading over the valley. It looks like they'll camp there for the night, closer to the road." Abishai nods toward the rocks. "Get out of sight. I'll send the rest of the men after you. The watchmen are in place above us. They'll be able to see the paths and report to me without showing themselves."

"Good." I sheath my sword, trying to shake off the feeling of being watched. The eerie sensation has been growing around me since Adullam, and I almost wouldn't know what to do without it. "Let's go, Uriah."

The young man stays beside me, glancing up and down the paths with his sword drawn. When we reach the mouth of the cave, Uriah steps in front of me, heading into the dimness first, testing every step. We follow the twists and turns into the darkness, and I bend down to strike a flint against the stone. The sparks catch my torch, pushing shadows across the jagged walls.

In the back corner, several of my men are already waiting, sitting on the ground with their weapons across their laps or leaning against the wall within reach. When they see me, every one jumps to attention. I wave them back down.

"Saul is camped below us. We won't be able to leave tonight without being seen. Get some rest. The watchmen will tell us if we need to move."

"But you'll face him? If he comes up here?" a man named Ethan questions, his knuckles bulging around a battle axe.

I swallow. "Yes."

Uriah turns to face me. "I'm going with you. If you leave this cave, you're not going alone."

The torch only lights half his face, but I'm gripped by the unbroken resolve in his eyes. How else can I answer that except with my own willingness to take action? It may not be the action I wanted to take, but such is war. It drives us to things we wouldn't have chosen. We don't always get what we want.

Thirteen

I touch Uriah's shoulder. "Just wait for my orders. I don't want you to risk anything without cause."

Uriah straightens more than I thought possible. He's almost eye level with me. "You are our cause."

I restrain a broken laugh, turning away. I don't deserve him. Since we met, I can't bury the feeling. Sitting up against the wall, I drape my hands over my knees and lean my head against an uncomfortable point of rock.

What else would you have me do, Adonai? You know I've always been yours to command. But Eliab's right. Maybe you've already given the orders, and I've been too stubborn to see it.

Too busy wishing Saul was someone he's not. Hasn't Jonathan spent his whole life wishing the same? If the king wouldn't change for the love of his son, why should he change for me?

I close my eyes, remembering the Philistine note I'd pulled from the arrow that took Jonathan down years ago. *And so it begins, Melek Israel.*

Even back then, I'd felt the pull of destiny drawing me into a much bigger battle. I hadn't fully understood it, but I'd known I would need more courage than I had up to that point. Yahweh chose me for this. All of it. And now he trusts me to make the decisions I wasn't able to make as a boy. Why else would Yahweh tell me I could do as I chose and then bring my rival to the very cave where I've been hiding?

I steel myself against the tide of pain, keeping my eyes shut as more men enter the cave and settle in to rest. The eyes of Adonai are on me for good, to help me fulfill my calling. He has turned His face away from Saul. I'm done fighting the truth.

Barely moving my lips, I let my murmured prayers fold into the shuffling sounds of feet and shoulders adjusting on the cave floor.

"Adonai, you have seen everything Saul has done to me. Turn him back from pursuing me. Let his way be dark and slippery, with the angel of God pursuing him. He hid a net for my life, but he will fall into it himself." The words taste bitter, and I clamp my teeth against the sting. "Contend, O Lord, with those who contend with me. Draw the spear against my pursuers, for you are my salvation."

I rest my head on my arm, my free hand wandering down to my shepherd's knife. I grip it in the dark, resolve snapping into place like a fresh piece of armor. I would rather Yahweh take Saul down Himself. But if He does not—if Saul comes up here to do us harm, I will do what I vowed I never would.

Thirteen

Kill the king.

* * * *

"My lord!"

The strained whisper rouses me, and my shoulder pops when someone shoves it up against the cave wall. I blink into absolute darkness, barely able to make out the shape of Uriah's face and the glint of a sword. "My lord, he's here."

Uriah glances back nervously. Behind him, every man is on his feet, facing the empty blackness leading to the cave's mouth.

I lean forward, returning my knife to its sheath. "Saul?" The word barely catches my vocal cords, but it heats every vein.

Abishai steps into view, bending down. "He's out in the cave, nearer the front."

Sick dread washes over me. "With Abner?"

"No. He's alone." The whites of Abishai's eyes are nearly eclipsed with black. He grips my shoulder. "This is the moment, David. The moment Yahweh spoke of. Do what you must. We'll stay back. Once you've killed the king, we can deal with whoever comes after him, one by one, until all of us are able to escape."

The handle of my blade turns cold in my hand. I feel a sharp edge creeping up my throat, restraint squeezing my lungs. The men behind Abishai are clasping arms, gripping weapons with fresh fervor, every face lit with hope. I already planned what to do. I can't back down now. Not when Yahweh's brought him to me.

Joab steps around the corner, followed by his watchmen. His hand at my neck pulls my face close enough to see the sparks in his eyes. In all the years I've known him, I've never seen him look so alive. "Go on, Melek. Adonai is with you."

Several men touch me as I turn my body toward the front of the cave. I can't be dreaming, but I feel like I'm on the outside watching myself. My own words from every song I've ever written dance across my mind, distracting me.

Turn away from evil. Seek peace and pursue it. The Lord is my rock and my salvation, my fortress and my deliverer.

I arch my shoulders, tossing hesitancy behind my back. Sometimes the best way to turn from evil is to face it, head on. Saul has chosen the path of destruction for himself. I adjust my footing, moving forward carefully.

By the time I reach the mouth of the cave, I'm crawling, hand over fist, measuring each step to avoid scraping my feet or dislodging rock. The cave's quiet amplifies every sound, flinging it at the king's back. My heart jolts up into my throat when I see the huge shoulders, the six-foot-five form bending over. It's definitely him.

Unbuckling his belt, he drops his sword at his feet and leans his spear against the wall within reach.

I lock my muscles, considering. The sound of my sword pulling free will be too loud. Bending deeply, one knee pressed into the ground, I slide my dagger from the leather pouch strapped to my leg. It's still long enough to do the job. And thanks to Jonathan's training, I know exactly where to put it. I can easily leap to Saul's side and slice his throat. In the darkness, he won't even know it's me.

The handle turns moist, and I grip it tighter. My vision won't hold onto Saul's frame. Every time I blink, his shoulders smear into the cave wall, mixed up in shadow. Irritation teases my nerves. Why would he come so far inside such a deep cave, alone? He knows better. Abner knows better.

I adjust my grip. I have to think of Nob. All those innocents, dead. I have to think of all the attempts he's made on my life. The way he's cast me out, turned Michal against me.

Tilting his head back, Saul fiddles with the clasp on his heavy scarlet robe. Freeing the garment, he flings it over his shoulder without looking.

I wait, one fist pressed into the ground while the king relieves himself, then starts to pull his clothing back into place. Arching his back, he studies the wall in front of him before bending to adjust his leg greaves.

A clawed fist seizes my stomach. I'm taking too long. I've done this hundreds of times. To Philistines. But we're in no less danger here. More than a hundred families depend on me. I'm their shepherd, and Saul's the bear who wants to kill us.

I'm the shepherd. My vision shifts, and I see myself crouched in the corner of Saul's chamber with my harp. Singing over his torment. Looking into his stricken eyes and telling him it would be all right. Telling Jonathan the same while he'd wept over his father's condition.

I lower my hand, all the fight gone out of me. He's a sick man, but he's still my king. And what of my vow? I'd promised Yahweh I wouldn't be the one to strike him. I'd made a promise on the same day Jonathan offered me his respect.

My trust is rarely misplaced, and Yahweh's never is. You have both.

Thirteen

Jonathan's words burn like fire inside my head. The sting spreads through my eyes until I can't see. Feeling in the dark, my fingers clasp the edge of Saul's robe, and I turn the blade on the fabric, slicing through the hem until a strip of cloth pulls free. Exactly like the piece the men of Keilah took from me.

Saul tenses. Even without looking up, I feel his head turn. His body slowly rising. I don't know if he can see me yet, but his eyes have been adjusting for several minutes.

Sudden fear douses me in a cold sweat. I've hesitated too long. Like I did in his chamber the night he almost speared me. Except this time, I've endangered everyone in these caves.

Saul reaches for his spear. "Who…?"

Before I can move, someone springs to my side, stretching a bowstring. "Touch that spear, and you die."

"Uriah, don't!" I respond to the voice, grasping the boy's wrist, but he doesn't change his stance. "Uriah, stand down. Now!"

More of my men scramble from the depths, and Saul whips around, right and left, trying to make out the others who are now trained on him. Joab and Abishai, if I had to guess. Saul's spear clatters to the floor, and one of my nephews swoops down on it. "Move, and we'll shoot you," Joab snarls.

"You won't touch him!" My voice echoes in the cavern, and Saul's outstretched hands start to shake.

"D-David? Is that you?"

Still clutching the piece of Saul's robe, I bend into the cave floor, touching my forehead to it. "It's me, my lord."

Saul exhales, spinning from side to side again, thinking he's about to die. He still doesn't see me, on my knees, without a weapon. Pain digs through my chest, twisting the words in my throat. I sit up, my voice quivering.

"Why are you here, my lord?" I didn't intend to speak, but I'm suddenly anxious to know this before one of my men attacks him. "What have I done to make you pursue me this far? What have I done except fight your enemies and make your family my own? I put you above my own father! I thought you knew me."

"David—" Joab protests, but I talk over him.

"I thought you knew I wanted to serve and honor you as long as you lived. Haven't I proven my loyalty? But instead, you follow the counsel of men who call me a traitor, those who say I want to kill you and take by force what can only be given by Yahweh. Why do you listen to them?!"

Thirteen

My own words unbuckle my defenses, and I start to shake, feeling exposed. Desperate for him to hear me.

"You've seen it over and over. I could have risen against you so many times, and yet I chose not to. Even tonight, I could have killed you. I got close enough to cut your robe." I fling the piece of cloth at him, and he steps back. "But I would not take your life, even though you're hunting mine! Can't you see that there's no treason in my heart?"

I want to shake him. When will he see? How can he press me this hard, to the point where I was ready to kill him to be free of all this?

"May the Lord judge between us and avenge me all the wrong I've suffered. You were my father once." I sink lower on my knees, feeling winded. Bereft. "And yet you come out against me as though I'm a treacherous monster. Isn't it enough that you've crushed me into the dust like a flea?"

A heavy hissing sound cuts the air, reaching out to touch the edge of my words.

"Is it really you, David?" Saul bends over, wheezing, his hands grasping the side of his robe where I cut it. "How…how can you be like this? How does a man let his enemy go away safely when he has the chance to kill him?" He shakes his head several times. "You're much more righteous than I. The Lord will surely reward you for this, David. I know He intends to give you the throne and establish Israel in your hands. I know it, I just…"

He's rambling again, caught up in the panicked recrimination that seizes him after a rage. I steady myself, backing away. We still have to get out of this. Saul's army won't be so easily persuaded. And the king is a different man when his soldiers are watching.

Saul shudders, his hands outstretched again. He's still feeling the presence of my men, the bows and swords aimed in his direction. "Just please promise me you won't cut off my name from my father's house. Swear before the Lord that you won't destroy my family."

"I swear it." I've sworn it before.

Joab spins Saul's spear. "Your weapons stay with us. You're going to walk out of here and lead your men home. Tonight. If you're planning to send them in here to kill us, think again. We are hundreds, and half of us are already watching your army from the rocks. Just take your men and return to Gibeah." He steps forward. "My archers will follow. If your men attack us, we'll cut you down like the lying serpent you are."

Thirteen

"I'll go." Saul backs away, nearly stumbling over his dragging robe and the protruding rocks edging up from the cave floor. His hands are still stretched out before him. Still shaking. He glances behind him, then pivots around, refusing to turn his back. "I'll command them and we'll go."

I watch him carefully, my eyes burning. Does he realize how close he came to death? Does he know the folly of trying to cheat it now? I don't breathe until he's left the cave, and Joab's men return with the report that his men are clearing out of En-Gedi, the retinue heading north back to Gibeah.

Burying the point of my knife into the dust, I lean my forehead against the hilt. We'll have to leave soon as well. Head up to the stronghold before Saul can change his mind and double back. My men file past me, returning to the back of the cave, but I can tell which one stops in front of me.

Joab's voice is trapped in his chest, refusing to lift. "I would ask what's wrong with you, but I won't get a satisfying answer. I didn't realize Saul was so deep under your skin."

I lift my head slowly, keeping my eyes closed. "He's my father. And my king. I won't go against him." There's something relieving in the decision, even as it consigns me to more wandering.

"So, this is what we are to expect?" Joab speaks to me like I'm a stranger, all the fervor flattened out of his tone.

"I told you before. I'll defend whoever comes to me for sanctuary. But I won't kill Saul." I open my eyes, letting the pain enter my voice. "Don't you see what you're trying to get me to do? You're trying to make me like him! The Lord forbid that I should stretch out my hand against His anointed."

"*You* are His anointed." Joab points vehemently in my face. "And your enemy was two feet away from you, alone. Yahweh couldn't have made it any simpler for you."

I stand up sharply. "Watch what you lay at the door of the Lord! He never told me to take Saul's life. Would you have me chasing the same murderous frenzies Saul is caught up in? Is that what you want for my kingship?"

Joab angles closer, his face inches from mine. "I want you to live to see your kingship. Saul doesn't deserve the crown he wears."

I soften my voice. "He won't have it forever. Either the Lord will strike him, or he'll die in battle. His time will come, as it does for all men. But I won't be the one to kill him. I've made my decision, and I won't yield. Not to you or to anyone!" I strike his chest, driving him back apace.

Thirteen

He gapes at me, but I keep talking. He's going to hear me. "From Saul's own lips, Yahweh will judge between us and vindicate me for the honor I've shown to His anointed. I have chosen Adonai as my salvation." I breathe, settling myself. "Do you trust Him, Joab?"

Joab closes his mouth, lowering his arms. "I trust Yahweh. I'm no longer completely sure about you."

FOURTEEN

Jonathan

Pain stabs my eyes the second I open them. I shrink away from the slice of sunlight inching through my father's heavy curtains and cover my face with my hands. At the moment, I don't remember why I'm in Saul's fortress chambers and not at home. I have no idea what time it is, or why the sun is so bright, but I have to sleep. The moment I think it, though, I can't do it.

Eema's final words wrestle with my father's screams of rage in my mind until I can't close my eyes. I shove off the floor, the aches in my body deeper than physical pain.

After my mother's death, I should be in mourning.

Instead, I have to keep fighting at Abba's side.

The darkness has returned, crawling back into Gibeah with the king after his time in En-Gedi. For weeks since then, the death grip of torment has rivaled anything I've seen before. Abba's back to the old succession of fuming and exploding, then dropping into a dazed sleep of exhaustion. Except this time, David and his music are far away. There's nothing for me to do except come when my father calls and listen to him rage.

"My son…my son, spare me," he mumbles across the room, tossing and sobbing into his bedclothes. "Spare me!" His shout tears into my half-sleep, and I rush to his side, gripping his arm to stop him from swinging around while dreaming.

"Abba, I'm here! I won't harm you!"

He whirls around, his huge, empty eyes devouring my face before dissolving into a fresh fit of tears. "No…he spared me. My son David. He…had my robe, but he…he wouldn't take my life." He collapses back across his bed, his voice mounting into a howling cry. Pulling his arm free, he punches the wall over his pillow. "Cursed shepherd! Humiliating me before my men!"

Horrified, I ease off the bed, feeling safer on my feet. "Abba, what's…?"

"He took everything from me!" Saul roars, grasping the front of my tunic. "He couldn't even face me with a sword in his hand! He should have fought me. I would have brought his head back with me! I'll do it, too! I'll kill that pretender with my own hands…"

Fourteen

His words bend and break off into nothing, his exhaustion taking over. Groaning, he falls flat across the bed, the mattress sinking under his weight.

Relieved, I back away, regaining the rhythm of my own breathing while I watch his chest sink lower and lower. The heavy sleep holding him prisoner after his dreams is the only mercy we've been experiencing in this confusion. No one will venture an opinion, and no one can help the way David used to.

Easing through the door, I step outside and run into my new armorbearer, Nadab. The youth Abner employed in Ezra's place is standing there trembling, with his sword drawn.

"What were you going to do with that?" I demand, torn between gratitude and offense.

Nadab's eyes are enormous. "Whatever you want, my lord."

My mind pushes Ezra's image over his, and the contrast is painful. As a young warrior, Ezra had made me promise I'd fight back if the king tried to hurt me too badly.

"You know how to knock him out without killing him. And if you won't, I will."

It's a heavy memory now that Ezra's been sent into exile. I grind my teeth. I should have kept him by my side until I was able to kill Doeg myself. Only Sheva's poor health after the miscarriage prevented me from leaving Gibeah to follow Ezra.

I point Nadab down the hall. "The king is asleep now. Go find Abner and tell him I need to speak with him before we meet with the council."

"He's with the council now, my lord," the boy says.

"Now?" I crane my neck to see out the nearest window, searching for the position of the sun. The king's chamber shuts out light like a tomb. Time of day doesn't matter in there. I wince, thinking of the way my father howled in rage. "Please tell me they're assembled in the fortress." Not the antechamber beneath Saul's rooms.

Nadab winces, his discomfort mirroring mine.

I sigh, covering my eyes with my hand. "Just get Abner."

He was the closest to Saul during those weeks they spent in En-Gedi. He can tell me what the king is babbling about.

The army he'd taken after David came home wearing the same heavy cloud darkening the king's brow. They all refused to

Fourteen

look at me, refused to talk about what had happened. My father's voice was already hoarse, no doubt from venting his frustration during the journey.

I've seen the signs before. He was ready to break, but only so many things can trigger him. I'm willing to bet Abner will know what pushed him over the edge this time. The general has been avoiding me since he returned, and now he's holding council without me. Not a coincidence.

Abner follows Nadab outside the council room, looking annoyed. He pulls the door shut behind him. "What is it?"

I glance over his shoulder. "Hiding something in there?"

Abner's face flinches. "Just discussing a plan the king set in motion when he first got back. Before…this." He lifts a weary hand toward my father's chamber.

"And nothing about this plan includes me?"

I'm tired of confronting him. After all these years, you'd think I could trust my father's general. But suspicion and mistrust are pressed into these fortress walls like mortar. And I can only imagine how the commanders of Benjamin are interpreting my actions in Ziph. Saul made sure they heard about what I did.

249

Flustered, Abner looks up and down the corridor. "What can I do for you, Jonathan?"

I fold my arms. I won't be dismissed. I'm still the Hassar. I follow Abner's aimless gaze until I have his attention. "You can tell me what happened in En-Gedi."

The cloud drops from Abner's face, revealing everything he was trying to hide. "Nothing happened."

I uncross my arms. "That's what you told me after Amalek. And the same torment took him by storm, except now, we have no shepherd boy to soothe it away." I fix my eyes on him until they start to burn. "Talk."

Abner's forehead creases. "Did the king say something?"

"He said his son spared him. His son David." My voice tightens. "Then, he said something about his robe. And a shepherd humiliating him before his men."

Abner's chest rises and falls rapidly. He opens his mouth several times, trying to speak, then reaches inside his cloak and pulls out a scrap of red cloth. He places it in my hands. The edges are frayed and torn, but I can see the gold fringe from my father's robe.

Fourteen

"David?" I ask, flicking my eyes up.

Abner's throat bobs up and down. "We think so. We were encamped below the crags by the sheepcotes where the path winds up into the cliffs of the wild goats. We'd planned to search the caves in the morning, but Saul went up alone around midnight to relieve himself."

I clear my throat, wrestling back the urge to slam Abner against the door. In over twenty years, he's never let the king out of his sight.

Sweat slides across Abner's brow beneath his hair. "When Saul came back, he had a torn robe and no weapons. He told us we had to leave immediately and return to Gibeah. He seemed incredibly shaken, so I obeyed without question. I knew he'd likely been threatened, but I was too frightened to ask him about it. I figured he would talk when he was ready."

I laugh harshly. "Well, he's talking now." Leaning my elbow into the wall, I grip the torn cloth against my head. "So, David spared Saul up in those caves," I summarize. "He cut his robe but let him go free?"

Abner scoffs slightly. "I wouldn't say that."

I lift my head, my eyes snapping back onto him. "What would you say? My father is here, alive, and more shaken than I've seen him in years. We know David was hiding in En-Gedi. What else could have happened up there?"

Abner's voices bites, disdain tightening his face. "David humiliated his king, sneaking up on him in the dark and terrorizing him with those renegades he calls his mighty men. Your little friend is the reason for your father's torment."

"Is he? So, the years before David came were just our imagination?" I'm too tired to fight with him, but I'll have him remember how things used to be and how David changed them. I press my finger into his chest. "You were there. You saw how Yahweh's presence walked into this house with that boy and gave my father…a second chance."

My voice breaks as I realize that Saul isn't taking it. Probably ever. By pursuing David, he's rejecting Yahweh a second time. Again and again. I pull my hand down my face, trying to remove the threat of emotion. "What was the plan my father set in motion when you returned?"

Abner fiddles with his sword, glancing down the corridor. "It's just a few campaigns to ensure our support in Judah, that's all. He's offered tax exemption to the wealthy nobles in Carmel,

Fourteen

Maon, and Hebron—the ones with the most to give and the most to lose. They'll be freed from taxation if they'll inform the king when David comes to them for help. Which he will. He can't keep that company in the cliffs forever. The summer harvest will draw them out to more fertile pastures."

Using David's need for food to trap him. Shameless. I chew my lip hard until I taste blood. "Anyone accept?"

Abner swallows. "Several haven't responded yet, but we've received word from Shaphat of Maon and Nabal of Carmel."

Two of the most worthless men I know of in southern Israel. I step back, sighing sharply, but Abner moves with me.

"This is a good development, Jonathan. Judah hasn't been in league with us in years. We'll finally have some support from Israel's fiercest tribe."

"I'll celebrate later," I sneer back at him, hearing Ishvi's voice within the antechamber. More and more these days, Abner and my brothers act like they don't know me, discussing how to trap David right alongside other matters of state. As if his followers are just another band of Ammonite rogues we're trying to run off. Not that my father pays much attention to our real enemies these days.

"Anything else?" I fold my arms, already certain I don't want to hear more.

When I see the hint of justification sharpen Abner's eyes, I feel nauseous. He gave the prophet Samuel the same look after we failed to destroy Amalek. He fidgets. "The other order concerns the Gibeonites."

My brow pulls into a frown, but I can't think of any recent problems we might have had with the Canaanite band. Descended from the Hivites and Amorites, the sons of Gibeon make up four clans who have been in servitude to Israel since the days of Moses' successor Joshua. They deceived our ancestors centuries ago, tricking Joshua's men into making a covenant with them. Since then, they've existed on the outskirts of Israel. No one really trusts them, but they're little more than dispatch riders, stonecutters, menials.

Abner's brow shines with sweat now. "The king was incensed that we have spent so many centuries bound by their deception. He dispatched Malchi's thousands to Beeroth to…finish them."

"Finish them?" I repeat, trying to understand. "Finish them!" I shout it this time, and Abner swallows, trying to explain.

Fourteen

"His wrath was burning when he returned, and he had to unleash it somewhere. We can all be thankful it wasn't on another holy city like Nob."

Just when I thought that would be the worst thing I would ever see him do! I slap Abner's shoulders with both hands, slamming him up against the door of the antechamber. I don't care if the others hear. The king had no right to give such an order!

"We had a covenant with them, Abner ben Ner! Joshua promised in the name of the Lord! That's binding!" I hit him again in the chest. "How can you continue to follow my father so blindly when you see what he's doing, where he's leading us?"

Abner's face is gray. "He's my king."

My eyes blaze with tears. "But Yahweh is your God! An edict of mass destruction against Gibeon drags Adonai's name through the dust. Before the *Canaanites!*"

Grinding my fists in front of Abner's face, I shove him aside, heading for the outer stairs built around the courtyard.

"Where are you going?" Abner raises his voice.

"I'm going home. I haven't seen my wife in two nights, and you seem to have things under control here." I stop on the top stair, my throat aching. "Think about who you're really serving with all this, Abner. We don't have all the time in the world."

I don't look back to see if he understands.

I take the long way home, circling around through my father's fields, desperate to escape my own horror. I thought I was finished being shocked by Saul's actions. His sin at Amalek was omission, failing to complete the task Adonai gave him to rid Israel of an ancient bloodthirsty enemy. My father wouldn't do that. But he'll destroy our neighbors in order to have extra plunder to tempt Judah with.

I'm so sick, I almost consider riding after Malchi's men, trying to stop them. But they're likely already upon Beeroth by now. I pull up next to the stream by Ezel, remembering how terrified David had looked hiding behind it. What's one ancient covenant to Saul if David's life meant nothing to him?

Bone weary, I ride uphill to my house and find the lower rooms filled with servants, each wearing a masked expression that disturbs me. The women dart back and forth from the back kitchen to the upper chambers carrying basins of hot herb-scented water and a few boiling pots. The distinct smell of wormwood crawls up the stairs after me.

Fourteen

Sheva never makes me come find her, always greeting me at the door or in the courtyard. But now, she's sitting by the window against three cushions while her maids beg her to lie down. When she sees me, her face lights up, but she doesn't stand.

"Jonathan." Her voice is slanted and heady, and she buries her face into a cloth before beginning to cough.

"What's wrong with you?" I move over to her, placing my hand on her arm. Her tunic is clammy, and her back is like a heated slab of rock under it.

Sheva shrugs, but there's a shadow taking over more and more of her face. "I don't know; it's just a little…"

"It's the Ammonite fever we started seeing last month," one of her maids interrupts, glancing at me while she loosens Sheva's garments. "She began coughing two nights ago, when you left to attend the king. Ammiel's son told me twelve others in Gibeah have become ill. Your mother-in-law advised us to send Mephi to one of your sisters for a while."

"Mephi isn't going anywhere," Sheva croaks, clenching the cloth in her fist. "Not yet. I'll recover. I'll be fine."

But the look in her eyes is saying the opposite. She's carving a hole in the floor with her gaze, and her dilated pupils are swimming in tears. Something's very wrong. My head aches while my mind races, trying to decide what it might be.

My wife has been withdrawn since we lost the baby. But once her seclusion ended, she'd seemed ready to go on. Whatever's troubling her now is different. There might be something to this fever.

"Give me a moment alone with her," I tell the maids. "And send for one of the physicians. Get Ammiel or his son Machir, not their apprentices."

Sheva shakes her head, forcing a smile as her maids leave. "Machir's been here. The maids have been following his advice since he left." She opens a vial, and the scent of wormwood bites the air again.

I kneel at her feet, my arms around her hips. "Where's Mephi?"

She nods at the bed where our son is sprawled asleep, one hand under his cheek, his curls hiding his eyes. "If you really think we should send him away…"

"We can start with having him sleep in his own bed," I chuckle, thinking of what an achievement that will be. The boy is attached to his mother's hip. And mine when I'm home.

Fourteen

I'm staring at the cloth Sheva's holding, and my eyes catch a sliver of red on the edge. My chest pinches.

Sheva watches her hands, picking at a nail. "How is the king?"

I sigh, every burden dropping back into place. "No better, but I found out the source of his raging. Abner told me Abba came across David in the caves of En-Gedi. He was in there alone, and David could have killed him, but he cut his robe instead and sent him home."

Sheva's mouth drops open, her chest falling. "So…why does he rage?"

I shrug. It's hard to explain. "Tormented by his brush with death, I suppose. It's been like this for years. He rages at David, but he's really angry at himself."

"But not enough to change," Sheva whispers, and a tear drips down her cheek.

Her unspoken anguish pierces a helpless nerve inside me. I grip her arms tighter. "What's wrong, Sheva?"

Keeping her eyes down, she murmurs, "I thought he would've given up by now. But then I heard what he intends to do to the Gibeonites, what he still plans to do to David. Doesn't he realize what he's doing?"

My throat thickens. "Sometimes I think he does. But it doesn't matter to him as much as ridding himself of David. He's convinced himself that David is the source of all the evil in his life. He forgets that it's self-inflicted, stemming from his break with Yahweh."

Sheva nods. Her mouth bends and pulls toward grief, overshadowing her usual bravery. It angers me to see fear settling over her. All I want to do is erase it from her brow.

She wipes sweat from her forehead. "I'm afraid of what all this might mean. I can't help thinking…with everything happening lately…" She pauses to cough, then continues. "You told me years ago that David is meant to be king. Adonai chose him. If Saul doesn't stop seeking his life and David won't fight back, then Yahweh will have to answer the threat Himself. And now, the king is going after Gibeon as well."

I wince, fresh anger turning my stomach.

Sheva's eyes finally find mine and overflow, her voice inching into a sob. "We had Gibeonite servants when I was a girl. My father told me we had a covenant with them. And now the king will destroy them in direct violation of a binding treaty! What else can our God do but answer his rebellion?"

Her shoulders heave, and she surrenders to tears, in between coughs. "I don't want to watch everything crumble while our son is caught in the middle. If Yahweh removes Saul, men will try to forcibly crown you or Mephi. Unless…unless there's no one left." She weeps, her face breaking apart in her hands. "Will Yahweh strike our son?"

"Sheva, no!" I say it before the full weight of her fear hits me like a millstone to the chest. I grab her, but the impact of what she's saying is tearing at me from the inside. It's something we should have talked about long ago. It's just too horrific to fathom. "I can't believe that," I say into her hair. "I won't believe it, and neither should you."

My mind writhes, desperate for hope. Yahweh is a faithful God, keeping His covenant of love with those who follow His commands. But He also visits vengeance on the third and fourth generations.

Sheva gulps, her sobs wild. She's never cried like this except when we lost our daughter. Now, she's afraid for our son. Not even for herself. Her fingers bite into me. "I want to know for sure. We're raising Mephi to be faithful, you and I. But how can he help it if he's caught in this quicksand Saul's created?"

She's so brittle in my arms, still too underweight since the baby. I hold her as tightly as I dare, my heart racing faster and faster while she clings to my robe, her sobs tearing me open.

"You have to find a way to save him. Please, Jonathan! Promise me you'll save our son!"

* * * * *

I meant to rest at home, but I'm up all through the night pacing, trying to find words for the anguish roaming around inside me. I've learned how to manage anxiety, but the weight of this responsibility is threatening to flatten me if I don't do something.

Sheva's right. My father will not be allowed to continue in rebellion forever. My wife sees it coming as clearly as I have for years, but now it's closer at hand.

Saul's recent bout with madness, his raging at David, and his move against Gibeon is all the proof I need that he hasn't gone back to the Lord. Hasn't even tried. I can't even remember the last time he celebrated a feast or honored a priest. It's foolish to keep my family here, waiting for something worse to happen.

But I need direction first. Strategy. And I can only think of one man I would dare approach with this.

Fourteen

By morning, I've composed a message six different times, rewriting it in my head until it's half of what I started with. It's a simple petition for wisdom, one I'm hoping the Roeh won't just toss in the fire. The prophet Samuel anointed both my father and David. He's been Yahweh's messenger to Israel for a lifetime, and I'm desperate to talk to him, but I don't dare ride to Ramah myself.

All I want to know is if I should take my wife and my son and forsake this madness. Leave Gibeah behind until I can see David crowned.

I'm glad I did this at night. By the time I put the message into a dispatch rider's hands, exhaustion is blurring the part of me that might hesitate. "Take this to Ramah, and put it into the hands of the Roeh's servant. No one less," I tell him before going upstairs and burying any misgivings in overdue sleep.

Any other time, I would worry about spies following him to report on me. But I've put that out before the Lord too, determined to know His will in this matter.

"I'll stay until I have clear direction. But if the messenger betrays me to Saul, I'm taking my family out of here. I won't wait." I whisper it into the sunrise before collapsing across my bed. Mephi's already sleeping there, but he doesn't wake up.

After several days go by with no word, good or bad, I'm astonished when a man from the school of prophets arrives. I'd expected the same messenger to return with instructions, but instead Samuel's servant comes alone.

It's been so long since anyone from Ramah came here. But he might as well be invisible, because no one at the gate stops him, and none of my guards ask questions.

Even so, I bring him into the inner chamber behind my armory, a place I go to pray in seclusion. The narrow room holds only a few cushions and a copy of the Law of Moses carefully rolled up on a table. If the young prophet sees it, he doesn't say. Now that we're alone, I notice how exhausted he looks. His expression is drawn and distressed.

"I'll have my servant bring you something to eat," I begin, ashamed. Why didn't I think to offer before?

"No." He shakes his head. "Let me say what I've come to say."

I step in front of him, my back covering the slant of light from the tiny window. "Yes?"

I suppose I should be afraid. It's the first word from Samuel I've sought in years, since I last went to him about David. But I'm

Fourteen

too desperate. And the young student's face is locked, refusing to betray anything.

"The Roeh Samuel has been ill," he begins.

"I was wondering how he's been faring," I comment, pausing to let the news settle over me.

Since the winter, the aged prophet has been struggling to recover. The strange Ammonite sickness left him wheezing and coughing blood. Like Sheva. Without telling the king, I'd sent a few of Gibeah's best healers to Ramah, but they'd returned without much to report.

I shift my weight, trying to conceal my eagerness. "I'm grateful for Samuel's response," I continue. The prophet hasn't seen my father since their break over our disobedience at Amalek.

The tightness in the messenger's face suddenly relaxes, softening into something like respect. "He sent me as soon as he'd sought the Lord." He steps forward. "He was eager to have you know that you are greatly beloved. Though you are bound to your father, you have chosen to walk in the light of Yahweh's face, and so He has not turned away from you."

I nearly gasp out loud, the pain ripping through my chest is so great. Emotion surges up between my ribs, and I grip the edge of the table behind me, unsure how to respond. I don't need to speak. I just stand there, letting the oil of the message make its way through my veins, covering everything that's been stripped raw by fear.

Whatever else he has to say, it's enough to know my God is not ashamed of me. It's all I've wanted to be certain of since I was a boy—that, and my father's love. The latter has been much harder to obtain. But if I have Yahweh's smile, I can withstand anything, face anything. David taught me that much.

I grapple for words, overwhelmed. "I—I'm…"

The messenger's face saddens, the unexplainable pain returning. "The Roeh knew how much Yahweh's trust would mean to you. But he only sent me because he knew you could be trusted with the rest." His eyes edge up to mine, grabbing hold of the militant honor that always waits beneath my exterior. "You are not to tell anyone what I'm about to say. It's not for anyone else to hear. That is why the Roeh didn't write it down."

Now I'm trembling for a different reason, my mind darting in a hundred different directions. Steadying myself, I exhale slowly and fold my hands. "Understood."

The young man's chest fills with air, his eyes lightening, and when he speaks again, authority strengthens his tone. My pulse quickens, listening. Drinking in Yahweh's words.

"David will never strike your father. You already know this. But the throne will not pass easily from one to another. It will be a struggle to maintain your faith in the days to come. The covenant binding you to David will provide your son with the safety you long for, but the cords connecting you to your father are just as strong."

The young prophet steps closer and grips my wrist. "You must cling to Yahweh's faithfulness and to the promises He has made to His people. Let His understanding direct your preparations for the future. Because when Saul dies, so will you."

The words crash into me, roaring in my ears, but then a powerful hush fills the room, like a storm abruptly ceasing. "When?" I ask, instantly regretting the question.

Fortunately, the young man shakes his head slowly. "Only Yahweh knows times and seasons."

I nod, all the years I've spent beside my father reopening before me like an unfurled scroll. I hear my own words standing out to me from a dozen different conversations.

I won't leave you, Abba. I will die by your side, fighting the enemies of the Lord. Achish will march into Gibeah over my dead body.

It seems obvious, if not inevitable, that I will die as I always unconsciously planned. Deep sadness opens in the center of me, but I don't recoil away from it. After hearing the prophet say it aloud, I realize I've always known.

Amid the strange peace filling my veins, questions start to emerge, disturbing the calm. How will it happen? In battle with our enemies? Or will one of David's men cut us down and live just long enough to regret it? My father is aging, but he still has plenty of strength left. When Sheva and Mephi enter my mind, I have to swallow hard to bury the pain. Will I live to see my son grow up? I shake off the thought. It's too much.

The Roeh is right. It wouldn't make sense to reveal the news of my death. Everyone must die sooner or later. That much hasn't changed. I force myself to remember the rest of the message. Somehow, in the midst of all the chaos and rebellion, Yahweh has seen my persistence, and He's pleased with it. He doesn't look with anger at my son. Sheva will find relief in knowing the truth.

"Thank you for telling me this," I address the messenger, gripped with a desire to lay eyes on Samuel and tell him the same

Fourteen

myself. "Are you certain I shouldn't ride up to Ramah?" I ask, a plan already forming in my mind. I could summon Ammiel and see what we can do for the old prophet's illness. Maybe get some wisdom for Sheva's while I'm at it.

Pain cuts the man's face. I see it before he lowers his head. "No," he says quietly. "By this time, there won't be anyone to receive you except a funeral procession." He folds his hands while I struggle to comprehend what he's saying. "The Roeh is dead."

FIFTEEN

David

Gray clouds slump together on the horizon, and the collective grief of Israel adds heaviness to the air. Concealed by a ragged disguise, with dust staining the color of my hair, I keep to the fringes of the multitude, but I can feel the passion that's been stirred. The people move like a slow, wailing wave, pressing through to the bier where the Roeh has been laid. Over the heads of the crowd, I can see the shoulders of the rocky cave where Samuel will rest.

Even for all the talk of his age, the news of his death had been sudden, stirring a powerful grief I hadn't expected to feel. Another layer of security has dropped away, and the weeping tells me Israel feels as vulnerable as I do. Even after Saul's rejection, Samuel still holds the heart of the land. The generations around me have grown up hearing how he was chosen by Yahweh as a boy to deliver the words of God, but few have heard them spoken over their own head in blessing.

The Lord sees you, David. He sees your heart.

I close my eyes to ease the sting. What else does Adonai see these days? What could Samuel tell me if I could speak to him once more? The hunger to know is almost painful. So much has happened in the past month, and it all should have meant more, given me precise direction. Instead, we're still wandering. Still in disguise, just to be here.

My muscles clench when Saul's voice reaches me over the crowd, even though we can't see each other. I don't know what he would do if he found me here. After En-Gedi, I should have been able to return to Israel. But I can't.

I shift my shoulders under the sackcloth, longing to push back the woolen hood. It's past midday, and in spite of the heavy clouds, sweat trails the back of my neck, dripping down my back like a long tear. I glance casually at the strategic points where my men are standing. It's time. We'll have to slip away, one by one, before Saul finishes his speech and starts moving through the crowds.

I wish I could stay, for Jonathan. He'd been there to strengthen me after the death of my own parents. After hearing about his mother's recent death, I want to do the same for him as he did for me. I know he was close to his Eema. But the rest of our company is waiting several days' journey south, in Paran. It's time we joined them. Before Saul finishes his duties up here and decides to come after us.

Blinking away the mist staining my vision, I squint at the sky.

Farewell, Roeh.

The phrase seems to lift my disguise, uncovering the relative safety I'd felt. With Samuel's death, Saul will feel even more unrestrained. Even though the Roeh's presence hadn't stopped him before. Either way, we have to leave. Before Saul realizes we're here.

* * * * *

The illusion of safety returns once I see our tents spreading over the southern valley. Our camp in the golden grassland of Paran is the closest we've come in years to a normal Israelite existence. Our people have turned into day laborers, working to scrape as much provision from these summer days as possible. Living completely off the land isn't easy, but we'll do anything to avoid the hunger of the previous winter, especially with more joining our ranks almost weekly.

One of them shocked me. Jonathan's armorbearer Ezra had arrived several months ago, banished for killing Saul's Edomite spy. His feat had earned him instant respect among my men, but Ezra still keeps to himself, unaccepting of the situation. I know he never would have left Jonathan if he hadn't been forced to. And he doesn't want me to rule.

He's been a Godsend though, fixing the oldest armor and honing the younger men's fighting skills. Uriah admires him, and Abishai is convinced he'll command one of my thousands one day.

He's alone for once, restringing his bow in the shade of a tamarisk tree. He lifts his eyes when I pass, but his hands don't stop working. The question in his face saddens me. He didn't accompany me north, fearing Saul might see him. He's not used to living under a death sentence, but I'm almost grateful he hasn't come to me for any advice. I'm still waiting for it to get easier.

Stopping at the edge of camp, I take a long drink from the brook, gathering strength before going to greet Ahinoam. The ice between us still hasn't thawed, and she's spoken even less since Saul trapped us in the caves. I hate admitting defeat where's she's concerned, but I can't give her the assurance she wants. The other women have done their best to lift her burdens. For that I'm grateful.

Fifteen

Emerging from our tent with a water jug, Ahinoam squints into the sunlight, her expression changing. Her pace quickens slightly, and she reaches out to me with a simple, "You're back."

"I'm back," I repeat, kissing her cheek.

"Did Saul see you?" she asks, her face tightening.

"No."

Ahinoam nods and bends over the water. "Then we'll have some more time here."

"I hope so."

I fill my lungs with the warm smell of the fields, my spirits lifting. Out here, it's almost possible to forget we're in exile. The owners of these extensive stretches of land live so far removed from their servants that we can be assured of solitude.

The open pastures are scattered with shepherds and their flocks, and we've guarded them before they even knew we were there, providing a barrier between them and the predators and thieves of the open grassland. Fortunately, the shepherds have been grateful and welcoming.

Ahinoam dips a cloth into the brook and dabs her brow with it. "When will your men receive payment for the season?"

"Hard to say. Joab was supposed to take some servants up to the main house this morning." I sigh, looking out over the southern pasture. In the distance, a handful of shepherds drive the flocks toward the far end of the brook. "It's been a plentiful season, but unfortunately, the shearing is almost over, and the servants have no authority to distribute payment for our services. We'll have to deal with the Calebite who owns all this."

"Who is he?" Ahinoam asks.

I bend down for a drink, hiding my grimace in the water. None of my men had reacted well when they'd found out who we've been working for.

Ezra comes up beside Ahinoam and answers for me. "It's Nabal. He's one of the richest men in Carmel." He thrusts a waterskin into the brook, disgusted.

Ahinoam blinks. "Is that a problem?"

"It's not ideal," I admit. "He has a terrible reputation."

"His name means *fool*, and that's exactly what he is," Ezra translates. "He's an abusive drunkard, and everyone who does business with him says it's a nightmare."

Fifteen

I splash water onto my neck, glancing at the angle of the sun. The longer my servants are with Nabal, the more I wonder how they're being received.

Asking for handouts is never easy, but we've earned it fairly. Very few Israelite men of property would turn their brothers away in a time of plenty. Perhaps since my servants are approaching Nabal in the midst of a feast, he'll be in the mood to negotiate fairly.

Watching the gold tinge of the fields against the horizon, I feel my thoughts unwind, trying to run free.

During another shearing season generations ago, my great-grandfather Boaz had reached out to his future wife, Ruth, who'd been gleaning in his fields as a destitute widow. He'd used his wealth and position as a kinsman to give her a life of dignity. And everything had changed.

"May you be blessed by the Lord, the God of Israel under whose wings you have taken refuge," he'd told her.

Boaz's words remind me to hope. Survival may be a struggle, but Yahweh is our refuge. And He never turns away those who need Him.

Uriah and Abishai join us at the brook, followed by several servants ready to fill waterskins. Ezra hangs back, but it's the first time he hasn't simply walked away from the others.

"You think we'll get out of this ahead?" Abishai wonders aloud. The slant of his voice tells me he doesn't.

I shrug, taking another drink as Ahinoam heads back to camp. "I don't know. I guess I'm hoping Nabal will be in a better mood with the feasting today."

"I met some of the household servants," Uriah interjects. "They were accompanying his wife back home from Maon. One of them said he doesn't allow gleaners to visit his fields. Which means he has little regard for the poor or the Law."

I turn around. "When did you talk to his wife?"

Abishai grins. "Relax. You know her. It's Abigail."

The name hits me like cold water being dumped over my head. "She married *him?!*" I explode, breathless, and then have to cope with all the sudden baffled stares trained on me.

Abishai buries the humor in his expression, but he can't keep it out of his voice. "Yes. Nothing in your life is fair." He glances back toward the tents, waiting for Ahinoam to make it inside. "Do you want to see her?"

Fifteen

"No! Are you mad?" I push past him, completely unwound. It's bad enough they had to see me react. "Just watch for Joab and Asa. We'll deal with Nabal and get out of here."

If these are Abigail's fields, I definitely can't stay.

I hate to leave the others behind to talk this over, but I'm already walking away into the south field. Straight into the memories. They're so old, they should be dusty by now, but their warmth is irresistible, pulling me into an embrace I hadn't realized I missed.

Abigail had been one of my first friends, back when I was still too young to understand why my mother was dead or why my father couldn't express any love for me. We had played in the fields every summer until the year before I'd been summoned to Gibeah. My father's old servant Aaron had teasingly said I would marry her one day, and I'd always laughed at him. But all I have to do is picture Abigail's face, and I know the idea never left me.

The last time I saw her, she was stretching over a ravine, clinging to a salient branch with one hand while inching down toward a trapped lamb. A clump of brambles was the only thing between her and the forty feet of open space plunging to a stony creek bottom.

"You shouldn't be doing this, Abi. I'm the shepherd," I had warned her.

But Abigail hadn't listened. She'd just slid farther down the slope, wedging herself against the rotting thorn bush imprisoning the lamb. "Almost there. Got him."

Her fingers digging into the rock, she'd lifted her other arm as high as it would go until I could reach the lamb. Tossing it to safety, I'd pulled Abigail the rest of the way up while the unstable ground crumbled under her sandals.

Now, half-hidden in her husband's field, I pull a handful of grass and work it through my fingers while the rest of the memory fills the meadow in front of me.

* * * * *

In my mind's eye, Abigail laughs gently, her eyes skirting our fingers still locked together after our escape from the ravine. "I'm fine."

"Why did you have to climb down there?" I swipe sweat from my forehead, concern battling with my admiration. "You know what your father would have done to me if anything happened to you?"

"It had to be me. I never get to do anything like that at home." She picks a thorn from her sleeve, giggling as the wind takes her hair in every direction. Giving up trying to control it, she spreads her arms, striking a queenly pose. "How do I look after a rescue?"

Her unbound hair dances behind her. Her clothes are dusty, and her forearm is scratched from the brambles. I try to come up with some way to tease her, but only one word comes to mind. "Beautiful."

She rolls her eyes. "My father says it's a useful trait in a daughter."

I wince. That's not what I meant. She stares out over the flock, something heavy creeping into her smile. "I'm going to miss these hills. It's almost over."

"What is?"

"All of this." She shrugs. "I can just feel it. Every step laid out before me. My preordained life falling into place." She looks up to the edge of the forest, drinking everything in. "Can't we just live up there?"

"You mean, run away?" The suggestion impresses me as much as it shocks me.

"People do, don't they? The resistance groups?"

"Yes, but they're not welcome in any of the towns. They can't worship openly or keep the feasts. They have to steal to survive." I shake my head. "Unless you want to spend your life with someone like Joab, I wouldn't recommend it."

She faces me. "Who says I would be with someone like Joab?"

"That's the kind of men who are up there. And many of them can't even support families. Believe me, they wouldn't welcome a woman all by herself."

"What if I wasn't alone?" The seriousness in her face makes me feel unsteady. Her voice comes closer. "Are you going to tell me that any town could give you what you have out here?"

"No." But it would take a lot more to make me walk away from my country. Fortunately, Abigail knows me well enough to hear what I'm not saying.

She smirks. "You've heard too many stories. You want to fight for Saul. But he has plenty of soldiers he can command to battle at a moment's notice. Why do you want to fight beside him?"

"I don't know. I just…have to."

The intensity of her stare makes me panic a little. She's my best friend, and I don't want to lose her. But our friendship has been based on songs, and stories, and sheep. And she's a woman now. Destined for things I can't give her.

I don't realize how close we're standing to each other until someone shouts her name across the field.

"Abigail!"

I step back, but she moves with me. Her casual manner is gone, her ease scattered.

The two men storming across the pasture are probably six or seven years older than me. They both share physical similarities with Abigail, but their manner doesn't convince me they're related to her. Instead, I feel myself readying for defense, like with Eliab.

Abigail murmurs, "My brothers…Kemuel, Abiram." She doesn't have time to say more before the older man jumps down her throat.

"What are you doing, girl? Eema's been looking for you."

"She knows where I am." Abigail threads her fingers together. "I always spend time among the sheep at home."

"You're not a child anymore. It's unfitting for you to be wandering the pastures distracting Jesse's servants."

"This is Jesse's son," she says icily.

"What happened to you? Where's your veil?" he demands, ignoring her tone.

Remembering, she looks around for it while her brothers make sure I feel every bit of the contempt in their eyes.

"Nothing happened to me. I took it off. It's hot." Flustered, she yanks it off the branch where she'd left it.

"Well, put it back on," Kemuel commands. "Abba has someone he wants you to meet."

"In Bethlehem?"

Her brother snorts. "He's passing through, like us. No one of any importance actually lives here."

Abigail wraps her veil around her hair. "Jesse is descended from Boaz. Even the king knows about him."

Her brother's next comment is aimed at her but meant for me. "If I recall correctly, Boaz had a foreign wife and mother.

Fifteen

If you think Abba's going to waste you on some half-Moabite, you're mistaken. Now, let's go."

* * * * *

My watchmen's signal horn startles me back to the present, and I shudder, sickened understanding slashing the memory to pieces. Nabal had been the traveling merchant, the rich man they'd insisted she meet that day. They'd probably promised her to him already, before she'd even seen him. And all this time, she's been married to a man no one speaks of without grimacing. A man who abuses his servants and ignores the Law. My stomach turns over.

"My lord!" Uriah calls, halfway across the field. "Joab's returned."

I approach him, apprehension staining my alertness. Why did any of us think Nabal would receive my messengers? Nabal is loyal to Saul. He's maintained his wealth with no tax increases because of his neutrality over the years.

Joab's group has reached the edge of our tents, and they're already surrounded by my other men, all rumbling complaints while my nephew's voice crackles with offense.

"What happened?" I elbow into the group, annoyed when several of my servants fall abruptly silent, looking away. "Did you speak with Nabal?"

Joab spits in the dust. "He's everything we've heard. A selfish fool."

Heat fills my cheeks, and my heart stumbles over beats, unsteady. "What did he say?"

A familiar heaviness clouds Joab's face. "We should never have said a word to that pompous drunkard. We should have taken what was rightfully ours."

"He's not going to help us," Asahel summarizes. "He knows what we've done. He just doesn't care."

"What did he say?" I hold myself steady, trying not to picture Abigail sitting next to Nabal while my men asked for food.

My nephew looks away, and my defenses stir, shaken awake. "That bad?"

Asa tries to soften his words by aiming them at the ground. "He said you were a nobody, a worthless runaway. He said there are a lot of slaves breaking away from their masters these days, and he's not going to waste his bread on someone with no country."

A collective groan builds among the men, but I don't hear it. A fist enters my chest and tightens, sealing off everything except the ugly words. They dig into me over and over.

"It's barely afternoon, and he was already drunk. He said he would send word to Saul if we didn't get off his land by nightfall," Asa adds, agitated.

Joab curses, decapitating a nearby shrub with his sword. "He's an idiot! Who does he think he's dealing with? Any common raider would have robbed him blind already, especially if he had a family to support."

My men murmur agreement, but I barely hear them over the pounding in my head. It's not the first time I've heard words like this. And not just from Nabal. From everyone. My father, Eliab, the town elders, Saul's men. Even Abigail's family. Despising me, beating me down. Trying to find ways to hurt me. And I have to swallow my pride and take it while my friends sit helpless, bound to the people who hate me.

Fugitive. Bastard. Traitor.

I stiffen, a new edge slicing through the softness in me. If they want to see me as a lawless brigand, then so be it. I'm clenching the weapon at my belt, my hand sweating while redness eats away at my vision.

I wait for the chatter to settle so my words hit their mark. "If Nabal wants common raiders, he's going to get common raiders."

Joab blinks. "What?"

I address the others, my jaw clenched. "Everyone, strap on your swords. Every man in Nabal's house will die tonight."

"You're serious?" Joab hesitates.

I turn to him, my throat hardening. "Do you have a problem with that?"

His face tightens. "You know I don't."

"Good," I snap, my tone cutting through my torn pride. "Then show him what we're made of."

Leaving a handful of servants with our women and children in the shepherd's caves, we move from the outskirts of Nabal's property and head straight for his main compound nestled at the center of his sprawling fields.

The sunlight drops away behind the farthest hill, but my anger only builds as we approach. Jonathan had been a boy when the Philistines had torched his father's fields. Without protection, it can happen to the wealthiest in Israel.

Fifteen

Tonight, Nabal will learn what it's like to have our protection removed. And Saul won't be anywhere nearby to help him. My men can make short work of this place before the sun even sets. None of his gold or his flocks or even the king's favor will save him.

"What if the servants ride out to meet us?" Abishai inquires, moving up next to me. "He won't just let us ride up to the house."

"Then, we'll start with them." My fingers bite into the leather of the reins, and my mule shakes its head, feeling my tension. A few feet away, Ezra looks down, avoiding eye contact. I stiffen, disturbed. I understand why Ezra would hesitate, but I've never known my men to hold back before.

"If you're ashamed to fight, then go wait with the servants." I can barely believe the harshness coming from my own mouth, but I've walked too far in anger's grip. I can't take back my orders now, especially when it's the first proactive direction I've given in months.

I'm tired of hiding out, expending energy on others' welfare and expecting them to be grateful. Israel doesn't want me. They had put up with me for Saul's sake and sung my praises with Jonathan, but now, I'm just another castoff, and they'd rather see me trampled. They don't want me to rule. They'd rather Saul killed me.

I kick the mule's sides, urging him faster up the last hill. I'll be able to see Nabal's house over this one. And someone is coming to meet us. Several servants on donkeys and camels, with one riding out ahead of the others. My mule slows without my direction, and my sight clears.

"I'll meet them," Joab growls, but I grab his shoulder before he can ride past me.

"Hold it. It's a woman." With the last breath I can manage, I wave at the others. "All of you, stop. Stand down a moment."

The servants below us have slowed as well, coming to a stop behind the woman. She slips off her mount, and the sunset deepens the gold thread in her purple headdress.

I'm on the ground as well, without realizing how I got there, but before I can reach her, the woman reaches up and slides her veil aside. Completely. Revealing the gorgeous fall of thick hair I remember. Her eyes grab my breath and imprison it in my chest.

Abigail.

I barely have time to read her expression before she goes down on her hands and knees. Bowing. Her voice pulls tears into my eyes.

Fifteen

"My lord, let the blame for all of this fall on me. Please listen to me and spare my servants." Her hands tremble around her veil. "Don't pay any attention to Nabal. He's a worthless man, as you say. A fool, just like his name implies. His eyes are closed to everything but his own concerns."

She catches her breath and continues, "He said he doesn't know you, but he does. Everyone in Israel knows who you are and what you've done. But Nabal has ignored Yahweh's hand for years. Please don't give heed to anything he said." She lifts her eyes. "I swear to you, I didn't see your servants or I would have given them what they asked for."

Winded, Abigail pauses to breathe, rising to her feet. "All of your enemies are like Nabal. Foolish. Misguided. But they won't stop you. God has spared you from the burden of bloodguilt. You've never had to save yourself, David."

I feel pinned to the ground, unable to move. I'm close enough to see the pulse jumping in her throat.

Her eyes won't leave mine, even when she turns to gesture at the men behind her. "Please accept this gift for your company as payment for the service you gave our shepherds. And forgive us for the insults you received."

My men are already commenting under their breaths at the amount she's brought with her. The donkeys are laden down with at least two hundred loaves of bread, clusters of figs, baskets of grain and fruit.

But I can't stop looking at Abigail. Listening to her. I'm refusing to breathe, afraid I'll wake up and this won't be real. Because she's speaking to me the way only Yahweh does.

Abigail's eyes find mine and hold on. "The future of your house is more certain than the ground under our feet because you are fighting the Lord's battles," she says, her words fumbling with the lock on my heart. The added depth and maturity in her voice is holding me captive.

"It won't be like it was before," she declares. "Israel will not find evil with you as long as you live. If men rise up to kill you, your life shall be bound to the land of the living in the care of Adonai. And He will fling the lives of your enemies away, as from the hollow of a sling. You won't have to avenge yourself or carry the grief of shedding needless blood."

I feel her words in the pit of my stomach, in the curve of my heart. Everywhere. I'm seeing it too. The open valley of Elah, and my stone streaking toward Goliath to smash his skull. My own voice flinging Yahweh's praises to the skies, only willing to sing about Him.

Fifteen

Yahweh was my advocate, my shield, my fortress long before I ever had the promise of a throne. Abigail saw it all those years ago when we were only children. And now, her words have brought it all back into view, pushing through the fog that covered my vision.

It's been so long since anyone's counsel has been able to do that.

Abigail finishes, holding out her hands. "And when Yahweh has made you a prince over Israel...remember me, my lord."

I finally exhale, but nothing disappears. Abigail is really standing there, trying not to react to my reaction. I don't know how I dare, but I take her hand in mine.

"Blessed be the God of Israel!" I drag my eyes downward for a moment, grappling for control. "He was the one who sent you out here. I would have—there would have been nothing left after tomorrow."

And I would have left grieving, carrying a new burden. Taking on everything I hated about Saul. But Yahweh had saved me from that. By sending *her*.

I wish to God the eyes of my whole army weren't on me. How is it possible that I was about to make life so much more difficult for a woman who's…Abigail? It was a mistake to look in her eyes, to take her hand. As grateful as I am, I'm already fighting a dozen other emotions. How can I let her go back to such an evil man without knowing she'll be all right?

Retrieving her hand, she bows again, drawing her veil back around herself. "My lord," she barely whispers before turning to walk back down the hill. Atop her mule, she kicks the animal into a faster canter than I've ever seen a woman ride. Her servants approach my men with the provisions, but I still can't move.

Abishai whistles softly, coming up behind me. "Your childhood friendship was worth something after all. Who would have known?"

Tears stab my eyes, spinning my vision until the sunset covers Abigail's retreating form with gold. "Only Yahweh."

*****

Ten days later

My stomach tosses, wound with more joyous anticipation than I've felt in years. I don't even remember being this way with Michal. Or anyone. Just Abigail. I hadn't been able to erase her words from my mind. I never wanted to. I hated to think I would never see her again.

Fifteen

Now, I can hardly believe I will. Every day for the rest of my life.

In just ten short days, I was avenged of Nabal without lifting a finger. Flying into a rage after hearing what his wife had done, the man had collapsed, clutching his heart. Later that day, Asa brought me word that Nabal was dead. I had bowed facedown before the Lord, shaken by how close I'd been to taking vengeance into my own hands.

After that, there was only one thing to do. Abigail was the first woman I ever chose for myself, out in the pastures, without any king in the way. Asking her to marry me felt like something I should've done long ago, but to hear that she was willing to consider it seemed like a miracle.

"She's not considering it, David. She's coming," Asa reminds me, reading my thoughts on his way past. He shoves my shoulder, not even trying to hide his grin. "You're lucky you have servants, or you would've had to go down and face her yourself."

He ducks away from my attempt to punch him, sprinting off down the path. My behavior has them all talking, but I'm still too stunned to argue with anyone.

I have no idea how long I've been standing here, hyperventilating, watching the road like...well, like the old

David. Unbound youthfulness dances freely in my chest. The boy who'd shared dreams in the pastures with Abigail isn't dead. And praise Yahweh, the girl I loved isn't either.

When I see Abigail approaching with her maidservants, my heartbeat dances out of control. Now that she's here, hesitation is shaking my confidence. She's been a rich man's wife for years, and now she's coming home to a cave? To a would-be king on the run, with another wife already?

Joab's gentle hand on my arm startles me. I didn't think his gruffness was capable of warmth. "You're allowed to be happy," he says, his stubborn smile surfacing. "Yahweh brought her to you long ago when you were both stupid enough to love sheep. You deserve each other."

He shoves me, and I head downhill to meet Abigail, a laugh bubbling in my chest. Joab's right. We've belonged together for a long time. It's so good to see her smile the way I remember it. Unhindered. Exuberant. She sweeps into a stately bow, but I can see her joy dancing past her politeness.

"My lord," she murmurs, beaming.

My own smile trembles, and I spread my arms. "Welcome to the resistance. I would be more careful what you wish for in the future."

Her smile jerks slightly. "Is that any way to greet a bride?"

Then, we're in each other's arms, laughing and crying while my men shake the hills with their cheers. For the first time since leaving Gibeah, I feel the promise leaning close. Smiling deep into me.

Far into the night, we dance and celebrate like we haven't in years. When the stars burn brighter than our fires, my men and their families retreat into their tents, leaving me alone in a back cave with my new wife.

I try not to seem tentative watching Abigail. She's dressed simply, without any of the ornaments she'd been wearing ten days ago. The few maidservants who accompanied her have moved into one of the tents with Ahinoam. Her small collection of belongings rests at her feet, still packed, while she sits on a flat rock shelf, calmly looking around.

"It's nothing compared to what you had," I venture, joining her.

"That's a good thing," she sighs, releasing a strange heaviness into the cave.

Up close now, I see the bruise on her cheek more clearly, and I have to bury the simmering anger, reminding myself Nabal is already dead.

I cup her face toward mine, smoothing her hair back. "I'm so sorry. We probably should have run away when you wanted to." I half-chuckle, but she places her hands over mine.

"But then who would have killed Goliath?" Her eyes fill, but she smiles through the tears. "David, if anything, my years of marriage to Nabal prepared me for the wilderness. For daily dependence on Yahweh through impossible things. Like your days in Saul's court did for you."

My heart aches with admiration. Yahweh has shepherded her too. She's waited years in a prison of her own, and yet her heart hasn't become hard. She's older and stronger. But my Abi's still alive in her eyes and in the words Yahweh sent her to say.

I wrap her in my arms, awash with gratitude. It's so freeing to have my heart hurt for a good reason.

"I'm sorry it took me so long, then. To find you," I whisper. "As God is my witness, I won't let anyone hurt you again."

SIXTEEN

Jonathan

The abrupt knock breaks into my troubled sleep. I straighten abruptly, pain chewing through my neck. I'm slumped against the wall, dozing in the same position all day across from my wife's sickbed. Ammiel glances at me and reaches over to touch Sheva's forehead. I wonder how long he let me sleep, if you can call it that.

I don't have time to get up. Nadab doesn't wait for my command before entering. "My lord prince, the king is here."

Alarmed annoyance jolts my heartbeat into rhythm. Saul hasn't come to see me in weeks. To be fair, I haven't seen him either. Not since my mother died. I couldn't look his indifference in the eyes again, not after losing Eema.

I wince, rolling my shoulder until it pops. Why would Saul come here? I'm fairly certain he hasn't said more than six words to my wife, but today he comes to our house? When Sheva hasn't risen from her bed in seven days?

Ammiel mouths, "I'll stay," nodding at Sheva's sleeping form.

I get to my feet and touch his shoulder, hoping the physician sees gratitude in my weariness. Since the infection took hold of my wife, Ammiel's been kind. Too kind. Which tells me all I need to know. I've seen that practiced calm enough times on the battlefield. It's the same look he gave my father when Abner carried me home from Geba after I'd lost half the blood in my body fighting Philistines.

Trained alarm. Uncovered just enough to warn you.

And it makes me want to do exactly what my father did back then. I want to grab Sheva's shoulders and beg her to fight. *Don't let go! Don't leave!*

But I don't know how much I can ask of her. Her face hasn't held color for a week. She's barely eating, dehydrated. I haven't seen much of her eyes lately, either closed in sleep or strained beyond recognition. The women say it's the baby she lost. Her strength never returned. But every time she's awake, I see her being brave for me. So, I'm relieved when she sleeps.

I pray. Bring Mephi in when I can. Walk out to the fields when the fear threatens to choke me. Last night, I almost broke down, but I saw the restraint in Ammiel's eyes. *Save it.*

Sixteen

Outside Sheva's chamber, Nadab stumbles out of my way as I nearly run into him. I'm not seeing much. My wife's face is filling my mind with questions I know this boy can't understand. Was I wrong to marry her? Seeing the lengths my father has gone to kill David, it's hard not to wonder if the destruction of our house has already begun. And I've dragged an innocent, beautiful woman into it.

"He said it was urgent, my lord." Nadab follows me, rambling, but I'm barely listening.

My new armorbearer is nothing like Ezra. Young and inexperienced, he's terrified of the king and uncertain of me. But I don't bother trying to get through to him. Since Eema died, I haven't spoken much to anyone, and with Sheva so ill now, I've had more reason to withdraw. I've spent my days at her side, sometimes with Mephi, and my nights poring over Torah until my eyes fail. I don't know what I'm searching for, but I know what I need.

Our people live by the Law of Moses, hundreds of rituals and sacrifices designed to keep Yahweh's precepts fresh in our minds. But Adonai's mercy also breathes in every stroke of ink on parchment. The fierce God who drowned the Egyptian army and sent plagues on the Philistines also proclaimed His goodness to Moses, forever transforming our ancestor with the abundant reality of His character.

If there's any future for my family, it's in Yahweh alone. Still, my mind edges away from every promise, afraid to hope. Afraid to believe they're for me.

My own promises to David haunt me, leaving me wondering if I was hasty to speak them. I believe he will be king, but my place beside him wasn't mine to promise. After years of trying to prepare my family and Israel for it, I've given up hoping for a peaceful transition into David's rule. I may not fight it, but there are plenty of others who will. And now I have the prophet's word affirming the same. But it's becoming harder to wait things out, believing for the best while continually experiencing the worst.

Back when I'd seen Yahweh's anointing on David at Elah, it had been easy to throw my lot in with his. Throw my robe around his shoulders and put a sword in his hand. In those days, I'd known clearly how I could help him. But now, I'm not certain what my place is. Beyond maintaining a position that stopped being mine long ago.

It isn't just grief that keeps me quiet. Not anymore. I won't speak because I'm afraid of what wanders around in the back of my mind. I'm afraid Yahweh is almost finished with me, and there's nothing more I can do but step out of the way.

Sixteen

I had gone to the wilderness to lift my friend out of discouragement. But who will do the same for me?

Wandering through the tangle of my thoughts, I've somehow made it to my armory. My father is watching me, his body angled away from the window, and I wonder how long we've been standing here like this. I blink and realize he's dressed for battle, freshly polished armor gleaming over his riding clothes.

He pushes his cloak aside, revealing his sword. "You look at me as though you don't know me."

I don't. Not really. I'm tired of straining my eyes looking for someone who isn't there. Tired of imagining it and having my hope betrayed. I'm not a boy anymore.

When I stay silent, Saul clears his throat. "I saw the plans you laid out for the defense of Gibeah's armory. It will be effective if Bosheth has enough smarts to implement it. We can use the money we plundered from Gibeon."

My expression tightens. I hate remembering what he did in Beeroth, destroying most of the Gibeonites and sending the rest running for the wilderness. And now he wants to use their meager wealth to build up Gibeah? What is he doing?

Saul faces me squarely. "I have need of you. I've been lenient, but seclusion is no place for you. The time of mourning is past."

As if I'll wake up one day and forget about my mother's death. Forget that my wife is soon to follow. I tense, unable to drag my eyes from the floor. I hear my father's heavy step across it, moving closer. I'm not looking at him, so I recoil when he tries to touch me. He's only softening now because he wants something. And he's wrong. The time of mourning is only beginning.

"I miss her too." He curls his hands around my shoulders, then abruptly lets go. "I know you were close with your mother. She saw too many of my faults, and she sowed her bitterness into you. But I know she wanted you to rule. She would want you by your king's side, making sure that nothing could stand in your way. In Mephi's way."

So, it's about me and Mephi now. Not you.

When I lift my head, I see it all over him. Why he's come. And I can't make myself believe it.

Saul steps in front of me. "One of Nabal's old servants sent word. David's back in the wilderness near Jeshimon. A dozen of my spies have verified the report. He eluded me last time he was there, but I'm not going to let it happen again. I'm taking three thousand men back to Ziph. You're coming with me."

I'm too tired to act as shocked as I feel. But at least my response is easy.

Sixteen

"No." The first word I've said to him in weeks.

The king acts as though he didn't hear me. "He's back in the same location he was before, near the hill Hachilah. Where you found him."

I feel the accusation in his statement, but it doesn't trouble me anymore. If he wanted to kill me, he would've done it long ago. He wouldn't do it then, and he won't now. I'm too valuable.

I fold my arms. "I can't leave, my lord. Jehosheva is getting worse. Her fever won't come down, and her breathing is shallow. The physicians are worried."

Saul tilts his head at the door as if remembering my wife is under the same roof.

I nod. "Ammiel's with her."

The king sighs heavily, letting his agitation propel him across the room. "These women die far too easily. Unlike that traitor David. If you really want to protect your wife and son, you will come with me. Abner has sent Hittite spies to Hachilah with messages to lure David out of hiding."

"What makes you think I would be part of that?" Is he blind?

"I have sent a list of articles throughout Israel urging the elders to sign it." Saul produces a long document, and the first thing I see at the bottom are my brothers' signatures. And Abner's.

The king continues, "It declares David's so-called anointing as unlawful and names you the next king of Israel, with Mephi to follow you. Several men of Benjamin have already complied. Once David's band of renegades sees this, they will disband or be destroyed. I am confident that they will come to nothing once David is dead."

He looks at me. "Naturally, some of the people are hesitant. As long as you remain divided with me on this matter, Israel remains uncertain about her future. But if they see you ride out with me to protect what is ours, they will support you in keeping the throne."

I stare at the paper without reading it, struggling to find words for what my father won't understand. He still doesn't see it. He's not just setting himself against David, but Yahweh.

I lift my head. "Has it ever occurred to you that killing David shouldn't be this difficult? If he were just a rogue brigand inciting men against you, then stopping him would be simple."

Saul snatches the document back. "He's stolen the hearts of the people. He's made things complicated."

"What about Yahweh's heart?" My words freeze the blood in my own veins, and my father's eyes turn black. I hear my voice from far away, my heart pounding outside my ears. "Do you remember when Samuel told us Adonai had chosen a man after His own heart to rule Israel? Can a man fight against Yahweh and win?"

"What do you know about fighting Yahweh?" Saul whispers.

"I know you can't."

The king releases an incredulous huff and leans closer to me. "What else do you know about David's anointing that I don't? Did you speak to Samuel?"

"I know David is a gift to Israel. I will not set myself against the one our God has chosen. We swore an oath before Yahweh, and I will not be the one to break it."

Saul chews the inside of his mouth, turning one way, then another. Deciding what angle he'll use to lash out at me.

"I see what you're doing. I've known it all these years." He smirks, pointing. "You resent me. You hate me because I hit you, and I made a vow that you broke, and I didn't listen every time you whined about Samuel. The Philistines stopped you from running away from me after Amalek. But you've been watching for another chance ever since. You couldn't wait to throw your lot in with someone else just to see me fail."

"That is *not true!*" I've never heard him acknowledge what he did back then. And we've never really talked about why I left the war camp after Amalek. We were too busy making sure I'd live after running into the raiding party. But he's wrong about me. Still.

Saul scoffs, triumphant in his anger. "You think you're so much better than me, but you dishonor me at every turn. Choosing your own way over mine while I fight to protect the status I gave you. You chose David over your own father! Your own family!"

I clench my fists. "No—"

He advances, spitting. "Did your mother know about your covenant with the shepherd? Did she realize her own son was a traitor?"

"Stop."

"You love him more."

"Abba!" I grab his shoulders, my fingers digging into the space beneath his armor. Restraint is in pieces around our feet.

His eyes are enormous. But all I want to do is make him see me. Make him listen. My jaw shakes around the words.

"I have given you my whole life. Everything I am, everything I have is yours." Too much. "What I have done for David, I was compelled to do. I saw the presence of God on him, Abba. Like I saw it on you once."

I relax my grip, breathing through a frozen sob. "And yes, I love him. He loves Yahweh. He loves you. He's my brother and your son. Why would he come against you now when he's already spared you? He only stays away because you've hunted him, made him fear for his life. But I know him better than anyone. And God is my witness, we have never sought your death."

My father's chest finally moves. "Then how does he intend to take the throne? Would you have us locked in a stalemate—his nephew's arrow aimed at me, yours aimed at Joab, and David simply standing there waiting to see who dies first? Unless I protect what is ours, we're headed for a bloody impasse."

"David was yours. And yet, you never protected him." Or me.

"I suppose you would rather I place the crown on David's head myself!" He drops his arms, annoyance returning. "We're going to Ziph. Are you coming, or should I assume you've deserted me?"

Has he heard nothing I've said? "I will ride with you to Ziph if you wish. But it will be a fool's errand."

"Not if your friend hears that you're coming." Conspiracy creeps into his tone.

"What?"

Saul's eyes glitter. "I've told the men of Ziph that my son Jonathan is on his way there to meet with David. You wouldn't want him to come all the way out of the wilderness for nothing."

He never ceases to amaze me. To think I used to be afraid of being taken by the Philistines and used against my father. Now, I'm just a different kind of hostage.

Saul paces, grinning. "He will come to you, and then I will kill him. And nail these articles to the wall of his cave." He waves the parchment in my face before pushing toward the door.

I call after him over the thump of alarm in my chest. "David carries the *ephod* and has the support of many priests. He will inquire of the Lord and find out it's a trap."

Sixteen

Saul laughs over his shoulder. "He thinks he's a king, doesn't he? Kings don't inquire of anyone."

* * * * *

There's no sign of David anywhere in Ziph, but I'm not surprised.

With every step of the journey, I've prayed for my friend to see through Saul's perverse game. For my father to give it up and go home. But if surviving a night trapped in a cave hasn't convinced Saul of David's innocence, I don't know what will.

I watch Abba's thousands, fully armed, spreading out at the base of each hill, setting watchmen at posts along the escape routes. Some of the men from Ziph have even come out to help us.

My father looks satisfied. Even relaxed. He's hoping to snare David in multiple ways. If David believes the reports, which he won't, he'll come close enough to risk death. If he sends men who are taken by our guards, the king will have real hostages. And if David's men kill or capture me, Saul will have a blatant act of treason to answer. Something he's had to fabricate until now.

But none of the scenarios he's imagined will happen. I can feel it. There's something in the air here. A heavy silence lurking among the rocks. It's as though Yahweh is brooding, smiling at our attempts to alter His will.

I tighten my fists, terrified at the way His mercy waits, giving us chance after chance. My eyes locked on the glow of sunset painting the ridge, I murmur quiet prayers.

"Adonai, you know I have not come down to seek the life of your anointed. Show mercy to my father and to my brother David. Show mercy, and do not allow the king to heap more sins onto our family's shoulders. We are all in your hands."

"There." Saul's eyes change, locking onto a distant upper tower of rock. "We'll camp within sight of the ridge blocking the pass. They'll have to cross over it to escape." He stabs the ground with his spear and points next to it. "Jonathan, you will sleep here, beside me."

I smile grimly. He chooses bodyguards so well. He knows I'm probably the only one who could make David think twice about whatever move he's planning.

"Have the spies returned?" Saul asks.

"They spoke with a few men who certainly belong to David," Abner responds. "It is very possible we will see him in another day or so."

Sixteen

My father's cousin wears his age with exhaustion. His life has been consumed with this hunt, and he has to see how futile it is. The country has all but flocked to David, with only the wealthiest fearing Saul's anger. It's not difficult for the people to see the difference between the king and his rival, especially after the Gibeonite massacre. David equips and aids his countrymen, while Saul threatens and maims them.

The king nods, sighing. "Abner, you will keep watch tonight. At the first sign of someone approaching, alert the guards. Even if David doesn't come down himself, he'll be sure to rescue any of his men if we capture them."

Like Ezra? I fold my arms, resisting a shiver. He's another man I won't see die. "It doesn't matter what you do, my lord. Yahweh will not give you David's life."

Saul turns on his heel. "Are you saying He might give David yours? Or mine?"

"David will not harm either of us." I'll say it until the day he hears me.

But Saul shakes his head, looking ten years older. "Then he cannot mean to be king."

He gives me his back, refusing to speak again. I prop myself against a boulder and watch the soldiers making camp around me. Laying a trap for the man who used to be their commander. A man they've seen fight the battles of the Lord beside them.

Whispers slither toward me on the night air, and I hold my breath. I'm awake behind the eyes, but I refuse to move, shutting everything out to focus on what I'm sure was a voice. I watch Abner and his guards, their eyes combing the hills like birds of prey. They're experienced. If David's men choose to approach, I don't see how they'll be missed.

"Make them invisible, Adonai," I whisper. "Let David leave this place without a trace, as though he was never here. May the king's plans come to nothing."

The moment I lie down, my eyes snap onto my father's spear, and worry digs through my head, fighting sleep. Even if David's men want to spare me, they won't care about the king. They could pin my father to the ground, and no one would even hear anything. All they would have to do is wait until everyone's asleep. Is this the moment the prophet spoke of? The moment when we die? *Adonai...*

Before my next breath, the silence warms, pulling close around me like a blanket. Speaking directly into my mind.

Sixteen

Stay still. Rest.

And my entire body relaxes, every edge softening, every bit of tension dropping away. My vision fades, and the hills become the walls of my father's fortress. Where I slept unafraid years ago, stretched out on the floor with David's music winding hope through my veins.

I settle back, gratefully drowning in the memory. The sweep of sleep is the reminder of Yahweh's closeness, even in times of trouble. Something David could always bring back into focus. I could stay there forever.

* * * * *

The strange cloud doesn't lift from my body until sunlight touches my eyelids. I stretch and turn onto my back, drinking in the feeling of strength being coaxed awake. I haven't felt so rested in years. Whatever I slept under last night was God-sent. Like the peace that always came with David's music.

The sounds of the waking army reach my ears, and I sit up, smiling wryly. Abner looks dazed. He was supposed to be keeping watch, but instead he slept. Everyone did. Even the guards are rolling over, catching themselves awake. I wonder how incensed my father will be when he notices. But it isn't the king who yells down at his general.

"Abner!"

The cry grabs hold of my chest. Everyone scrambles to attention, looking around for the source of the voice, but I already know it. I get to my feet slowly, my eyes grabbing hold of him. David is standing on the far side of the opposite ridge, out of reach, but not out of shooting range.

Abner adjusts his grip on his sword. "Who's calling? Who are you to call out to the king?" he shouts while his servants ready their bows.

Even from up on the ridge, David's voice pulls, emotion shaking it to pieces. "Will you not answer me, Abner? You're supposed to be one of Israel's best! There's no one like you in Saul's army. And yet you failed to protect the king from the one who would have killed him last night. Perhaps Saul should be seeking *your* life for failing to guard him. Just look and see."

Abner gapes, looking around frantically.

"Abba's spear and water jug are gone," I say quietly. My eyes meet Abner's once, and then I look back at David. For a strained moment, no one speaks. No one answers him. Just like at Elah, the army holds its breath. Waiting.

My father's response is ragged. Unrecognizable. "Is that your voice, David? My son?"

Sixteen

My heart turns over.

"Yes. It's me. Just like last time." Still not aiming any weapons, David holds his ground, but I can see his chest heaving. "And you are still seeking my life. Why? If it was the Lord who sent you to kill me, I would gladly give myself over. But if you've been listening to the false accusations of men, may the Lord God curse them for turning you against me." Bruised passion maims David's voice, keeping it unsteady.

"These evil reports you believe have driven me from my home, forcing me away from the land of our people and away from the presence of the Lord. Do you know how long it's been since I've been able to worship in the temple? Walk freely in the streets of the town where I was born? And now you would shed my blood in a foreign place? Make me die homeless? What am I to you? I'm just one common man. I'm nothing compared to who you have at your side now. But you've made me some animal to hunt. Why, my king? Why?"

The anguish between my friend's words pulls all of mine to the surface. Mist encases my vision, and I blink it away so I can see clearly. In five seconds, David has reached deeper into my father's heart than I've ever been able to. And this time, the whole army has seen it.

Spent of words, David's grief escapes in the fall of his chest. These are questions he's been wanting to ask since the day my father commanded his service after Goliath was killed. They've been building in him with every spear thrown since then.

I can feel the tremors coming off my father without looking. His strained response barely carries across the hills. "I have sinned, David. You know I've sinned. Everyone knows it." His frayed breath doesn't give any power to his words. "I have acted the fool, and yet you have treated my life with honor." He lifts his hand. "Come back to me, my son. Come home to Israel. I have clearly been mistaken in you."

Mistaken? Is that what he calls it to take a man's home and reputation? To make him desperate enough to flee to foreign lands, begging Philistines and Canaanites for help? I'm so ashamed, I can barely keep my head raised. I'm not surprised when David doesn't buy it.

"Mistaken is one word for it," my friend says, not bothering to lift his voice. "Here's your spear. Have one of your servants come and get it."

After a frozen second, Abner snaps his fingers, and Nadab and Gera scramble to retrieve the king's items. David watches with his fists clenched at his sides. He doesn't move, but when

Sixteen

Abishai hands over the spear, my eyes open to the lines of men edging the rocks above us. A hundred arrows trained in our direction.

They won't shoot. But David knows who he can trust and who he can't. He nods after the spear. "You tried to kill me with it twice. And now, I've spared you twice with the same weapon. We're even."

When the spear is back in Saul's hand, David breathes deeply, closing his eyes on the exhale. Letting go. His voice sounds lighter when he speaks again.

"The Lord rewards every man for his righteousness and his faithfulness, my king. He is witness of what's happened between us. He gave you into my hand today, and I did not harm you. I only pray my life will be counted precious in His sight, and He will save me from all this trouble."

Crestfallen, my father stammers, "Yes, of course He will, David. You've always had His favor. No doubt you will do many mighty things and walk in success all your days."

David lifts his chin, refusing the compliment. "Go home, my king."

Saul fumbles for words, confused. "You will not...?"

Reaching out, I stop him with a hand on his arm, a gentle shake of my head. One day, David will come home. But not today. Not like this. The truth burns my chest. There's only room for one king in Israel. Perhaps there is more reconciliation to come. But repentance will have to take a much stronger hold in my father before David can rule. "Abba. Let's go."

His gaze still pulling toward David, Saul turns to me. His eyes are different, empty without the confident arrogance. Speechless for once, he covers my hand with his own and turns away to walk beside me.

He understands. David might not kill him, but he won't come back and submit to continual abuse. He won't stay where he's haunted by the threat of death. For a second, I let myself wonder if the burden will ever be lifted from my shoulders. If I'll ever be free of what binds me to Gibeah, free enough to join David in what He's doing.

But for now, my wife and my son are waiting. And Yahweh will never leave my side. After the way His peace enveloped me last night, I realize I can hold onto His nearness no matter what happens.

Before turning away, David locks eyes with me, reaches up to his shoulder, and touches his lips. I nod and do the same,

Sixteen

raising my hand in our familiar salute of fellowship. "God go with you, my friend," I mouth softly.

My father says little on the way back to Gibeah, trailed by an unfamiliar calm. It encourages me, however unsteady it is. When I glance at him, I catch the glint of a tear trailing into his beard, and my heart shoves into my breastplate.

He was impacted by what happened today, even if he won't speak of it. His words to David still push warmth through my veins, filling in the coldness that had settled.

I glance at the king again and try to feel relieved when he smiles sadly in my direction. Something ended today. I'm sure of it. My father will stop hunting David. There will be respect, if not peace between them. We can set our minds to uniting the tribes and holding back the Philistines. And wait to see what God will do through David.

I lift my shoulders in a deep breath before letting them drop. I should be grateful. Yet, the strangest feeling lingers in the unused corners of my heart, an odd anxiety that troubles me as we travel home.

There was something even more final about this meeting with David. Something unnerving and undefined. Like our salute was a farewell. Like it was the last time I would lay eyes on him.

SEVENTEEN

David

"My son. David, my son."

Days later, the king's wails of repentance still linger in my mind like smoke lifting from a burned fortress. I pace in front of the wreckage, waiting for something to make sense.

I've considered, pondered, and handled each word, waiting for relief to accompany them. But there's nothing. Just the same emptiness that's been killing my trust ever since Saul threw the first spear. Even after the king's armies had ridden off, voluntarily giving up the hunt, I'd heard only one thing clearly in the caverns of my mind. *This isn't over.*

No matter how much I want it to be.

I refuse to move, even as the campfire deepens the sting in my face and the haze above me shifts into heavy darkness and starlight. I've been out here for hours, gripped by Saul's parting words and the changed landscape of my own heart.

He'd called me his son. Something I've longed to hear for years. But now the words feel hollow, voiceless. The first time he'd called me his son was after choking me in his chambers when I was fifteen. After throwing a spear at me, he'd tried to placate my fear and revulsion by telling me how he loved me like he loved Jonathan.

But Jonathan has suffered at his hands. And now, so have I.

I get up abruptly and turn my back to the flames, letting the cool openness of the ridgeline touch my face. The heat building behind my eyes has nothing to do with the fire.

I've seen Saul's tears before, felt the weight of his sorrow as he grieved over what he'd done to me. As heavy as it's been, he's worn it like clothing. Surface deep. Shaken off in an instant. His jealousy is stronger than his repentance because he's spent too long feeding the wrong thing. He doesn't have the will to fight these inner battles the way Jonathan does.

And I've changed. Maybe not as much as I'd feared. But I'm no longer willing to believe him. I'm not willing to live in the shadow of uncertainty, wondering when he'll threaten me again. I'm not Jonathan. I pick at the fraying edge of the scarlet robe I still wear.

Seventeen

I should have seen the warning signs back at Elah. Jonathan had wrapped me in the robe of friendship while Saul had treated me like a possession and tried to kill me later. I'm finished with the grip of his control. I belong to the One who anointed me. I'm done serving a king who doesn't want me to.

So, where does that leave us? I shift my attention downhill at the tents spreading over the valley, each one aglow with firelight. It's a relief to camp in safety, knowing Saul isn't pursuing us, but I'm still responsible for these people.

My six-hundred warriors with their wives and children are still waiting to return to Israel. They all pray for Yahweh's wisdom to give me direction, but deep down, I know what they want. Security. Peace. An end to wandering.

Even Abigail wants it, though she hasn't uttered a word of complaint since marrying me. She's shared her courage with everyone she encounters, even softening Ahinoam's taut exterior, but everyone has a limit.

And I fear Saul has brought me to mine.

Something's opening up in my mind, expanding it in errant directions, and I close my eyes, trying to convince myself I have other options. I don't like feeling trapped.

Do we return to Israel and try to content ourselves with Saul's capricious mercies? Even if I could trust him with my life, will he spare the people who've followed me? When he's been trying to capture some of them for years? Where would my unruly warriors fit in Gibeah? The runaway orphans like Uriah? The foreigners?

When Joab comes to find me, he doesn't speak. Not at first. He just shoves my sword out of the way with his foot and sits in its place, looking at my back. "Abigail wants to know what you're thinking."

Does she? I'm about to brush off his comment, but the truth lifts from my lungs instead.

"I can't do this anymore. Always running. Being betrayed. Never sure of who we can trust. If we go on much longer, Saul will eventually kill me. And then the rest of us."

It sounds perverse to say it out loud. Jonathan would protest if he were here. But he isn't. The strange hope lifting in his face had brought tears to my eyes. Hopefully, he'll have some rest now. Time to focus on his wife and child. For whatever time he has left. I'd been grieved to hear the reports that Jehosheva is dying back in Gibeah.

Joab's eyes don't move from the fire. He nods several times. "And what of Saul's impassioned speech on the hill?"

"You know him, Joab. He was showing off in front of Jonathan and his men. But he'll forget he ever said any of it. He can't be trusted."

My pulse crashes, emotion stirred. No one wants to believe him more than I do. I want to go home. I want to strategize with Jonathan and take my wives to the temple for the feasts and walk freely in the streets of Bethlehem. But Saul is a liar, and I refuse to let our people suffer for it. I refuse to be betrayed again.

I fold my arms, muttering, "Saul barely tolerated me as a shepherd and a singer. He isn't going to accept me the way I am now. It's time for us to gain the upper hand."

I steal a glance at the side of Joab's leathery face, but I don't have to look too deep to know what his response will be. He's always been the bold predator type. One step ahead of everyone else with radical plans. Acting before thinking. Stirring my anger with his rash decisions only to leave me consumed with gratitude later. And so many of my men are the same.

I still remember what Joab did back when we wandered in Judah's wilderness to escape Keilah, forced to avoid Bethlehem because of a Philistine garrison in Ephrath.

Hiding so close to my childhood home and being unable to enter had been too hard on my spirit. I'd made the mistake of voicing my struggles aloud. Less than a day later, Joab and his brothers had approached me, covered with the sweat of battle and holding a clay jug as though it were filled with priceless incense.

"What is that?" I'd asked. It wasn't like them to disappear without orders.

Joab had set the jug down triumphantly. "Water. From the well of Bethlehem. The one I'd race you to as a child." He'd grinned like an idiot, and I'd jumped down his throat.

"You went down there? The Philistines have the place on lockdown, Joab!"

"Hence, the swords."

I'd stared at him, aghast. "Let me get this straight. You fought your way through a Philistine blockade *to get water?*"

"Yes. Half the guards by the gate are dead, and they never even saw us. The commanders are probably scrambling to figure out what happened." Joab had shared a smirk with the others while I struggled to comprehend it.

"You risked your men's lives for an *errand?*"

His wry shrug had tossed my concern back into my face. "Welcome to my life. Besides, I don't think you understand what you sound like when you want something. You don't, because you're inside yourself, but we all have to hear it, and trust me, death would be a relief."

"How was I supposed to know you would actually go there?" Embarrassment was stinging my face. It wasn't the first time I'd regretted being honest with him.

"You fight with me. You live with me. You should have known! Just drink it."

I had stepped back, horrified. "How can I drink this after you took such a risk? It would be like drinking your blood. Just give it to me. I'll pour it out before the Lord."

"You can't be serious," he'd blanched, the humor leaving his face.

"Watch me," I'd grabbed the jug, but Joab had smacked it out of my hands.

"You're insane! That's your problem. You're crazy."

The memory pushes a soft laugh to the surface, and Joab frowns, waiting to understand.

His fierceness used to frighten the steady people of Bethlehem who feared fanning the flames of Saul's wrath or antagonizing the Amalekites. But my brothers and I saw different. All Joab's fervor needed was clear direction. These last few years have turned him into a tested weapon, delivering results beyond what most kings would dare to request.

Before I was anointed, Joab and his brothers had led the charge with the resistance, believing in what they could be even before they did. Their trust in my anointing has stirred others to join our cause. They've helped my men polish their skills and keep their eyes on the prize—the day we will return to Israel and take our positions in the plan that still makes me catch my breath. My kingship.

Remembering what's ahead of us makes me even more doubtful about the direction I'm considering. Can I really offer my people such a crazy solution as the one that's been dancing around me for days? It doesn't lead to Israel, and it doesn't leave much room for failure.

Weary of fighting with myself, I decide to give up. I sit next to Joab, folding my hands over my knees. "We need to strengthen our position in the region, but we need a change. Something more permanent until we can come back to Israel to stay."

Joab blinks. "What do you have in mind?"

"You may wish you hadn't asked."

He shrugs. "You've had a plan for a while. I've seen the smoke hanging around you."

I wince. "It's a terrible plan. At least, it's not smart." I'm already seeing the bloodstained walls of Goliath's city, remembering the spiked collar I'd worn there.

Joab's brows simply lift.

I wait one heartbeat, long enough to feel the pressure on my spirit. The slight weight is enough to make me want to hesitate. But the thought of waiting any longer for Saul to regroup drives the words out of me. "We're going to Gath."

* * * * *

We arrive at Goliath's hometown before I'm ready to. Alongside twelve of my fiercest warriors, I approach the fortress walls with heaviness pulling from every direction. Achish's gates reach out to me in jagged shadow, and from behind, I can sense my hidden men waiting in the trees for a sign that I've ventured too far into trouble.

Like the last time I was here.

Even deeper in the forest, Abigail waits with the women, praying that my journey results in sanctuary, not attack.

I try to blink her face away, but it's still lurking behind my eyes, asking the questions she wouldn't. *Are you sure about this?*

I grip my sword, wondering how long I'll be allowed to hold onto it. Where is Goliath's sword being kept in this glorified dungeon? I swallow tightly, wishing I could be more certain that this will work. But I left the comfort of easy decisions behind years ago when I set out on my own.

I glance at my nephews, pulling our plan back into view. We've agreed there are two ways I can play this. Desperate or bitter. Both might be needed if I'm to convince Achish to listen. He might just attack me where I stand. Which was the first scenario Joab had planned for.

"We have to consider the possibility that he might not receive you," he'd reminded me. "I will have eight units hold back outside the gates, some visible, some hidden. If there's trouble, Abishai will shoot a flaming arrow over the wall to alert them to attack. We should be able to fight our way out from the inside."

"We're only taking twelve inside the fortress," I'd informed him.

"Twelve units?"

"Twelve men. Achish can't see us as a threat. I have to be able to convince him that we're done with Israel and willing to fight for him. I'm hoping he'll allow us to camp outside the city so we can make plans in private while appearing to be mercenaries."

I steady myself, recalling our discussions. We've rehearsed this, poring over every angle multiple times. It's a good plan. It'll work. But the sweat coating my body is saying otherwise.

"You're not alone, you know." Joab's mutter barely makes it to my ears. "This time, you're not a captive. We have the upper hand, whether Achish thinks we do or not."

Instead of nodding, I lift my head higher, mentally preparing to deal with the approaching guards and the spears pointing in our direction. But my nephew's accidental wisdom is buried in my chest now and won't budge. *You're not alone. Why do you act like you are?*

"What are you doing here?" The lead Philistine guard must be at least half-giant, seven feet or taller, his spearhead nearly touching my throat. His men are fanning out around us, grabbing those in the back to search them.

"You're from Israel, aren't you?" The guard snarls in my face.

"Yes," I answer, pretending not to care when they snatch at my sword. I dig my fingers into the handle. "We have come to speak with your lord the king. And we will keep our weapons. We mean him no harm."

"And I mean you no harm." The Philistine grins through a mouth that's been split by a knife. "How about I bring your heads to Achish instead?"

"He knows me," I insist, making my voice rougher. "We've come to offer our services to him."

By a miracle, the man hesitates long enough for the others to start goading him. "Let them go! Maybe Achish will let us have them when he's finished."

The guard's brows knit so tightly that his forehead disappears. "Follow me. Stay behind them, men," he orders the others. "Keep them in line."

I swallow several times on our way through the fortress doors. It's built like a tomb, the darkened entrance curving over our heads. Torches scar the walls with soot, making the faces of the carved idols dance. The incense is cloying, staining the memories pushing too close. I only remember the throne room. I'd been dragged in here unconscious the last time. But this meeting has to be different.

Achish is waiting for us now, draped over a throne at the top of four short stairs. The fins of his god Dagon ornament the edges of his dais, and the extra age in the king's face makes him seem grotesque. Shadows gape from his eyes, and for a second, I wonder if he's ill.

An attendant is whispering in his ear when we approach, already edging away from the king's reaction. But Achish just heaves an unconvinced chuckle.

"More cast-off Israelites for me to deal with?" He addresses the servants, barely looking at me. "It's been years since Saul sent any of his spies into my territory. I'm not sure if I should be insulted."

I take one step forward. "Do you know me, my lord?"

His laugh breaks off mid-breath, but he doesn't lift his elbow from the chair. "Umm…"

"I am David, the son of Jesse. Goliath's killer." My words snatch every sound from the room, even stealing the echoes.

The king's breathing halts, then resumes shakily. "You're the real David? Not some drunken imposter?"

"I was the real David last time," I admit quietly. I can tell the moment the news works its way through him, releasing the poison in his eyes.

"That was you?" he hisses, as though his lungs are full of water. He pushes to his feet, leaning forward like a panther about to spring.

I hold myself rigid, hiding the way his voice makes my skin tingle. The threat of danger pulls around me, but I refuse to reach for my sword.

Achish's anger is stone cold, pulling all the air from the room. His councilmen don't even draw breath while he takes two measured steps toward me, stopping at the edge of the dais steps.

"You have five seconds to explain to me why I shouldn't kill you."

That's all I need. I don't even bother to breathe. "Because Saul wants to. I thought you of all people would be interested in exploiting my situation."

Seventeen

"Ha!" Achish snaps loud enough to clap explosive echoes through the room. "Do you think I'm fool enough to believe you'd turn on Saul? You're more knit to his family than to your own."

I look down, covering my wince. He sees too clearly, and he's heard too much. Anger will be the only way to hide the whole truth. I take a half step forward, clenching my fists over my sword so he doesn't think I'm attacking.

"I'm no family to Saul. He took everything from me. All I want is to return the favor." I force a self-satisfied smile. "And he's too much of a fool to notice, as I predicted."

"So, you've been…working against him all this time? Undermining him?" Achish chews on the implication, unconvinced. "That's hardly what the rumors indicate. You've become Israel's hero, a hunted vigilante fighting the battles of your God while Saul chases you around the country."

I shrug, mocking the idea. "My people sang my praises in the beginning, but at the first test of loyalty with Saul, they betrayed me. I would put no trust in what they say. You know how their stories grow, how false they are. At one time, they led me to believe you were a poor general, content to hide behind giants."

I see the sparks in his eyes. The injured pride waking up. I have seconds before it ignites and lashes out to burn me.

Achish shifts his weight, struggling to restrain himself. "And I'm supposed to help you now?"

I breathe in, holding the air until my chest aches. I slip my hand into my cloak, my fingers closing around the blue stone Jonathan brought back to me in Ziph. It's high time I was rid of it. Keeping my eyes down, I kneel and hold it out to Achish. *Forgive me, Michal.*

Achish takes it, his breathing picking up. "This is from one of the temples." I can sense the change in his voice.

I nod, leaning into the unsteadiness that upends me when I think of Michal. I don't miss her the way I used to, but losing her had hurt worse than anything else Saul had done to me. Hopefully, Achish will misinterpret my bitterness.

"It's from an old battle. Back when I believed Saul cared what I did. I killed Tyrian for him, not realizing my own king was hoping for my death." I lift my eyes, willing them to burn. "But you know my skills. It's all I have left that Saul hasn't taken. Command me, and I'll make sure you get whatever he's kept from you. Saul's greatest enemies are the ones he creates himself. And my men know this. He will regret underestimating us."

Achish drops his head to one side, trying to hide his unruly smile. He's enjoying this, but also trying to decide if he believes

Seventeen

it. I know where he's going next, and I breathe several times, preparing for it.

"And what about the prince?" The king descends one step, leaning over me. "The one they say is bound to you with the hand of your God? He is just as much our enemy as Saul is. Even more."

His hatred heats the air between us, and I have to resist choking on the flames. This man has tried to kill my brother dozens of times. But what I'd said about Saul was the truth. I can't lie about Jonathan. I drop my eyes again, feigning hurt. "Betrayal only comes by the hands of those you love, my lord."

"Indeed," the king spits. "Which is why love is for fools."

I clear my throat. "I did not come here to discuss love, my lord. It has become my mission to take as much from Saul as I can before he breathes his last. I march on the Negeb in a fortnight, and I can do it for nothing. Or I could do it in the service of a king who will appreciate it."

A dozen considerations push and pull in Achish's eyes, but finally a hearty laugh breaks through them. He bends over, clapping his hands. "It's brilliant, really. You've made Saul hate you so much that he's made your life torture. All of which brought you to me. And I thought I was favored by the gods before…"

He shakes his head, dropping his hands onto my shoulders. I almost flinch at the sharpness of the incense hanging around him. He grins deeply at me. "The bold young stripling from Elah has become his own man. And Saul is enraged to see it."

I swallow. "Truly, I would love to give him something to really rage about, but it's become complicated over the years. My men have families, and they slow us down, having to follow us from place to place. We are so many, and we need somewhere to…"

"You can have Ziklag," Achish interrupts, startling everyone. Several of the commanders shift in place, but no one contradicts him. "It's an old training camp, but no one uses it since I've put garrisons in Endor. There's a spring nearby, houses you can inhabit. Even a high place and a guard tower."

I have to conceal my shock. "I-I'm stunned by your generosity, my lord. As soon as we can move our families into the city, my men and I will leave for the Negeb."

The southern desert of Israel is populated with as many scattered Canaanite clans as Israelites. The rogue bands have been harassing my Judean brothers my whole life, burning fields and kidnapping women. It should be easy to deal with them while making Achish think we're killing Israelites.

Before I can move, Achish claps his hand down on my arm, his fingers digging in deep. "You will report to me each time you return. Next time, I want a detailed description of where you intend to raid and what you hope to collect. Estimated times and other things. You will direct a portion of the spoils back to me, and you will eat at my table every ten days that you are home. Understand…my champion?"

I nod, grateful beyond words for my men. I would never be able to pull this off without my spies, but with Asa's direction, they'll keep Achish thinking exactly what I want him to think, concealing my movements while they're at it. And when we raid, we will leave no one alive to report on us. Joab's idea.

"Understood. You will see what your servant can do." I bow my head, amazed. This is the most twisted scheme I've come up with yet. The young and inexperienced part of me—the part I've repressed is still shocked that I'm back at Achish's feet, deceiving him a second time.

My stomach still clenches with the memory of our last meeting, a story I've only shared with a few of my men. But at least I'm not chained this time. I'm being offered a city. A defensible position. A place to make the most of my skills on Israel's behalf while assuming the outward position of traitor.

Saul will pounce on the news. Once he learns where I've gone, he'll help my cause unwittingly, spreading the rumor that I've deserted Israel, thus strengthening Achish's belief in the same. Only those who are paying attention will notice the truth. And hopefully keep quiet about it.

I'm halfway to my feet when Achish's gloating stops me.

"And you have more than just battle skills, if I've heard correctly. Didn't you used to entertain Saul? With the harp?"

Excuses scream through my mind. *No. No. No.*

"As a youth, I wrote songs of praise to Yahweh," I hedge cautiously. "I hardly think your men would appreciate that."

Achish heaves a laugh, unconcerned. "Well then, write something else. Something to commemorate your victories here. It's a new day, son of Jesse."

"Not on your life," I mutter soundlessly, turning away.

Suddenly, the throne room is closing in, the spiked walls edging over like claws ready to snatch me up. Enough. What we came here for is done. We won't be living here with the king. We've agreed to fight in exchange for Ziklag. Hopefully, the city's distance will help us keep our identity.

Seventeen

The oppressive clouds of incense are the heaviest entering and exiting. Once we're outside, I fill my lungs with the open air, knowing I won't really breathe until we're back in the forest. My men keep their formation close behind me, maintaining a steady march all the way through the outer courtyard.

The guards gape openly, not bothering to hide their outrage that we're allowed to walk freely. I stare right back at them, and my men mimic my level gaze without speaking. I can see several expressions closing, several throats bobbing. They know we've been accepted by their king. And that we're not afraid. But I'm not stupid enough to think they'll welcome us.

Handfuls of guards crowd closer as we approach the gate. Weapons unsheathe, aiming in our direction. One Philistine leans over, barely letting me pass. "What made you crawl out of your cave, giant-killer? Tired of begging your own king for mercy?"

My heartbeat pushes heat into my face, and I can feel Joab tensing beside me, but I've told them not to do anything. They know the difference between mockery and real danger.

The taunts grow more ribald as we approach the gates, but the men drop behind us, giving us space.

"Why should we raid anymore?" they jibe. "When Israelite slaves come to us?"

"The Hassar will defect to us next."

I barely hear Joab over the buzzing in my ears. "Regretting this already?"

I tighten my teeth. "Just imagining all the ways I'd like to kill them when this is over."

Abishai chortles. "Careful, or it may be over sooner than you planned."

"Well, I won't wear the Philistine colors. And I'm not attending their feasts. Not a chance. We'll do what we have to do and keep to Ziklag."

Even as it is, we'll have to purify ourselves every sunset. I can only pray Yahweh isn't offended by our presence here. Surely, He can see what I'm trying to do. This is survival. Nothing more.

"You mean you're going to refuse your lord's generous invitation?" Joab purrs.

I elbow him where his armor vest stops. "He's not my lord. He'll never be my lord."

My words break off, hitting someone else in the chest. I straighten up and look into the colorless eyes of Ittai, the brutal executioner I'd served under during my last visit.

Seventeen

The old Philistine commander is blocking our way through the gate, his massive arms folded. Every scar wound around his biceps stands out in deep carved detail. Behind us, his men hoot and cackle, encouraging him to teach us a lesson. But the half-giant saved my life once, guiding me out of the way of the mercenaries who would've left me for dead. I still don't know why, and neither of us have told anyone.

He lifts his chin, but I keep hold of his eyes, letting the years since our last meeting drift between us.

When he speaks, his mouth barely moves. "So…we're the next step in your wanderings toward the throne."

The moment he says it, I know he sees deeper than he'll let on. As he did before. I allow weariness to leak into my expression. "What do you know of my wanderings?"

Ittai's shoulder lifts. "I know what you were promised, and it isn't in Gath."

"The throne of Israel belongs to someone else. Someone I can't trust, but would rather not kill." For some reason, admitting it to him carries much more weight than what I told Achish.

Ittai's mouth slants with disbelief. "So, you're giving up?"

"Just altering my course."

Ittai's tone rumbles, his eyes watching the guards over my head. "More men want to kill you here than in Israel. Trying to make Saul jealous by turning to another king is hardly worth your life."

"That's not what I'm doing," I assure him.

But it won't hurt to make Saul realize what he's lost by casting me out. We could have been fighting together, side by side, all this time. But I'm finished waiting for him. He has Jonathan.

If I take up arms against the enemies of Israel and leave no one alive, the way Saul was meant to, then Achish will have no cause to suspect me of treason. No one will escape to tell him what I'm doing.

Fortunately, Jonathan was right about the Philistine king. His pride clouds his judgment. He sees me as a trophy, a chance to mock Saul. Let him think it. At least we'll have roofs over our heads and a defensible fortress while we're fighting. Then someday, we might be able to come home. My heart tugs, imagining it. How many years will it be?

Ittai's gravelly voice grabs my attention back. "You're no rogue soldier, David. Achish isn't the smartest man in the world, or he'd see what you're doing."

I look at him. "I'm hoping to capitalize on that."

"On what?"

"What Achish doesn't know." I wait for everything to take shape behind his eyes. When it does, I can't tell whether admiration or horror wins out.

"You're crazy, son of Israel," he mumbles, stepping back to let me pass.

"You already knew that." I move around him, walking backwards through the gate.

A sliver of humor cracks Ittai's rocky expression. "I did. But if you survive your ruse a second time, I'm leaving with you."

EIGHTEEN

Jonathan

A year later

I tug on the reins, easing my mule's pace as I approach Gibeah's gate. While my guards shout up to the watchmen on the battlements, I pause, studying the familiar mile markers, feeling like a wanderer. Stranded. Weary, all the way down to my bones.

I'm slumping on my mule's back, every shouted greeting bouncing off my shoulders while my mind pulls right and left, looking for a safe place to rest. I shouldn't have left. I shouldn't have come back.

Riding back into Gibeah after a journey used to relieve me. It usually meant I'd survived another war season. I was returning to my people in triumph with David beside me and my mother and sisters waiting at the fortress to celebrate our latest victory. But it's different now.

My father's city hasn't been home since Sheva died.

After my wife stopped breathing, everything about Gibeah angered me. The helpless grief that took hold of my heart. The maidservants' wailing in the lower rooms. Mephi's innocent questions and my lack of answers.

I'd fled the emptiness before my days of mourning were even completed, taking the king's men east to put down an Ammonite threat. What was meant to be a brief assignment stretched into several weeks while I battled an illness that assaulted me on the way home.

Fearing it was the same sickness Sheva died from, my father had sent his physician's son to the war camp. Ten years younger than I, Machir has been a skilled healer in Gibeah for years. He stayed by my side while I burned with fever, refusing to leave me until I was strong enough to travel.

Machir rides up next to me now, smiling gently as we circle around the market. "You're finally home. You can rest," he says, leaving me wincing. Rest is dangerous. The grief I don't know how to battle is waiting inside it.

"No." I clear my throat, failing to lighten my tone. "After I make my report to the king, I'll go join the others at the camp outside Aijalon."

Eighteen

My brothers will be preparing to go there soon, and the war council is gathering today to strategize for another battle season. The king will want me in the center of those decisions. Things have been in so much disarray at home…

Machir interrupts my drifting thoughts. "My lord, you're not a youth anymore, but…"

"I know that." I look sideways at him, offended. Does he think I can't feel the deep ache in my bones after a week of riding? The way my wrists burn after swinging my sword even in practice? But the worst of it is how tired my heart feels. I swear there are marks on it, as though a cart has driven across it. Over and over.

"I didn't finish." Machir's voice holds a smile even though his face doesn't. "I was going to say that your life isn't over. Your son needs you. Yahweh spared you from the fever for his sake. I say, choose life while you're alive."

Life. My heart cringes, feeling the grind of the wheels driving over it again. My face stings. "You lost your wife, didn't you?" I ask Machir, remembering an old conversation.

Machir's voice remains steady. "Six years ago. I felt it was my fault. I'm a healer, and yet I couldn't save her." He angles a self-deprecating smile down at the reins in his fist. "But then one day, I felt myself breathing again, and I realized that wishing for my own death didn't honor Yahweh. And it wouldn't bring Havah back."

No. It wouldn't. I feel the weight in my chest shift, dropping slightly. But it won't completely leave. Not yet. Because Sheva used to be there, and she won't return to the space she left empty. All that's left is for me to go to her. Which I will, at some point. The only question is when? And how?

Machir's hand reaches over and grips my arm. "Promise me you'll go home."

I stiffen, edging my shoulder away. "I'm at the king's command."

Machir's quiet voice somehow keeps reaching me over the bustle of the streets. "You've answered to Someone much higher for years. Don't give up."

The words of Samuel's servant ride into my mind on top of Machir's advice. Filling the air around me while the unsteady wind rumbles toward a storm.

Hold onto your faith. Hold onto the promises.

Eighteen

Why do they seem so far off? I'd give anything to be back at Elah, watching giants fall and believing Yahweh's plan for Israel was being fulfilled. It was easier to see back then.

I reach up to my brow, touching sweat. I'm still not right, shifting between hot and cold. Waving Machir away, I slow my mule to a stop in the shade of an olive tree. The branches lean over the market's edge, enclosing an old winepress in a shelter of green. I stare at the crumbling stones, thinking of the round, smooth one that broke Goliath's skull before my eyes.

It's been a while since I've prayed for David aloud. When I heard that he'd returned to Gath, I'd felt betrayed. He's not a lone wanderer anymore, desperate for food and shelter. This time, he went as a warrior, placing his whole army at Achish's disposal.

Many believe he's been double-crossing the Philistine king, but I haven't looked into the reports coming out of the Negeb, which is where Achish supposedly sent him to raid. I shudder against a deep chill. I'm sure David wouldn't turn on us now. Not when his kingship is so close.

My hand wanders through my hair, catching the thin gold crown on my head. It won't be there much longer. I can feel it. *Where are you, God of my fathers? You said I was beloved. You said you haven't turned your face from me. So, where is your peace? What do you want from me?*

With the next rumble of thunder, the sky slowly rips open and the gentlest rain I've ever felt falls like a curtain from the bruised clouds overhead. A warm wind comes sweeping up from the fields, and I sit there enveloped in it, the water drenching my hair and bouncing off my shoulders.

Palms up, I close my eyes and inhale the scent of sweet earth, the first time I can breathe without a catch in my chest. Small progress, but I'll take it.

We will be well, my love. Everything will be all right.

After avoiding it for weeks, I let myself picture Sheva's face when I'd said those words with Mephi sleeping in my lap. She'd relaxed into a deep smile, her countenance smoothing out right before her breathing stopped. I'd run from my wife's death, but Machir is right. Mephi still lives. And he needs me for as long as I have left.

Drawing on that, I shove my mule back into the road.

I've sent word ahead, so I meet my father in his antechamber as the war council is gathering. Saul's commanders have had their first respite in years, no longer out chasing David. And though my father demands regular reports from his spies on David's movements, he won't ride out against him anymore. I suppose something good has come from my friend's move to Gath.

Eighteen

Drenched and exhausted, I steel myself to make a full report to the king, expecting his usual dry acknowledgement of my efforts, followed by a litany of further duties. But Saul takes one look at me, and his face falls. He glances at Abner. They both watch me closely while I speak, and when I finish, Saul leans forward, studying me. "What does Ammiel's son have to say about your illness?"

I adjust my posture, making sure my shoulders are still squared. "Machir says I'll be fine. I can meet Ishvi at Aijalon in a few days."

Saul shakes his head curtly. "No. You're going home."

I'm shocked. Apart from my wedding, my father hasn't demanded I rest in...well, it's been decades. "My lord..."

Saul stands to his feet, shoving his chair back against the wall. "You heard me, didn't you? You're going home, and you'll stay there until I have need of you. Discussion over. Everyone, get out."

The commanders stand to leave, and Saul surprises me by coming over to place a hand on my neck. "You have to know I need you here. If anything happens to me..." He inhales, his eyes finding mine. "Mephi isn't ready to be king. Jonathan, you're my heir, and I want you well. Your brothers can handle things for a while. Now, go home to your son, and take care of yourself. That's an order."

He squeezes my neck and moves away, his weak smile tugging at my heart. I haven't been paying much attention to how much silver has worked its way into the dark brown and black of his beard. My father is aging, but he could have had a longer life stretching before him if he'd chosen to remain faithful. Fruitful old age is something our people value like inheritance or children. Our God always rewards those who keep after Him through the years.

Adonai, is it too late for him to see it?

Praying under my breath as I leave the room, I barely see the armored man approaching until he almost runs into me.

"Forgive me, my lord," he says, bowing. "But my servant wants to speak to you. He's refusing to give me a message. He says it's for your ears only."

I blink, registering the face of my father's captain of the guard. "Who is it? What's his name?"

"Ziba, son of Ebal, my lord." Another voice answers abruptly, and Naamah's brother appears at his master's side. His

Eighteen

arms are folded, his eyes blazing with a confrontation I'm sure I don't want to have. Holding my breath, I nod for the captain to leave and watch him follow the last few commanders from the room.

Ziba's eyes won't leave mine. Agitation seethes off him like humidity. "You know who I am?" he demands as soon as we're alone.

I release my sigh. "Yes. Talk."

Ziba exhales tightly and starts to pace, his neck muscles grinding over each word. "I have kept silent all these years, but no more! Your family has taken too much from mine. Your father is the reason my sons will never know their grandfather."

I sigh again, inwardly this time. I know all this. Ziba has always held a grudge against my family for everything that's befallen his. When he was a youth, his parents were killed in an Amalekite raid while he and Naamah hid in a well. Afterwards, they'd been taken by Saul's tax collectors to pay outstanding debts. They'd ended up in our house as servants, and I'd fallen in love with Naamah.

It was a lifetime ago, mixed up with my first battles and my father's break with Samuel. And I'm too weary to deal with those memories.

Ziba's tone turns sharper, his breathing heightened. "You're that madman's favorite. The crown jewel of Benjamin. For years, you had the power to make an honest woman out of my sister, and you did *nothing!*"

My face burns as pent-up emotions sour into fury. If by nothing he means secure a good position for Naamah and then take a beating when my father found us kissing…then yes. Nothing. I'd pushed her behind my back, afraid Saul would hit her. Naamah was the only woman who'd ever witnessed my father's rage unleashed on me.

Blinded by the violent images, I tower over Ziba, backing him into the wall. "What right do you have to accuse me? How do you know I won't call my guard and throw you out of here?"

Ziba doesn't even flinch. Unblinking, he stares me down, and I find the deepest pain waiting in the center of his hatred. "Because my sister still believes I can come to you."

I fold my arms, bracing myself. "What have you done?"

"Me?" His voice cracks around the words. "It's that dog your sister married. The Sarrah hasn't given him a child, so he took Naamah to his bed. Forced her! Now, Michal is a reasonable, compassionate woman, so naturally she sent Naamah away when

Eighteen

she found out. My sister came to me weeping, with only the clothes on her back. Ruined! Do I have your attention now, you worthless prince of Israel?"

I bury my finger in his chest, restraining anger. "If you want my help, you'll keep your insults to yourself, or I'll shove them down your throat."

Pushing past him, I pace with my hands clasped behind my head, trying to comprehend what I just heard. Waiting for it to chase me down. When it hits me and I start imagining it, my blood turns to fire. I grind my fingers into my hair, remembering Palti's arrogant confidence. "I'll kill him."

The moment I say the words, I know I'm angry enough to follow through. The air is turning to smoke around me, the way it does in battle when I face an enemy on a more personal footing. But Ziba's sneer reaches me through the flames.

"Temper. That's all you men of Saul understand."

I turn to him. "You're telling me he raped your sister! Why did you come to me if you didn't want action?"

Ziba rubs his forehead. "He's claiming he did nothing wrong, believing I won't go to the king."

"You didn't. You came to me."

"Because the king will do nothing!" Ziba holds out his hands. "Palti told Naamah himself. As far as the king will understand, he slept with a maidservant, and Saul won't uphold any law preventing that."

Gritting my teeth around a curse, I start pacing again, but there's nowhere to go, no easy solution for this. The fact is, nothing can erase what was done. But that's what I want to do. Erase the pain Naamah suffered as an innocent victim. Palti's exaggerated smile stabs me behind my eyes. Why can't I protect anyone from that man?

Ziba moves closer to me. "Naamah knew you'd want to go after Palti. She begged me to stop you from tempting the wrath of the king," he mumbles as if mimicking her.

I unclench my hands. "Where is she now?"

"At your house. She insisted she'd be safe there." His tone implies he doesn't believe the same, but I'm already halfway to the door. Ziba calls after me. "Where are you going?"

"Home to find her," I respond without looking back. "No harm will come to her. You have my word."

Eighteen

Ziba's scoff chases after me, scalding my ears. "You're too late, Hassar."

I ride into my courtyard with my heart pumping in my temples, and I spot Naamah right away. She's sitting against the side of my house under a curtain of vines, her knees drawn up to her chest.

I pause at my gate, amazed by how the image of her sitting there pulls me all the way back to our childhood. Those brave, innocent days are so far behind me, I'd started to think they happened to a different person. But here they are, at my door, waiting for me.

I dismount and walk over to the house, with only two servants approaching to retrieve my mule. Naamah is one of the few people I can slip easily into conversation with. Even now. But pain bites through my throat this time.

It's maddening, these invisible enemies I can't fight. It's why I ride out against Philistia, Ammon, Amalek. To prevent them from taking ground, infiltrating our affections, stealing our virtue. And yet I come home and find a fellow Israelite casually doing the same.

I clench my fists around my belt. The Law is woven into the fabric of who I am as a son of Israel. But something in me wrestles with the futility of perfection. When will we achieve what Yahweh really intended? True justice. Lasting peace. When will completion come?

I know David's dreamed about it. But it's something I can't begin to understand.

"You should come inside," I say hoarsely, tired of thinking.

Naamah lifts her eyes, keeping her arms around her knees. Her lips part. "You came back."

My heart digs into the side of my chest. "Yes. And I'm not leaving this time. Not for a while." On impulse, I move closer and bend to her level, place my hand over her cold fingers. "I'm right here."

Naamah's body jerks, and she ducks her head. "Your servants…"

"No one will say anything," I assure her, letting my voice drop gently.

She trembles, fixing bloodshot eyes onto my face. "Are you certain?"

"You can say anything you want, Naamah. I've promised your brother I won't reveal this to anyone."

Emotion overflows in her face again, and she nods, trying to control the tears. "Ziba told you?"

I nod, rubbing my face as though I can scrub the reality from my mind. I hate apologizing for what I can't change. I want to go back and fight harder against my sister marrying that man.

"I'm sorry, Naamah," I murmur, resenting how powerless the words sound. "I shouldn't have kept you so close. With everything happening with my father, I should have found a safer place for you, away from our family."

Naamah's eyes open wider. "I never wanted to leave. It's not your fault."

A child's lilting voice distracts us both, and I look over Naamah's head to the south field where the servants are bringing Mephi back to the house. His little bow is clenched in his fist, and he's lifting his knees up high, making his way through the tall grass. Stray pieces stick to his legs from the rain.

Naamah turns her body. "Is that your son?"

"Yes." My heart smiles, filling up as it always does when I'm near Mephi. His innocence soothes away all the rough edges that keep me flinching through every day. How have I stayed away so long?

Naamah hugs herself again. "He's beautiful." A tear slips over her eyelid, and she catches it.

My heart turns inside out, and I open my arms, then drop them again, backing away when she notices my attempt to embrace her. "I'm sorry. I—I'm..." I rake a hand through my hair, resisting the pull of shame. "I failed you. Everyone I try to protect...I can't." My mother and father, my sister, my wife. Now Naamah.

"Not David," she says quietly.

"No. Not David." I look up toward Mephi. "But I'm already unable to protect him. He's everything to me, and all I've done is take his mother and then disappear in the king's work. I'm failing." My voice slants dangerously around the words.

"Abba!" Spotting us, Mephi flings himself across the yard toward me. I catch him under his arms, and he clasps my neck. I barely have time to set him down before he's talking, his hands gesturing wildly as he attempts to get words out.

"Abba, I did the bow, and I put the arrow like this, and it hit the tree like this!" His lisping baby voice spins in my head, dancing on my heart. His brown eyes glowing, he tugs at my hand. "C'mon! Lemme show you!"

Eighteen

"Hold on." I restrain him gently, turning him around to face Naamah. "Do you know who this is?"

Mephi shakes his head, holding onto my hands over his shoulders.

"This is my friend, Naamah." I pat his arms, prompting a response.

"Shalom, Ama," he murmurs, shortening her name, and I can see Naamah's countenance change, opening up so I can see her eyes again.

She bends down. "Shalom, little one. What's your name?"

"Mephi." He stretches himself up, using every inch. "I'm not little. I'm four."

Naamah smiles. "I see. And you're an archer, like your father?"

Mephi falters until she translates, "You can use a bow?"

"Yes, I can!" he exclaims, his exuberance returning. He grabs Naamah's wrist. "C'mon. I'll show you. C'mon, Abba."

I smirk in her direction, lifting my shoulders. Mephi's an expressive child, but he's not at ease around everyone. He's been more withdrawn since his mother's death, and seeing him open up so easily to Naamah feels like a gift. If he can heal, so can we.

We follow Mephi to the garden where he attempts a few shots with his little bow before growing bored. He swings from the low-hanging branches of the tamarisk tree while two servants hover around him, glancing nervously at me.

But I'm more relaxed than I've felt in years, watching him. I knew I shouldn't have run to the army, trying to bury myself with my wife. It's feeding my soul to be here. Mephi needs me, and I need him. Machir was right.

"You're not failing." Naamah kneels next to me on the ground. "I've heard people talk. They all marvel at how you've kept your word to David and Saul, even at your own cost, but they expected nothing less from you. You've been put in a winepress of suffering, but you kept faithful and defended your brother because you trusted Yahweh's choice." Her cheek edges into her shoulder. "It's because of you that I'm not alone in Israel."

Before I can hold her gaze too long, she looks across the yard. "And that precious little warrior loves you. I would know." She catches her breath, her voice unsteady again.

Making sure the servants are occupied with Mephi, I touch Naamah's shoulder, relieved that she doesn't flinch away. "If you want to stay here, I'll make you Mephi's nurse. You won't have to see Palti again."

The terror filling her eyes eats at me, making me reconsider my promise not to hurt him. Naamah's lips tremble. "What if he goes to the king? Will Saul make me go back to him?"

"Not if my sister sent you away. And just to eliminate any confusion, I'll make sure Palti knows you're under my protection."

"Will he care?" Her forehead wrinkles.

I lace my fingers over my knee, letting her see my seal ring. "I'm Saul's son. Trust me, I can be just as frightening."

Naamah looks troubled for a moment, then her eyes catch mine and her smile breaks through.

"Don't waste another thought on Palti," I tell her. "Mephi will be glad for your company. I reduced my household after Sheva died, so the servants have their hands full with him."

Naamah smiles again, considering deeply before responding. "I always wondered what your son would be like."

Warmth enters my cheeks. There was a time we'd talked about it in a different context, believing Saul would allow us to marry. Naamah keeps her face turned away, and I study her profile in silence until she whispers, "What will the king say? About me being here?"

I tense up, remembering his rage, remembering the way I'd cried out to Yahweh for the strength to be a better father. Praise be, Mephi has never had a reason to flinch away from my touch. I face Naamah. "I'm not telling him."

* * * * *

Saul is pleased at my request to gather my brothers for a feast before things get busy in preparation for the next war season. I expect the king to raise some snide question when I include Palti, but he's too distracted with the latest reports about David.

"My spies are saying Achish wants to make him a permanent member of his court. Can you believe that? The shepherd we all thought would be on our side forever. It seems I was right about him." Saul has the decency not to say more.

I ignore him and spend the rest of the afternoon shooting as many arrows as it will take to prepare my nerves for the next several hours.

I don't identify with my brothers anymore. Their conversations reveal the direction of their hearts, bound up in

Eighteen

dreams of what Saul plans to accomplish before the throne passes to me. I sit at my own table while Ishvi, Malchi, and Bosheth toss pointless plans back and forth over my head. Plans for a future that will never happen. They've pushed Samuel's words aside, just like our father has, choosing to believe something else.

I'm pleased to see Palti drinking far too much. He's playing right into my hands. If the Law didn't forbid lying in wait for someone, and if he wasn't married to my sister…

I flex my muscles, reminding myself what I have and haven't planned to do.

At dusk, I summon Palti away from the group and then wait for him to stumble out onto the upper terrace of the garden, above where the others are gathered. I'm impressed that he made it up here alone. He slurs my name through a grin, staggering in my direction, but he doesn't make it far.

Grasping the front of his tunic, I lift him up onto the back ledge of the balcony, enjoying his shock that I can do it with one arm. He clutches at my sleeve, unable to get a good grip. Inert fear bounces around in his eyes. "My lord, what's…what are you doing?"

"Something you've never done in your life," I snarl, restraining my rage.

His head flops back, and I tighten my grip, lifting him up until we're nose to nose. Reaching around his waist, I remove his dagger from his belt without looking and slide the flat of it up his chest. "I've killed hundreds of troublemakers in my time, men who've killed our sons and stolen the virtue of our daughters. Uncircumcised men. But you…what am I to do with you, *brother?*"

I say the last word through my teeth, and Palti pants, too incoherent to really fight back. "You're mad," he puffs. "You've gone mad."

"No," I let a dark grin slip through my anger. "You don't know what mad looks like. But I do. Do you believe me?" I flick the knife up to his throat, pressing just enough to free a bead of blood.

Palti shrinks back, gasping when my grip just gets tighter and there's nowhere to go. "Yes! Yes, I do—please—"

I bend him over the stone railing, my forearm pressing down on his windpipe. "Listen to me, son of Laish. I brought you here so you could look into the eyes of the man who is now responsible for Naamah bat Ebal. If you so much as lift your eyebrows in her direction or if you breathe a word of this to anyone, I can and will bury you so deep in *Sheol* that your father's bones won't be able to find you."

Eighteen

I shoot my hand up around his neck and slam his back against the stone again. "Do you understand me?"

He nods wildly, gripping my wrists, and I pull him down and drop him on the pavement. I storm back to the house, stopping once at the threshold to look back. Palti's shaking, swallowing convulsively, checking his sides for blood. Still in shock, he looks up at me, and I hesitate long enough to see startled hatred push through the fear in his eyes.

But I'm finished dealing with him. I no longer care who dislikes me. Turning on my heel, I slam the door, leaving him alone out on the terrace floor.

NINETEEN

David

Four months later

I hold my hands in the stream until the cold bites into my fingers, dragging the Amalekite blood into the current. When I can see my own skin again, I cup water and toss it over my face and behind my neck, willing myself to believe it's enough. I'm a few miles outside of Ziklag, and I have to be clean enough to face my wives and the others who wait for my command. Even here, I won't appear before them soaked in the blood of war.

It's fortunate that all blood looks the same, whether Israelite or Canaanite, because I wear it like a second skin, spending hours after each battle trying to cleanse myself of it so I'm able to breathe easier. Pray the ancient prayers and keep the feasts of our people without feeling like an imposter. That way, by the time I have to stand before Achish again, I'm anchored, my feet firmly planted in my heritage. It's been a challenge, but we're doing it.

I glance up at my men, reining in their horses and mules around the brook, filling waterskins. The loyalty that used to warm me grips my gut like a sickness now. My men will follow me anywhere. Even to Philistine territory. They came believing that this move will be temporary, like every cave we've occupied. One day, we'll go home. But it's been more than a year.

It's become second-nature, departing as a group, then splitting into smaller factions to cover more ground against our enemies while Achish thinks we're raiding Israel. Leaving no trace of our movements, no survivors to report on us. What's been harder is fabricating cover stories elaborate enough to appease Achish.

The Philistine king has a voracious appetite for conquest, and he never tires of hearing about our exploits. I've gotten used to spinning truth into lies, changing only names and nationalities, not numbers, presenting him with fake spoils from our Canaanite neighbors. The pagan king doesn't know the difference. He barely has a grasp on what we believe, having only heard stories about his father's brush with Yahweh's power.

I swirl my hands in the water, letting the stories wash over me while I watch the sunlight spinning in the current.

In the days of Samuel's youth, King Maoch had seen the image of their god Dagon fall facedown before the Ark of the

Covenant, which they'd stolen from us. He'd seen the tumors and violent sicknesses taking hold of his people while the symbol of Yahweh's power dwelt among them. He was the one who'd sent it away on a cart with golden images of the plagues our God had sent.

But Achish was young at the time, already planning his father's assassination.

It's another reason he doesn't think my betrayal of Saul is so strange.

"Take as much power as you can without leaning on anyone too much to obtain it," he often says, making me wonder if he's chiding me for trusting him. Every other day, I wonder if we're right to be here.

I expected inner battles to increase when we came to Gath, but the constant threat to safety is often hard to distinguish from spiritual oppression. We regain our national footing in the Judean desert to the south, fighting the mixed remnants of the Amalekites who'd harassed our people since our flight from Egypt. But studying my men now, I see the same shadows on every face. The Philistine lands are undeniably different.

Open idolatry and flagrant immorality thrive in Gath and Ekron, winding poisonous fingers into the earth until the atmosphere itself seems tainted. The same evils are restrained in Israel, bound back since Saul banished sorcerers and necromancers from our borders.

I spend as little time in Goliath's city as possible, departing as soon as I've made my regular reports to Achish. Gath distracts me. With its remnant of the *Nephilim* and its bronze monuments to gods resembling the giants, I'm constantly looking over my shoulder, unsure of what's real.

An uncomfortable feeling teases the back of my mind every time I cross Philistia's border. Whatever dark spirits lurk there know who I am, and it'll only be a matter of time before their king does as well.

Uriah kneels beside me, tilting a waterskin into the current. "The sun will be down in an hour or so. Do you want to camp here?"

I wipe the excess water from my face. "No, let's keep going. We can get to Ziklag by dark." I'm not sleeping in these woods.

Uriah's shoulders relax, and I watch him while he takes a drink. He's always been a fighter, but over the past two years, his youthful exterior has toughened to match the steely resolve inside him. His cheeks wear a deep brown beard now, and since I've known him, he's never lost a fight.

He stares into the water for a moment before looking at me. "My lord, I meant to ask you if I might stay in Ziklag the next time you ride out."

The sheepish slant of his smile uncovers something familiar in my chest, and I restrain a laugh. There's only one thing I can think of that's distracting enough to keep a young man like Uriah from battle. "Who is she?"

Uriah holds my gaze, even as pink emerges beneath his beard. "Bathsheba. She's one of Eliam's daughters." Pride gleams in his face before hesitancy returns. "Do you think I'm foolish to pursue her now? Before we're back home?"

"No," I chuckle. "I married twice while on the run."

"True." Uriah nods, trying to convince himself. "And Eliam's daughters grew up out here. They don't expect…well, they're not Sarrahs."

I drag a breath through my teeth, feeling the thorn burrowing deep. The days when I would count the steps back to Gibeah, yearning to see Michal, seem like a lifetime ago. I lean back against the bank, facing him. "Eliam. Isn't he Ahithophel's son?"

Uriah nods again.

"Ahithophel has become one of my closest advisors. He's one of the wisest men I know."

"He is," Uriah agrees, and just like that, I respect him more. The young man fidgets, playing with the straps on the waterskin. "Do you think they'll approve of me?"

Taking his shoulder, I grin into his hopeful eyes. "You can have any woman you want, Uriah."

He smirks. "No, *you* can have any woman you want." He tightens his sword at his belt, changing the subject. "I'm grateful we have Ziklag. I can't imagine trying to do what we're doing with Achish watching."

Neither can I. The abandoned city Achish gave me is still within his jurisdiction, but it's far enough from the Philistine capital that I can't sense his control. Which is probably why I don't feel much pressure to leave.

I pick at the edge of my sword. It's better this way. Gath would never welcome our families unless they conformed to Philistine culture, something we're shielded from within Ziklag's walls. I'd burned the images from the doorposts, and we'd purified every structure, relaxing once we realized Achish wasn't interested in supervising us. But he could show up any time he wants. It's his city.

Nineteen

The thought isn't even fully through my head when Uriah straightens up, his manner changing. "Achish's men," he says into the clearing, and I look up to see a dozen or more Philistine warriors riding into the glade, crossing the stream to surround us.

Their heavy robes match whatever the king is wearing these days, setting them apart as the nobility. They ride out beside Achish in battles requiring the whole army, but they rarely fight with the foot soldiers.

I start walking toward them with Uriah following, his hand on his sword. Not far behind us, my nephews sharpen their guard, moving into position. Since we came to Gath, we've fought separately from the Philistine lords. The wealthy commanders have vehemently opposed our presence with their king.

Achish has made a game out of their dislike, using my skills as perverse motivation to bait them. A few times, he made me spar with his closest warriors, laughing and drinking the whole time. I'd won, confident that Yahweh wouldn't let me fall on enemy soil without completing what I've been anointed to do. But I'd felt dirty afterwards. There's no honor in fighting for Achish's amusement, and the games only made the commanders' hatred burn hotter.

Since they don't often face direct combat, the nobles ride unbroken stallions, lavish gifts from the king. It's a matter of pride, but clearly not all of them have a firm grip on the animals. The nearest official allows his horse to rear up, its hooves kicking the air within inches of me.

"The king has summoned you to his palace in Gath. You must come with us." The man's gray eyes pinch beneath the rim of his helmet, shifting over my shoulder. "Not all of you. Just your shepherd."

Ironically, when he calls me a shepherd, I remember his name. "We'll make our reports as usual in a fortnight, Allu, after we've been home," I hedge, hoping he'll be satisfied with our usual practice. He isn't.

Allu's face turns a darker shade as he spits a response. "This isn't a request, Israelite! It's a command. Achish has decided to answer the complaints he's received about you."

I squint at him, recognizing a bluff. The men of Achish's court have whined constantly since my arrival, but I've been content to bury myself in battle and let the king handle the sycophants. So far, they haven't been able to sway him.

I fold my hands. "What complaints? The king hasn't shown any displeasure with me since I've been here."

Nineteen

Allu sneers, "You haven't been here. You still think like a rebel, wandering the land with no ties to anyone." He looks deeply, trying to uncover something he has yet to find. "Achish sent us to bring you before him. Alone," he says pointedly. "You've chosen your king; now obey him."

I shift my weight, refusing to break eye contact. He's trying to make this sound like a threat, and I'm not sure if I should take it as one. It's true, I've avoided the main cities, and Achish has never voiced any disapproval about my movements. But kings can change.

I try one more excuse, sweeping a hand across my dusty clothing and blood-stained armor. "I'm hardly fit to see the king like this."

The men scoff while Allu snaps vehemently. "Achish isn't an Israelite, fool. Your ritual washings mean nothing to him. Follow us now, or we'll treat you like the Judean rat you are."

Joab's shadow moves behind me, and I hear Uriah's sword sliding in its scabbard. I lift up my hand, turning around. Allu's right. They may not be the king's fiercest warriors, but they carry his support and authority, and even though we outnumber them, we'd be signing our own death warrants if we killed them. I touch Uriah's shoulder and lock eyes with Joab.

"Camp here, and wait for me. I'll follow Allu to Gath and meet you on the way back to Ziklag."

I see the question glaring in Joab's eyes. I've never approached Achish alone. Not since I was dragged before him at the end of a chain years ago. Within the fortress, it won't be easy for me to get word to my men if I run into trouble.

I slide my hand up the front of my breastplate and spin my fingers in a slingshot motion. Joab lifts his chin, understanding my signal for a group of them to follow me in secret. They'll camp outside Gath's walls, watching and listening. I'll sling a stone over the gate if I need them to attack.

"You heard him. Make camp here," Joab bellows orders through the clearing.

Once the Philistines turn their horses around, Asahel approaches me and winds a small ram's horn into my belt under my robe. He's the fastest runner I know; he'll be one of the first to reach me if I call for help. I clasp his hand over it and swing myself up onto my mule.

I ride north in silence, and Gath's jagged walls scar the landscape within four miles. I try to stay ahead of the men, showing no hesitancy, but the nobles keep shadowing me, one riding in front, three behind, and the others crowding around on either side.

Ittai is waiting outside the guardhouse, but he feigns disinterest, not reacting when several of his soldiers spit on the ground in my direction. With a face like stone, he signals the watchmen to open the gates. I ride through them, refusing to look back.

Ittai hasn't approached me since my arrival here, but the air is always thick between us, filled with everything we aren't saying. Everything he knows.

For an instant, I wonder if he's behind Achish's sudden desire to get me alone. Trusting him with my true motives is probably the stupidest thing I've done yet. But then, he doesn't know my exact movements. Unless he's sent men to follow me.

I move through Gath's courtyard, ice climbing my throat. Achish's palace sits adjacent to the high places, up against a sacred clearing where he worships. Incense-laden clouds smear the air around every grove, and the carved faces of their gods leer at me from the trees. I don't keep track of the Philistines' festivals, but their symbols and rituals are becoming disturbingly familiar.

Fertility prayers are scrawled across every other column and pole, while the rest of them are decorated with images of the half-fish Dagon or their mother-god. Dusk drops over the sun almost instantly when I touch the edge of the hill. I glance at the other riders, but they act like they don't notice the chill writhing in the air.

My foot touches ground, and a dozen curses dart through my mind. These walls are stained with the evil pronouncements Achish's wise men level at Israel before each war season. My fists tighten against the deep tremors being stirred awake. I'm not here to fight. But I'm remembering Goliath's eyes, gripped by the way I'd seen straight through them into the depths of *Sheol*.

The old fear turns over, waking up in a dark corner of my spirit. Yahweh was my obsession then; every part of me chased after Him for all I was worth. But now I've taken refuge in the land of the giants who oppose Him. Does He think I've chosen them over Him? Will He leave me here?

I twist my neck, trying to shake off the heaviness mounting over me. Yahweh sees more clearly than anyone. He knows my heart.

Someone shouts, and the palace doors open. The noblemen crowd around, herding me through Achish's door and into the arms of a dozen court servants. When they start grabbing at me, I shove them off, resentful.

Nineteen

"Do I go before the king as a prisoner?" I demand.

Allu's smile smears the dimness. "You yourself said you were in no condition to see the king. We'll make you acceptable."

Pressed against an inner wall, I have to let them remove my weapons and armor vest. They line up the metal on the ground and toss a garish tunic with a gold fringe at me. "Put this on," one of the servants orders me, and the lords stand by snickering while I do it.

Allu steps forward when the servants back away. "The king has a gift for you. One you left behind the last time." He drapes a heavy gold chain over my head, and when it drops onto my chest, I see the outline of Dagon's image on the pendant. Never.

I yank it off and drop it at Allu's feet. "I've never worn his gold before, and I won't now. I'm a warrior, not an ornament."

The triumph filling the lord's face intensifies the fear growing inside me. Am I failing some sort of test?

Allu's tone is frosty. "You're a mercenary, Israelite. You belong to the king."

My stomach winces, the pain reaching up into my chest. "Then let him command me."

The men keep behind me, directing me down the confusing corridors to an inner chamber. I can feel the length of the room. Our steps echo in the emptiness, but it's heavily dark. Even the torches on the wall don't seem to burn at full strength. At the room's center, I barely make out a low table spread with unclean food. Swine's flesh, goat's meat swimming in its mother's milk. My senses burn. This is a test, one I probably won't win without a fight. Footsteps shuffle down the dark hallway, leaving me alone.

I reach for my sword, but it's gone. I'm an idiot. What am I doing here without a weapon? Furious at myself for walking into a trap, I breathe Yahweh's name and step across the threshold.

A flame touches a basin of oil at the far end of the room, and fear turns a blazing dagger on my insides as a familiar sound crackles over my head. Trapped within the stone walls, the lion's growl makes the floor vibrate under me. A man's laughter barely reaches my ears over the deafening sound.

"Come now; you're not afraid."

My attention pulls to the left. Achish is sitting on a gold-edged chair, draped in a pale robe with a scarlet fringe. His hand is clasped around a long leash, and my gaze follows it to the neck of a huge beast, its head bent while it paws at the ground. I blink a few times, but it's no vision. Achish really has a lion beside him.

Nineteen

The tawny fur glistens in the torchlight, angry muscles writhing underneath.

Achish crosses one leg over the other. "You've killed these before. Didn't you tell Goliath how the hand of Yahweh saved you when you were just a boy?"

His mockery echoes in my head before he abruptly lets the leash go. Danger claws at my limbs, every defense screaming when the lion springs forward a pace. But it stops halfway across the room, a frustrated growl breaking in its throat. Horrified, I watch Achish raise his hand, his fingers tickling the air in the lion's direction. He stands up and strolls past the animal, his smile wide.

"I'll wager you've never seen Saul do that. We command things you Israelites would never dream of."

I straighten, trying to settle myself. Sorcery is part of the air they breathe in Gath. The mediums of Ekron routinely visit the king, spinning whatever webs he desires. But it'll turn on them eventually. The darkness always does. I've seen it.

An old story pricks my mind, our ancestors' account of Moses' dealings with the magicians of Egypt, when his staff-turned-snake swallowed the ones used by the sorcerers. I drag my gaze off the lion, fixing it on Achish instead.

Let him mock. The fact remains, he saw his father tremble before the Ark of the Covenant. He saw Goliath fall at the hands of a shepherd boy. He knows Yahweh always wins.

"The lords said you wanted to see me alone," I say, my voice too loud in the room. "I was planning on delivering my reports within a fortnight. We raided the Kenites' camp within the Negeb. No one's left."

Achish rubs his beardless chin before responding. "Your success is unmatched, my champion. You're always indispensable to the ones you serve. And yet, one thing puzzles me. Can you guess what it is?" He pauses, letting me think for a moment. "You fight my battles; you live in the city I gave you. Yet, after all this time, you still look like a Hebrew."

I am a Hebrew. My nerves clench, but it would be unwise to answer. I wait while the king moves toward me, his scrutiny choking the air.

"Up till now, I've turned a deaf ear to the lords' complaints. I've found no fault with your battle skills. But my men have made me realize you're still ungrateful. You never wear the gold pieces I've sent you, honoring our gods." Achish's soft shoes scuff the stone floor as he circles me. "You don't stay for our celebrations."

Nineteen

Turning on his heel, he grasps my hair from behind, combing his fingers through the thickness. Abhorrence grips my body, winding up into my throat.

"Why haven't you cut this?" he demands. "Are you going to pretend you don't notice how my soldiers keep themselves clean-shaven?"

Fire climbs my neck, charring my senses until I have to dig through the ashes for an appropriate response. I haven't missed the distinctions between myself and the other mercenaries, not to mention that they're branded with the symbol of Dagon's curled tail. I'd put it out of my mind, assuming Achish wouldn't want an Israelite to resemble his men so closely.

I steel myself, pushing innocence into my voice. "When I came here, I didn't expect you to treat me kindly, let alone accept me as one of your people. I'm not used to feasts and wealth anymore. I've been content to fight."

Achish chuckles. "Yes, always the man of war. But a bit of revelry at the end of a bloodbath pleases the gods."

"I suppose my thirst for blood is greater than my thirst for pleasure," I mutter, forcing a smile.

A deep shadow reaches out to me from Achish's face. "Then let's see you drink."

My body clenches with each step closer to the table. There's a good chance the wine has been offered to Philistia's gods, but maybe it'll distract Achish from my inability to eat anything here. I sit down, and shame drops over me like a heavy garment.

Achish fills a cup and murmurs, "This was just brought in from the winepress in my grove. Even the gods haven't tasted it yet."

A breath of relief fills my lungs for a moment. It has yet to be offered to the demons Philistia entertains. But one sip tells me they don't cleanse off the dregs before serving it. I have to bite down hard against the urge to spit it out. I force it down, gulping too much. The sting stabs my nose, dragging a knife down my throat. But the faster I can satisfy the king, the sooner I can leave.

Achish keeps pouring, and I watch him over the rim of the cup.

"Your success on my behalf has reached Israel, I hear," he ventures, watching for my reaction. "Saul must be eating up the rumors. You're finally the traitor he always thought you were."

Nineteen

My head is going to explode. The wine is heavier than I'm used to, and whatever Achish has laced it with is knife-edged, imprisoning my veins with something like helpless rage. I was no traitor before, and I'm no traitor now. But my mind argues, accusing me. *Then why are you here, drinking with an enemy of Israel?*

On the hills outside Bethlehem, Yahweh would come so close it would feel like I was breathing with Him. How I long for that safety and assurance now. My heart turns inside out, imagining it while the king keeps talking. The slow drone of his voice opens a dark pathway, dragging me along it.

"You've proven yourself a capable mercenary, one of the fiercest warriors I've ever seen. But my men are not convinced of your loyalty, since you've made no effort to become one of us."

Achish pours more wine, his voice folding gently into the sloshing sound. "Saul no longer hunts you, but we both know he would have your head if you returned now. You're tainted already, so why do you hesitate to prove yourself to me? How long do you think you can deceive me?"

I squint across the table, wondering how much he's saying and how much is just roaming around in my mind. In my doubled vision, Achish has several heads, like Leviathan, the serpent-monster of old. His grin shows the teeth of a predator, and I can't tell how close he is.

He bends forward, his voice slinking toward me. "Where did you really raid, Israelite?"

I grip the table's edge, but it keeps turning to liquid, pulling away from me. "I—raided the Negeb of the Kenites in Judah," I repeat, refusing to think of it as a lie. He has to hear me believing it.

Achish plants his hands on the table, his face horribly distorted. "Your own kin? No." His voice drags, echoing into the chambers behind us. "You wouldn't really turn against Saul. Is it worth losing the support of the countrymen who have worshipped you?"

"I serve you now," I mumble. "You know that."

Achish's grin swims in front of me. "It's true. You've made yourself a stench to your people, and once you become fully mine, your God will forsake you too." He waits, sharpening his tongue. "You know Jonathan will never see your face again."

My arm jerks, and my wrist goes too far, knocking over a goblet. Wine spills across the table, pooling around my fingers like blood. He's baiting me, trying to get me to open up. But I can't let him. We've gone too far, my men and I.

I lean into the table and summon every bit of strength to stand up, leaning onto feet with no feeling. My mouth feels thick, but I try to speak as coherently as I can. "My lord, I have always honored our agreement. You will find nothing to condemn."

It takes far too much energy to reach inside my cloak, but after fumbling around the ram's horn, I finally retrieve the bag of torn Judean clothing, cut from old cloaks and soaked in the blood of our enemies. I drop it at Achish's feet.

"Another hundred are dead. My men have the livestock we took from them. I will have my servants send them to you for whatever sacrifices you desire to make." My temples pound, squeezing the muscles behind my eyes, but I refuse to wince.

"I would rather you attend the sacrifices." Achish stares at the sack on the floor, his eyes traveling up my body to lock onto my face. "You truly intend to continue in my service?"

"Yes," I gasp. My lungs are on fire, and the wandering of the king's eyes feels like the crawl of insects on my skin.

Achish leans forward, his tongue dragging over his teeth. "Then…you will follow me to Israel?"

Israel? My senses writhe, grappling for alertness. I'd known it would only be a matter of time before Achish forced me to march with him against Israel. But the news is still upending me. I had hoped to know with enough time to be able to instruct my men, work our own plan. The king is still waiting for an answer.

"Of course," I whisper. "It's the command I've been waiting for, my lord."

That much is true, at least.

Smiling broadly, Achish reaches behind his chair and lifts Goliath's sword into view. Placing it across his hands lengthwise, he holds it out to me. "Then carry this into battle alongside my commanders. Let all the men who accused you watch you finish what Goliath began."

My heart shudders, beating out of time while the heat of sickness stirs around it. I focus hard and take the weapon. "As I have said, you will see what your servant can do."

Satisfied, Achish clasps my arms, any suspicion slinking away to the edges of the room where the lion is still crouched. "Excellent. Go, then. I will arrange the necessary preparations, and when we return, I will make you my bodyguard for life. Prove yourself this last time, my champion, and you will have everything Saul denied you."

Nineteen

"Thank you," I mumble, staggering backwards as soon as he lets go of me. I'm still not convinced he didn't poison me. Sharp pain is devouring my stomach, and I have to get out of this palace before the walls crush me.

* * * * *

No one follows me outside. Once I've figured out the labyrinth of corridors to the outer courtyard, I stumble past the gate and vomit into the dust. The fist of shame digs into my neck, keeping me from lifting my head. Shaking on my hands and knees, I grip the ground, feeling like the earth will tilt and toss me off.

I should have fought him! The David I used to be would have noticed the sword of Goliath leaning against the chair and grabbed it to use on the king, lion or no lion. The old David was so full of faith, it spilled over onto the men around me. Now, I'm just a pawn. Again. I've defiled myself and my men, only to keep fighting battles I could have fought back in Israel.

Sweat claws my body as the wine's toxin slowly releases its grip. I drag my gaze to the indigo sky.

What am I doing, Yahweh? You know I don't want to be here. But we had to keep away. Saul would have come after us again, and I couldn't take it. I couldn't!

I can feel the old brokenness being stretched like a reinjured bone flexed too soon. I haven't touched it in so long, but the wound is still there. Those times I confronted Saul in the caves of En-Gedi, in the Ziphite hills, I'd had a moment of release, a chance to make him see what his hatred was doing to me. Otherwise, I've carried the burden around, burying it deep, afraid it would break the surface and foment the rage of my men.

I've expended so much energy protecting Saul. And now, I feel more exposed than ever. Look what he's driven me to! Even if he welcomed me home with open arms and repentance, how could he ever give me back those years on the run?

Tears emerge on my clammy cheeks, and I groan aloud. "Where else would we have found refuge? Where's home anymore?"

Before I finish, powerful chills explode along my arms and legs. Dust swirls around me, caught up in a fierce, mounting wind, and it's as though a hand reaches into me, finds the center, and yanks. Every shred of poison leaves my body, and my vision snaps sharply into focus, aligning with the lightning forking the horizon. Toward Israel.

Thunder rumbles around a terrible, audible voice.

I AM.

I collapse lengthwise on the ground, my limbs curled around myself, the breath fleeing from my body. Each heartbeat pushes every one of His Names through my head.

Yahweh. Adonai. El-Shaddai. El-Jireh. El-Roi.

Melek.

Instantly, I know how I've been able to forget who I am. By taking refuge in the enemy's camp, I've forgotten who He is. How we're bound together. Without Him, my anointing has no meaning, and I have no ability to attain it. How am I to be king when I'm a lost sheep myself? My mother's old admonition smiles in my head, soothing away the aches. *By following your Shepherd.*

I press my hands into my face before letting them fall forward, palms open. "Forgive me, my King."

The sensation of a hand runs along my back this time, gripping my collar and lifting me upright. *Ride to Jezreel. I will be with you.*

Yahweh's voice isn't audible anymore, but it's wound up in my heartbeat, and I know it's Him. I gasp, my lungs expanding and contracting around the relief surging through them. He hasn't left me. He won't forsake me.

"Thank you. Thank you." It's all I can say.

With the familiar flame back in my heart, I open my eyes and look toward the lower gate at the base of the hill. The two Philistine sentries are pressed up against the doors, no longer marching back and forth. The torchlight reveals the hugeness of their eyes, watching me in the dark. Whatever they saw is holding them hostage, impeding movement.

Ittai comes through a side door, looking askance at the other two. He leads my mule over to me, saying nothing about my condition. "Achish spoke to you." There's no question in his voice. He knows all about what happened inside.

I nod, and Ittai's brows leap up into his helmet. "You're sure about this?" he asks me.

I get up shakily. I'm not sure about anything. But Yahweh is with me. Somehow, He's willing to stay with me, even here. And if He's provided a way back to Israel, there has to be a reason. I can trust Him to reveal it as we go. I nod again, watching Ittai's expression close like an iron gate.

"You won't have time to return to Ziklag, but you can send a message back to your women. Your army can't be far ahead of you." His eyes skirt the tree line to the south. "Go and meet them. Bring them back here. In three days, we march to Israel."

TWENTY

Jonathan

The darkest clouds are edging the sun, shrouding the king's upper courtyard in shadows too ashen for evening. I pace as I wait for Ziba, my fingers curling into fists at my sides, my mind drawn back to the court.

The heaviness of my father's council room had filled every face, deafening silence stretching between the men who have defended the king since I was a boy. With the exception of the day Goliath showed his face, I've never seen the men of Benjamin look so dismayed, empty of solutions. Seeing them so bereft has sharpened all my old fears into something with teeth.

I've been summoned to battle before. More times than I can count. But a shiver of alarm has been creeping closer every day since the spies' latest report. It's been keeping step with my heart, pushing deeper until it's lodged permanently in the center of me. The place that's always so safe from doubt and dread.

This battle is different. There are too many Philistines this time. Too many. Achish has been toying with us all these years, keeping watch and building strength while Abba has ignored him, hunting David.

My mind buzzing, I feel along my belt until my fingers touch the rubies David took from Goliath's girdle on the day he slew the giant. I've carried the gemstones ever since as a reminder of our friendship. I fold my hand around them, summoning comfort from the memory of David giving them to me. Our bond was born out of the Elah battle and won't die with any other.

How many times have we strategized since then, camped out under the stars or walking the roof of the palace at dusk? I'd felt Yahweh's wisdom in David's words and his songs, the same wisdom that's completely lacking from Saul's court these days. What I wouldn't give to be waiting for him right now, not Naamah's brother.

I'd thought my friend's months of deception in Gath would have been enough to occupy Achish, perhaps give David time to send us information we would need to defeat them once and for all. But as always, reality is more complicated. David's spent sixteen months dancing on the edge of treason and living in the lion's mouth.

And now, the latest message from Achish has proven it. The Philistines are ten times more numerous than we thought. They're tired of waiting. They're coming with a rage we haven't felt in decades. Since I humiliated them at Michmash when I was fourteen, they've been planning how to use my father's weakness to seize control, gain a foothold in our land that won't be easily uprooted. They'd failed at Elah because of David. But now...

I shudder at the chill prickling along my skin. At this time of year, I can feel the storms brewing. The annual springtime rains are coming to pound the countryside and wash away the blood that is sure to follow this fighting season. Fixing my eyes on the slight strip of blue smiling in the gray horizon, I stand still and let the uneasy wind push through my hair before it dives down to toss in the garden below.

The memory of David and Michal kissing beneath those trees still closes my throat. I should find a way to talk to my sister, tell her goodbye. But I doubt she'll speak to me. I don't want to risk riding to Laish only to have her slam the door in my face. And I never want to see Palti again.

I shift my weight on the stone pavement, folding my arms. I need to go home. Just as soon as Ziba gets here. I sent him word by way of his master, the captain of the palace guard. He'll have to come up eventually.

I squint into the sharp air, watching the unsteady pace of Gibeah's market below. Saul sent word out among the people earlier, but he didn't try to control the information as much as usual. Fear is spreading faster than the old Ammonite plague, and I resist its pull, setting my jaw against the chill of doubt.

Am I doing right? How much can Ziba be trusted? He's certainly not the man I would have chosen to confide in at this moment.

Finally, I hear his sandals on the steps behind me climbing up onto the king's upper terrace. "What do you have to say to me?" he demands, stopping halfway across the large space.

I clench my hands around the railing. I'm so far from trusting him, it's laughable, but he's Naamah's brother. I have to make the most of that. Preparing an appropriate expression, I turn around to face him. "You've heard what they're saying in Gibeah?"

"About the Philistines marching to Jezreel? Yes." His words are tight, clipped. "For your information, I agree with the people already choosing to flee. I'm sending my own sons and servants across the Jordan as soon as the king leaves tomorrow."

I steady myself, refusing to imagine my father's city in uproar, my son having to escape with the rest of them. I stare

Ziba down, forcing eye contact. "I want you to promise that you will not go anywhere without Naamah. She is your sister, and without me, you'll be the only man she can depend on."

I already know what he'll say before it comes through his teeth.

"I *am* the only man she can depend on."

I lift my chin. "Therefore, I'm placing her in your care. Along with my son." I barely wait to see the disgust work its way through his face. "Naamah loves my son, and she won't go anywhere without him. This is important, Ziba."

I step closer to him, my hands lifted slightly, my voice dropping lower. "You remember what it was like to hide with your sister while our enemies destroyed your home. You cannot leave my son to the same fate. Naamah won't." I breathe past the catch in my voice. "Tomorrow, I ride out with the king to face Achish and his thousands at Gilboa, and whatever happens, I want you to help Naamah and Mephi get to safety. Once you have escaped, you can try to find a closer relative to take my son."

The names of a dozen servants and officials weave through my mind, and my desperation isolates the honest face of the physician's son. "Perhaps Machir ben Ammiel. Look for him."

Machir has known my family for years. Somehow, I'm certain he would be willing to help.

Ziba squints. "Why don't you ask him yourself?"

And reveal that we might not return? Not yet. It's bad enough I have to say this to Ziba.

"I don't have time to search for him before I leave. I'll write a letter and give it to Naamah. If you hear that the Philistines have…" I trail off, my throat snapping shut again. "Just get to safety and then give Machir the letter when you find him."

I reach beneath my breastplate for a thick leather bag. I hold it out, placing it in Ziba's hands. "I'm giving you enough to start over somewhere, hopefully give your sons a better future than they've been able to achieve under Saul. There's plenty for my son too."

Before he can remove it from my grasp, I tighten my hands around his. "Do I have your word, Ziba?"

Naamah's brother looks nothing like her. Or maybe it's just the way he's chosen to look at me all this time, mistrust staining the resemblance he might have shared with his sister. He still barely covers his disdain, even after everything I've done to help them.

Twenty

Ziba works his jaw a few times, then answers tightly, "I will get your son to safety."

I relax my shoulders, not bothering to hide my relief. "Thank you."

There's momentary triumph in Ziba's face, a realization that I'm now in his debt. But the hardness I'm used to seeing returns quickly to his brow. "You've made my sister into something no man wants," he grimaces, anger seething between his teeth. "But unfortunately, she doesn't hate you the way I do. Perhaps in time, I can clear that up for her. Or your boy."

He jerks the moneybag from my hands and walks away, leaving me grappling for a response. Indignance and wounded pride toss through me, but what wins out is what I've always tried with my father.

"Ziba—" I wait for him to turn back. "Whatever you have suffered at Saul's hands is not Mephi's fault. Remember, Yahweh sees what you do. You stand before Him, not me."

He tries to scoff, but instead ends up swallowing his contempt, stalking into the armory without answering. I head down the outer stairs to the courtyard, trying to believe I did the right thing. But Ziba's resentment glowers after me while I retrieve my mule and circle around toward home.

He's honest with me because he knows I'm too experienced to lash out at his grievances. Too many in Israel have suffered at Saul's hands, and I know it. David's ranks are swollen with them. I can only wonder why Ziba never joined him. He has fifteen sons who will make skilled warriors one day.

Nothing makes sense anymore. These days, it feels like we're bent in half, all our strength expended in holding up a crumbling wall like Samson of old. And it's just a matter of time before it collapses on top of us.

Unusual silence greets me when I enter my house. It hasn't been this quiet since Mephi was born. For the moment, I'm relieved not to see my son bursting through one of the doors to jump into my arms. I don't think I can look him in the eyes. Not yet. This could be the last time, and I need everything to sink in before I can turn it into something my son will understand.

Pausing at the threshold of the lower room, I breathe in, letting myself feel at home one more time. The sweet oils scenting the walls carry the image of Mephi's sweet, crooked smile and joyful abandon. It's a beautiful image, but the unfairness surrounding it hurts.

When I was his age, my days were alive with hope also. The valiant history of Israel's judges and prophets ruled my

Twenty

imagination, and I'd dreamed of being so faithful that Yahweh would have to take notice. Even at five years old, I'd known I would likely end up fighting, caught up in some war to defend Israel and strengthen her position in the region.

Ever since I saw his face, I've prayed Mephi would be able to avoid that existence. Abba's anointing was supposed to secure a better future for my son, a chance for him to live in peace, fully embracing the promises spread before Israel like a feast. But every day now, more and more, I doubt that Mephi's life will unfold the way I've hoped.

Flinging my cloak aside, I climb the stone stairs to the upper rooms, listening for voices. I feel like a stranger within these walls. The burden gripping my heart doesn't belong here. I don't even have words to describe it. I feel as though every step is labored, every breath borrowed.

I run my hands over the heavy tapestry covering Mephi's doorway, my mind sorting through all the arrangements I have to make. Before sunrise. My father had ordered all his sons to follow him, except Bosheth, something I hadn't expected he would do. He's kept me safe for a year, only allowing me to fight close to home and always beside him. I'm his heir, and when he sees me, he sees the security of his kingdom.

In the past, we've sharpened one another, feeding off of each other's courage. But now, I'm missing the certainty I've always worn with my armor. It's gone, and I feel as though I'm marching into battle injured. Something I've never done.

It's strange to see my father completely devoid of the arrogant pride that used to protect him. If the threat is serious enough to call me into a war that could last for years, then Saul is afraid. Very afraid.

I glance along the hallway, still looking for Ezra without meaning to. I'm running out of people I can really trust. Fortunately, one of the few is here with my son.

Mephi's lisping voice drifts through the curtain, followed by a woman's murmur, and I peek through the tassels. My little boy is more contained than I've ever seen him, cross-legged in a corner, pushing his wild curls out of his eyes with his fist while his other fingers follow the words on the parchment unrolled in front of him. Held by Naamah.

I edge back along the wall, not wanting to disturb them yet. I can't deny how natural it looks to see my son in Naamah's arms. Even in the midst of the sorrow following Sheva's death, I've never found it strange to have my old friend here. Naamah found her place easily, helping us settle back into ours.

Twenty

My attention sharpens, my ears honing in on the words filling the room. Naamah repeats them against my son's cheek, whispering them like anointing oil into his hair.

"The Lord our God is God. He is a faithful God, keeping His covenant of love to a thousand generations of those who love Him and keep His commands. And visiting His vengeance for sin on the third and fourth generations."

The words drift toward me like incense, and mist clouds my eyes. Without making a sound, I retreat to my chamber. I walk to the window across from my bed and watch the sky deepen, drowning the sun in a fiery blaze.

My father's words intone in the silence, absorbed by the sunset.

"There are too many at Aphek. If they amass this entire force against us, we will need all of our thousands to face them. I want each of you following me to Gilboa with your units. We leave at first light tomorrow."

He had waited for the news to sink in before snapping, "And no, Jonathan, I have not heard from Yahweh. I've had Ahijah praying for weeks while I waited for the spies' reports, but we've heard nothing. No dreams. No word. We're on our own now."

Even my father's bluster couldn't hide how much the admission had shaken him. I had tried to express my hesitation in private without sounding disrespectful. Or fearful. But the terrified anger turning Saul's eyes yellow had made me swallow my protests. Now, they're consuming me.

How long will this war keep me from my son? It's not like the usual fighting seasons where our strength is matched against theirs for territory. This time, Achish won't stop. He's done with petty raids, competitions with giants. He'll push until he has blood. Either mine or the blood of my father. Or both.

I sweep a hand across the cold sweat smearing my forehead. Samuel's prophecy was clear. If this is the end for my father, it's the end for me. But it's too soon. Mephi is too young. And I don't know how to ask for mercy. I don't know if I can.

Which is why I need to come back here. I've never felt drawn to my home more than to battle. I've always belonged in the forest war camps, fighting for the glory of Adonai and the honor of the men I revere. But now that I'm back in the house where I welcomed my bride and our son, I'm desperate to think of a way to stay. I'm afraid if I say goodbye this time, I won't return.

The absence of everyone I love groans around me, but for the first time, I'm relieved Sheva didn't live to see this. She

Twenty

didn't have to face losing me, seeing the threat to her son and her people. She'd begged me to save Mephi's life, but I don't know how much I can spare him from what's coming.

I've seen plenty of men die in battle. I've had to drag the grief aside, shoving it into a back corner of my mind. Over and over. Guarding myself and my strength so I could fight another day. When Sheva died, I'd allowed myself to feel. I'd wept with her, making every promise I could to ease her mind.

But now, I'm grasping the full reality of what she went through. Looking back from the end of her life at the ones she loved and having to let them go. It's terrifying. And yet, her dying words had been filled with a deliberate peace, entrusting everything she loved to Yahweh. Now, it's my chance to do the same.

Fumbling for a stray piece of parchment and an ink pen, I write a few shaky lines to Machir. If anything happens to me, Ziba will take my son into hiding. But I don't want him raising Mephi. Machir needs to find him as soon as possible. And help him get to David.

Mephi's voice grows louder in the next room, and my heart revolts again. How am I supposed to take his exuberant innocence and crush it with my disappearance? My mind starts to thrash again, pulling in hundreds of panicked directions. I have to decide now, make a plan for the servants to follow.

"Abba!" Mephi clatters into the room, and I spin around in time to catch him.

"Mephi. My heart." I hug him hard, burying my fingers in his hair. Crushing the letter in my fist behind his back. When I open my eyes, Naamah is staring into them. Too deep.

I set Mephi down. "Go get your bow, my son."

Once he's darted off, chattering to no one in particular, I face Naamah for exactly three seconds, refusing to break. Yet. Having her here has brought stability to a house that was fraying at the edges. Her presence has sheltered Mephi and stitched my heart back together. I don't want to rip at those wounds. Not again.

Facing Naamah, I wrangle every emotion into a back corner, forcing an invisible gate shut on them. For now.

"I'm taking him out to the fields," I tell her. "When I return, we'll talk."

* * * * *

Twenty

Mephi barely releases the arrow before he's prancing like a deer, crowing, "I did it, Abba! Look!"

I reach down and retrieve the arrow that hardly went anywhere, forcing a smile through the pain. Alone with my only son, the yearning is intense. To see him grow up, to have the pleasure of sharing life with him as I've done with my father. To continue showing him the acceptance and love I rarely felt from Saul. But for the first time, that certainty is slipping from my fingers.

"You shoot now, Abba." Mephi squints up at me through his curls, and my heart stops. Everyone says he looks like me. But occasionally, I'll blink and see Saul. Or my brothers. This time, it's Saul. Seeing my father in the angle of Mephi's smile is like seeing the chance Abba had to choose peace and have joyful light fill his countenance always.

I drop to my knees in the dirt. My arms fold around Mephi, and suddenly I'm shaking with intensity, holding back tears like my life depends on it. Mephi squirms a little in my grasp, clutching his little bow behind my back, and I will myself to relax. I don't want to scare him.

But the boy sees too deeply. Already. Still holding his bow, he places his hands around my face, his free fingers tracing my beard. "Why are you sad, Abba?"

The pain makes me want to tear at my clothes, but I restrain myself. "I don't want to leave you, Mephi." I set him on his feet and hold his wrists at his sides. "I have to go help Saba fight the Philistines. I might be gone a long time."

Mephi's eyes light up. "I'll come with you! I can fight."

I would laugh if it didn't hurt so much. My life has been consumed with war. But maybe it's not too late for my son to live differently. To never have to shed blood to protect his own life. I hope to God.

Mephi's already lost his train of thought, tracing the carved design on my bow, mumbling the words he'd just recited from Torah. I suck in another ragged breath. No one told me having a child would cause my heart to sing and ache so fiercely at the same time.

There's so much I haven't taught him, so much he doesn't understand. He's so young! And I have so little time. How much does he comprehend the truth that's already been sown into him? I lean forward and cup his face, steadying myself by making him focus.

"Do you know who we fight for, Mephi? Who goes before us?"

"Yahweh." He straightens his little back.

"Yes, Yahweh, the God of heaven and earth. The God who chose Israel out of all the other nations to be His own people. Promise me you will hold tight to Him, just like you're holding this bow. Honor Him, keep His commands, and never let go of Him. Will you do that, my son?"

Mephi nods, his eyes wide.

My grin breaking, I pull my son close and embrace him again. "Good." My fingers close around his bow. "Because when Yahweh is with you, your arrows will fly on the wings of the wind."

* * * * *

It's nearly impossible to extract Mephi from my side when I'm home, but the servants finally manage it, taking him into the garden to climb his favorite tamarisk tree. Just a few short years ago, he used to be afraid of the sprawling tree. Now we can't pry him off it. The maids used to worry, saying he would break his legs one day. But Naamah always laughs at his exuberance, taking delight in his spirit. My boy has fed her heart as well, helping her pick up the pieces of her life.

But she's not laughing today.

Usually, she would follow Mephi into the garden, but this time, she knows to stay behind. She waits silently in the corner of my chamber until we've been left alone. I watch the window, feeling myself unwinding from the inside out.

"What is it?" Naamah's voice always holds everything she's not saying, all the years we have in common. The sound of it curls into my chest, making my heart shudder. This is going to be harder than I expected.

Unlike Sheva, who'd always held a queenly steadiness inside her where I was concerned, Naamah has spent decades fearing this. That something would happen to me because of my father. She's feared it ever since she watched Saul knock me down after finding us together.

"You went to see the king?"

The moment she asks it, the hardness in my throat traps my answer. I just stand there while everything I thought I would say turns to ash in my mind. The fire building inside me reaches my face and burns through my eyes.

Naamah turns, calling to the guards at the door. "Both of you, out. Leave us. You too, Mirah," she says to the maid walking by. "Keep Mephi in the garden, and don't disturb us until I tell you."

Twenty

They all scramble to obey her. The calmness in Naamah's tone is bending over on itself like burning paper. The door finally closes, and the servants' footsteps descend down the outer stairs.

Naamah moves closer, her face's reflection filling the polished shield hanging to the left of the window. "The king's spies returned? What was the report?"

Bent over, I grab the edge of the window, feeling pain like a dagger in my chest. There's definitely something wrong with this battle. The frantic urgency gripping me is unlike anything I've ever experienced. Unspoken prayers groan through me.

Adonai, help me! I feel like my whole life has been a waste. Was I wrong to stay with Saul? Should I have joined David while I still could? What am I doing here now?

A flash of comfort comes with my next breath, that close and quick. A moment of quiet in the raging. It's the same inner witness that began with the prophet's recent message assuring me Yahweh was pleased with me. Telling me I had done right.

But everything else is very wrong. I've been wrong to pretend for so long.

Naamah is right at my back. Her voice drops deep into her chest. "Jonathan."

"I'm leaving tomorrow for Jezreel." The words cut my throat. "I don't know when…or if I'll be back."

"What?"

I snag a few breaths while I can. I may as well start at the beginning. "Abner's spies came back with a rough estimate of how many Philistines are gathered at Aphek. They're encamped at Shunem by now, marching north to meet us, and they're… more numerous than we thought. This war will not end with one battle. It may not end this year."

I can feel Naamah's horror without looking. I can smell the smoke of her understanding catching fire. She's grappling with the news, trying to decide what she wants to ask first. "What did he say? The king."

Lowering my arms, I turn around slowly and repeat myself. "I'm leaving. My father has commanded all his sons, except Bosheth, to fight. As I said, we leave for Jezreel tomorrow. We'll meet Achish's men at Gilboa, and…they will try their hardest to kill us."

Naamah's eyes turn black, terrified repulsion eating through the concern that was there before. Her hands lift to her face, and her breath comes with rough edges. She backs away, shaking

Twenty

her head. "No. What do you mean? I thought the king wanted you to rule. He's kept you close all this time because he wanted you safe. How can the king command you to battle now? *I don't understand!*"

She screams the last part, her broken sob leaping out between us.

I step away from the wall. "Naamah—God is no longer with my father. You know that, don't you? He promised long ago that my father's kingdom would not stand. Because of his rebellion, Saul is no longer hearing Yahweh's voice. He has received no direction for this battle, not in dreams, not from the priests." I let my voice shake. "I used to think I would stand beside David in his kingship. But I am not sure if I was hasty to believe that."

I hadn't planned on divulging Samuel's message to Naamah. But there's no merit in holding back anymore. Not with her. "I did receive one word from the Lord, a year or two ago, before Sheva died. According to the Roeh, Saul will likely not live to see David crowned. One of these battles will finish it. For my father, and for me."

Naamah heaves one sob after another, each sound weighing heavier with anger. "No. No, it won't. You won't…" She turns left, then right, trying to look for a different answer in the empty room. Finally, she faces me again, her teeth gritted. "Then *you* kill him!"

"Kill who?" My chest turns cold.

"Your father!" she wails. "Kill him now and become king. Then you can give the kingdom to anyone you please and show honor to Yahweh by deferring to David, but at least you'll live…Mephi will live…" She swipes her tears away, but they keep coming.

"Naamah…" I reach for her, but she pulls back, screaming.

"No!" She slaps my chest. "You're not doing this!"

I follow her as she continues to back away. "You know I can't kill him. He's still my father. He's still the king…"

"I don't care!" Naamah bends back and forth, swaying as though she'll fall. Her hands attack her hair, and she tears her veil off, flinging it across the room. "I don't *care* who he is! *He's taken your life!*"

I catch her arms and hold her while she flails, still trying to hit me.

Twenty

"Naamah, please listen!" Moving her across the floor as gently as I can, I press her up against the opposite wall. "I know what he's taken. I've been there for all of it. But Yahweh raised him up, and Yahweh will take him down." My heart twists and I have to pause until the pain subsides.

"I never wanted this," I continue through my own tears. "I would have left him years ago if I'd thought it would improve anything. But I couldn't abandon him and my place here. It wasn't right. If there was a chance he would change, I wanted to help him through it."

Her wet eyes are wide open, watching me, and I stare into them even though all I'm seeing are the crags of En-Gedi. When I'd looked up at David and known it was over. And that I'd made the right choice. I hadn't understood it then, but I do now.

I breathe heavily. "It wasn't for me to join David and leave my father here with all this. I'm a prince of Israel. Yahweh gave me this people. He gave me Sheva and Mephi. And you. That's what Yahweh gave me, and it was worth staying for."

I release her arms and cup her face, my heart breaking with thankfulness. She's here. I'm not alone. Then again, I never have been.

"I placed my life in Yahweh's hands when I was a boy. And He has never left me! His trust has never put me to shame. He will have mercy, and if He does not…" I grip her face tighter. "If He does not, He'll help me…" die well.

I don't say the last part for her sake. But she knows.

Naamah's eyes won't move from mine. Her tears drip onto my hands. "You can't go."

I smile, relieved to feel some warmth returning to my face. "Yes, I can. I can't follow Yahweh into Michmash and refuse Him at Gilboa."

She restrains another sob and grips my hands, gathering strength. When her eyes open again, there's fresh resolve in them. "What do you want me to do?"

I feel the dagger enter my gut again, remembering what she might face without me. What my son will face.

I take another deep breath. "As soon as I leave, I want you to pack. Take only what you need. Don't frighten Mephi, but get him ready. I've spoken to your brother. Keep him close. If you hear about our defeat, don't wait to verify the reports. Just leave. Get out of Gibeah and head for the hills. It's a longer way

Twenty

to Judah without using the roads, but the Philistines won't take their horses into the mountains."

Alarm jumps into her eyes. "Judah?"

My heart hammers, but I steady myself, hoping she'll believe this is the best course. "Yes. Judah. Hide there until David comes back. Don't tell anyone who you are or who my son is until you see him. Do you understand?"

She nods, but it's difficult with her face still in my hands.

I swallow hard. "You won't be able to take much with you on foot, but I've left money with your brother. There's enough for him to start over somewhere. He'll be able to provide for each of his sons. And mine." I retrieve the letter I wrote, pushing it into her hands. "This is for Machir ben Ammiel. I've instructed Ziba to send word to him if he needs more help."

Folding the letter away, Naamah pushes closer, threading our fingers together. I enjoy the warmth for a moment, then gently pull one of my hands free and slide my seal ring into her palm.

"Keep this for my son." I rub my thumb over her knuckles. "I know I failed you. I couldn't give you…what you deserved. But you're here now. And that means more to me than…"

I can't speak anymore. My throat hurts around the defeat I'm not used to tasting.

Naamah chokes on a breath. "I need to tell you something. I had no right to say it before, but I—" She sounds like she's going to be strong, but then her eyes lift and spill over. She covers her face.

Unhinged, I take her in my arms, kissing the top of her head. "I know. I love you too."

I can't tell which of us is shaking, but it's probably both. I kiss her, and then we stand there in silence while the sunset consumes the window, pooling red around us. Then we kneel, easing onto the floor. Just holding each other, our grief melting together. Between the two of us, it's easier to bear.

The next time I blink, we're surrounded by darkness. No lamps have been lit, and we're still on the floor. I'm slumped against the wall, Naamah's head heavy on my shoulder. When I shift my arm, she slides to my chest, asleep. Standing up carefully, I lift her into my arms and place her up onto my bed. She doesn't stir while I fold a blanket over her and trace the tear marks on her face.

What a faithful friend she's been. One of the few who's stayed by my side, unhindered by the tumult always trailing me. Perhaps this time, I'll draw the trouble away from her, give her a chance to have a decent life. I place my hand on her head and pray for Yahweh's *chesed* to protect and shield her. For His kindness to teach my boy what it means to be a true prince. I seal my petitions with a final kiss on Naamah's forehead.

Relieved to find Mephi sleeping in his room, I carry him into my own, placing him next to Naamah on the bed.

Then I sit back against the wall and watch my family sleep as long as my eyes will stay open.

TWENTY-ONE

David

I've been here before.

Asleep in the forest outside Aphek, surrounded by Philistine warriors, I dream about Aijalon. For the first time in years. My mind crosses the miles to the open plain west of Gibeah where the ambush found me as an untested armorbearer and took Jonathan down before my eyes.

The battle swells around me, every movement in slow motion, every sound muffled. Men stagger past me, bent over their wounds, while others wrestle for mastery, hands locked in armor vests and around swords. I wander between them, trying to summon back the old fierceness from years ago when I'd jumped into the fight to save Jonathan, even though I was only a servant and barely armed.

Yahweh's presence had taken hold of me like a physical command, sending me to Jonathan's side in time to use his spear.

This time, though, the Philistines aren't strangers. I've seen them in Achish's council house in Gath, around his throne during festivals. Their faces glower in my mind, each one turning to look at me as they cut through Israelite after Israelite.

The darkest feeling prickles along my spine like a frost, pulling my attention around to search for Jonathan. He's supposed to be here. And he is. On the ground. And Achish saunters between us, dragging Goliath's sword through the dirt. I can hear fire building, sparking up from the circular rut he's carving into the earth. Around my brother.

Blood from Jonathan's mouth trails into the ground, joining the crimson pool growing underneath him. His fingers move slowly, closing around his sword out of instinct, but the dullness in his eyes terrifies me. The coldest fist yanks my gut, but this time I can't move. Can't help him. The spear I'd driven into his attacker before isn't even in my hand. Achish's smile is pouring oil on the flames building between us. Inside me.

Rage flashes, fierce enough to shred my sleep, and I snag back a shout before I wake the camp. Harnessing breath after wild breath, I clench a fist around my cloak and run my other hand through the grass at my side. Trying to wake up.

We haven't reached Israel. Not yet. We're still several days' ride from Shunem, the northern city also called Endor, where

Twenty-One

Achish's Amalekite mercenaries have assembled. Jonathan is safe, helping Saul to gather Israel's thousands at Jezreel. And Achish has me marching with his cohorts to meet them.

My sides churning with a too-fast heartbeat, I lean my head against the tree at my back. The war camp is still asleep, slow snoring mingling with the sounds of the forest creeping toward dawn. But something sinister is awake, like a predator lurking in the trees.

I reach for my sword and my heart halts when I feel eyes on me. Ittai is leaning against a tree, his spear clenched across his chest. He unfolds himself from the shadows and speaks through the tightness in his jaw.

"They tried to kill you."

Once he says it, I notice the two men sprawled on the ground several feet off. From here, it looks like they're sleeping, but both of them have nasty bruises swelling on their foreheads. They've been knocked out.

Ittai bends down, crouching close enough to rumble a warning near my ear. "After the second watch, they tried to pin you to the ground. They'll be sent south to Ekron for punishment as soon as they wake up. But the mood is no longer with you, David."

"Was it ever?" I mutter, unfolding my limbs from the ground. It's a little too early to be turning betrayal over in my mind, but the rotten aroma is getting more familiar.

Ittai's darkened look weighs more than any words could. "You and your men have covered your tracks like skilled hunters. But this battle is different. It's personal this time, and the commanders aren't certain they can trust you with it."

They can't. Aloud, I ask, "Has the king told you his plans?"

"No."

Of course not. Ittai is an executioner. A trained torturer whose only job is to kill. And for more than a year, I've made Achish think I was the same. But my ruse was merely a cover, a way for my men to continue doing what we've always done. I knew my deception couldn't last forever, and it wasn't meant to. When Achish had ordered me to march with his full army on Jezreel, I'd only accepted because I planned to turn on him during the heat of the battle.

Which is exactly what the commanders fear.

Ittai keeps talking through his teeth, refusing to move his lips. "The Philistine lords fought hard for your death. They tried to send spies out to catch you in something. But your nephews

Twenty-One

are too vigilant." He smirks wryly. "When Achish summoned you, the lords were certain he would kill you. They were outraged to discover that he invited you to follow him to Israel." He looks directly at me, his eyes smearing black. "They're watching you."

No doubt. I'm not off in the wilderness with my men, able to do as I please. I'm marching alongside Achish's choice killers. The ones who have burned villages in my country, taken fathers from the children of Israel. And they see me the same way. In their eyes, I'm still the shepherd who killed Goliath, the one who's slain thousands of their warriors. For Saul. And they know I'd do it again.

I squint against the sharpness of my dream, wondering how much I should tell Ittai. Whatever I reveal, he's always seen several steps ahead. For a moment, I wonder if he'd ever be willing to join my men. He could be a worthy ally once we're able to get away. I hadn't planned on leaving until after the battle had been won and Israel had been saved. But now, I'm rethinking all my previous plans.

Ittai's voice opens chills along my spine. "He's tried to kill Saul and Jonathan before, but this time, it's his full mission. He's assembled all the rogue necromancers Saul has scattered throughout the wasteland from here to Shunem, and commanded them to petition any force within their control against the

Israelite king and prince. He doesn't intend to back down until they're dead."

He speaks without looking at me, barely moving his mouth. "Trust me, if it is your desire to save them, a covert betrayal in the heat of battle will not be enough. The commanders don't intend to let you get that far. One false move and you will watch your men be slaughtered. Achish may not kill you, but he'll make it so you cannot return to Israel ever again."

I nod, gripping Goliath's sword while everything takes shape on the periphery of my vision. I've ridden as far as I can on my old skills, fighting as a mercenary without direct supervision. But here, among the Philistine soldiers, it won't be long before Achish will demand more than I can give.

Across the brushy glade, Achish's tent broods in the morning stillness, the glimmer of lamplight staining the walls. Our last meeting made it clear enough. He doesn't want me dead; he wants me to fight for him exclusively, forever. But first, he has to possess me fully. If I stay, he'll design a trap where I'm forced to turn my spear against Saul myself, or face death. Why else would he have let me come on this mission?

I sit forward, every muscle in my body tensing. I was foolish to think I would get any further without being turned inside out

Twenty-One

for Achish's benefit. My men and I should leave while we can, before the king forces me to participate in some pre-war ritual to turn me into a full-fledged Philistine.

We should make up some excuse and head east into Judah's territory. We can assemble the elders in Hebron and formulate a more decisive strategy, then circle back and trap Achish from behind. Throw our full strength against him and reveal our true loyalties.

But how will Achish possibly allow us to leave? What excuse would I give? If we stay, it won't be easy to communicate any changes to my men. Strategizing has been hard enough with Achish's lackeys following us, honing in on every word. Even at the back of the army, we've been watched like prized champions. Achish isn't taking any chances.

Ittai slides his hands up and down on his spear, listening to my thoughts. "You know he's promised to make you his bodyguard." He watches the king's tent. "You don't understand what that means, being an Israelite, but it's a blood oath. Something you can't take back. He'll force you."

My throat closes, my eyes shifting to the deep black markings carved into Ittai's muscles. I've held to my deception thus far, boasting of my abilities while hoping I would have a clear moment to escape. But this battle isn't like the others. It's a test of loyalty, and he's definitely planning to make me prove myself. Publicly.

Ittai's eyes find mine. "Either you leave before we reach Jezreel, or Achish will make you a Philistine. Fully. You'll never be able to return to Israel once you've been forced to swear to Dagon."

"I won't do that. I'm not staying with him." I clench around the words, my eyes darting through the camp like a runaway stag, searching for escape. I won't betray Israel. I won't turn my back on Yahweh. But Achish will never let me go. After the assurance I've given him of my loyalty, he'll see through any excuse I try to come up with to avoid it.

I close my eyes, trying to recall the way the *hakkodesh* came for me outside Achish's palace. Yahweh's brought me up out of Gath before, but this time, I feel like I've gone too far to expect help. He told me to march to Jezreel, but then what? How am I to inquire of the Lord out here? I'm surrounded by Philistines, and the *ephod* is back in Ziklag with Abiathar. Panic bites through my muscles. I don't want to believe I'm trapped.

"I'll help you however I can." Ittai keeps his back to me, his voice no more than a heavy mutter. "But if you wait much

Twenty-One

longer, you will not be safe. Several commanders have already said they're willing to risk the king's anger to kill you."

My lips thin. It doesn't even surprise me anymore.

"Israelite!" Allu beckons to me across the camp from the door of Achish's tent. "The king would speak with you before the armies assemble."

No doubt to outline his plans for me. Or maybe he's trying to extract something, uncover my true motives. Either way, I have to be careful. I'm climbing a treacherous path, and at any moment, the stones under my feet could give way. I reach for my cloak, Jonathan's old one, but think better of it, grabbing the yellow one from Achish instead. I glance at Ittai, but he keeps his gaze firmly set on the space between the tents.

"I'll send your nephews to wait outside," he mumbles, and I realize it's the only help I'm going to get for now.

The guards pretend to ignore me at the door of Achish's tent, but I don't miss the contempt seething from their set jaws. They've hated me ever since I arrived. Hated the favor I've gained with their king without really trying.

I step inside and my lungs close around a metallic scent. Their incense smells too much like blood to me, and I want nothing more than to breathe free of it. I've been summoned one too many times to hear Achish drone on about Philistine customs and the superiority of his people to mine. Even his praises feel like curses. But so far, I've managed to escape anything worse. Like being forced to sing for him.

His robe only half-draped across his bare chest, Achish is seated behind a low table surrounded by cushions. A bowl of fruit and a golden goblet sit amid a pile of wrinkled maps. When I enter, the king waves his fingers at his servants, motioning for them to leave us alone.

I bow the way the Philistines do, one arm draped over my leg in the king's direction, anticipating anything but what I hear.

Achish sighs forcefully, slapping his maps down against the table and rubbing his face. He looks at me through his fingers, his expression agitated. "My champion, I have to ask you to leave."

"What?" I look up, my caution scattered. Fortunately, my shock works for me, covering anything else I might betray.

Achish spreads his hands, giving me a pained smile. "You can't stay here anymore. You and your men must return to Ziklag. And find somewhere else to go as soon as possible."

Twenty-One

"But...why, my lord?" I stammer, allowing the astonishment on my face to bury my delight. I have to remember to act betrayed, however providential this is.

Achish twirls the rings on his thick fingers, dejected. "David, you know not every one of my people is as open-minded as I am. I have found no fault with you since you came to me, but this isn't a raid on the Negeb, as you are well aware. We march on Saul this time, and many of my advisors are concerned that the sight of your apostate king and surrogate brother will cause you to turn against us."

"Ridiculous." I say it through a mask, hoping my eyes don't betray me.

"It's what they believe."

I push air through my lungs, pacing with fake aggravation. I have to be careful. If I overplay this, Achish might still side with me and move forward with his original plans.

I turn back to him, trying to sound wounded. "Did you tell them Saul's done nothing but try to kill me for the past several years? I've done nothing wrong, my lord. All I wanted was to prove my loyalty to you, fighting at your side."

"I know! I know; it's true." Achish pushes to his feet, coming around the table to place a hand on my arm. His rancid breath tickles my neck, and it's all I can do not to move away.

"It's nothing you've done," he assures me. "But when it comes to it, I have to trust the judgment of the men who have been with me the longest. I cannot afford to lose the support of my commanders just now. Perhaps when all this is over and Israel is in our grasp, we can find another place for you." He steps around in front of me. "Trust me. Go without a fight, and I will see what I can do for you in the future."

I can't hold back my relief much longer. I will be able to regroup with my men and take more decisive action to help Saul and Jonathan. We can strategize and prepare without the Philistines watching our every move. And I'll never have to hear Achish call me his champion ever again.

Achish chuckles to himself. "Who knows? When I return with Saul's head, maybe I'll give it to you."

I nearly punch him, hiding the urge in a deep bow. "Very well, my lord. I will gather my men and leave now. Before your armies assemble."

I turn my body away without straightening up. I need to get out of here before I do something I'll regret.

Twenty-One

But wait.

I halt in place, a wild smile nearly breaking through my restraint. Once I've controlled it, I turn on my heel and reach inside my cloak, finding the slip of parchment I've carried since my youth. It's worn thin, still darkly stained with Jonathan's blood, but the words are still readable—the message Achish sent into my brother's rib as a warning to Saul without knowing it was meant for me.

So it begins, Melek Israel.

The time has finally come to answer it. And end it.

I fold it twice and place it on Achish's table without kneeling.

"What's this?" He's foolish enough to look touched.

"A gift," I say without betraying any emotion. "For after the battle. Better fortune to read it once the war has been fought."

I don't dare look him in the eyes, but the lightness of his tone convinces me he's still deceived. He closes his hand around it, his eyes glittering. "Of course, my champion. May the gods preserve you."

I manage one last smile before turning my back on Philistia forever.

Go to Sheol.

* * * * *

We've barely cleared Aphek's walls before exultation erupts. My shoulders haven't felt this light in years, finally freed from the last and heaviest burden. My men celebrate, gloating over Achish's failure to recognize my subterfuge. I'm still marveling, amazed at how Yahweh keeps opening the way for me to escape any net I wander into.

Before looping around through Judah, we decide to head back south to Ziklag. We'll need every fighter we left behind, and the women and children will need to be moved to a more secure location if we're traveling all the way north to Jezreel.

With the Philistine forces moving in the opposite direction, we break into open worship, flinging praises at the skies and scattering our triumph along the pathways trodden by enemy forces for generations. I smile to myself, thinking of how hard the sons of Philistia have tried to end my life. Yet, my God laughs at them. He holds them in derision, His protection surrounding me like fortress walls.

I declare it over the triumph of my men. "Your faithfulness has found me yet again, Adonai. In your steadfast love, you have let me look in triumph on my enemies."

Twenty-One

By the time the path to Ziklag appears in the clearing ahead, my commanders and I have a new plan. We'll return to Israel by way of Hebron. Once the women and children are safely situated with the elders there, we will assemble any other fighters who want to join us. Then, we'll ride north and help Saul by striking Achish's forces from behind.

Joab's spies will keep me apprised on the status of the battle, and we'll inquire of the Lord to find out the exact moment to interfere. Once Achish sees my face in battle against him, the ensuing wildfire won't be quenched in a single armed conflict. It will be a war my men will have to fight for some time.

But I'll welcome it. This is the clear moment we've been waiting for, to prove ourselves as loyal sons of Israel and save our people. Saul's personal fate will remain in Yahweh's hands, but I'm determined to save Jonathan.

Immensely relieved, I breathe deeply, taking in a lungful of smoky air.

"David—"

My name reaches my ears before I can breathe again. My lungs and throat squeeze shut against the scent of ash. In the same moment, my eyes lock onto the missing gates of Ziklag.

They should be blocking the path ahead, but the road into town is empty now, gaping like a wound in the forest.

I slide off my mule, my body moving skittishly like I'm trapped in a dream where I can't respond as fast as I should. But I don't need to make it all the way there to notice the gates aren't completely gone. They've just been burned, mangled to a skeleton of their former strength. Along with every other structure beyond them.

The deepest black smoke coats whatever's left. Which isn't much. Almost every home has been flattened, as though a vortex of fire-breathing wind had blown through, splintering the pieces. A few boards hang loosely, like broken arms. The deadliest silence crawls out to meet us, and for a pointless second, I wonder where everyone is.

A creaking doorpost weeps in my direction—the only part of my house left standing—and my eyes immediately jump to the mark on its side. The horned outline of the Amalekite god is unmistakable. It adorns their armor, and it's often branded into the flesh of their soldiers. And their slaves. It laughs in my face now. Mocking my narrow escape from Philistia's Dagon.

"David—" A dozen men echo my name after Abishai says it. I turn and look at them, realizing what's taking shape in everyone's mind.

Twenty-One

They're gone. Taken prisoner by one of our worst enemies. And it's too much. The pain is like a branding iron being dragged through my head, disarming and torturing my senses. Frantic footsteps fill my ears while men run to their empty homes, screaming the names of wives and children who won't answer. Already in the doorway of my missing house, I'm trying to breathe around the images assaulting me.

Abigail's veil is on the floor, droplets of blood staining the boards around it. The amulet Ahinoam wears from her mother is crushed a few feet away. Kneading bowls and rotten food are scattered everywhere; the bed is tipped over on its side. Paths are carved through the ash in front of each house where our families were dragged off toward the wilderness. My mighty men are covered in the same dust now, stretched out on the ground, wailing.

The anguish destroying their features pushes up into my own heart, and I force a desperate gasp before I stop breathing. This pain is incurable. Unforgivable.

"Please, Yahweh! Don't let them be gone."

But even my prayer feels useless. Like the ash under my feet. They are gone. Probably being slaughtered right now. Raped. Turned into slaves. My stomach turns inside out, and grief attacks me like one of Achish's lions let loose.

I won't let anyone hurt you again.

My promise to Abigail takes the edge of the pain and twists it. And I fall flat on my face, the truth slamming into me over and over.

They're gone. They're gone. They're gone.

TWENTY-TWO

Jonathan

The darkness following my father through the door grips me with a cold that won't let me move. The sunlight is almost gone for the day, but even the oil lamps inside the king's tent seem to curl away, shrinking into dimness before the advancing shadows.

It's been a long time since I've felt peace or security in Abba's presence, but now the gloom around him has a voice. It's open rebellion. Accusation and mind-bending fear. It used to stay inside him, writhing and occasionally lashing out. But now, it's a predator that's hunted us down, breaching the safety of our camp with chilling authority. It's a thousand icy claws digging deep, devouring any hint of warmth.

Saul is holding the sides of the tent open with trembling fists, and I can see blood painting his knuckles where the skin has split on each of his fingers. Deeply cold, I push the maps aside on the table and rise slowly to my feet. I've been staring at the same drawings of our territory for hours, the rivers and borders smearing together without meaning while I prayed for the king's return.

When he'd slipped away from our camp two days ago with only Abner and his armorbearer Gera, a dozen evil scenarios poisoned my imagination. I've battled my own misgivings through the night, covering Saul's absence from the army and trying to dissuade the commanders against believing the worst of my father.

They all wanted to know why he would leave without more protection, without a word to me or my brothers, without summoning his other attendants. Where could he have gone, with our enemies encamped to the south and Achish's allies gathering in nearby Endor?

Just a few hours ago, I'd broken my fast, begging Yahweh to send the king back before I had to go after him. Any more time lost and the people would have concluded that my father had abandoned us. Too desperate to face what awaits us at Gilboa. I had refused to believe it.

But now, seeing him standing in the doorway weighted down by darkness kicks all my trust in the teeth. I know I could've lived a hundred years without seeing the abyss that's gaping from his eyes.

The terrible ashen presence on him confirms all my fears. His brow wears the same insurgent pallor as the day he offered the unlawful sacrifice when I was a boy. The day he justified his disobedience at Amalek and then turned on me when he was called to account. But now, everything I've feared and fought in my father has been multiplied. Stronger darkness and weaker resolve. Anger devoid of hope.

"What have you done?" I force the words out, though I'm sure I don't want to know.

His breaths shallow and labored, Saul doesn't look like he has the energy to respond, but somehow, my voice pulls an explosion out of him. "What have I done? You have gall to ask me that!" Wheezing, he flings his helmet down and overturns the nearest table, pacing away anguish he doesn't have the strength for. "What do you mean, what have I done? Who do you think you are, the prophet?!"

So that's what this is about. Samuel's been on his mind for years, and now that we're facing another war season without Yahweh's clear direction, all the old wounds are being torn open. But the prophet of Israel has been dead for years now. Unless…

The most horrible scenario fills my mind like a cloud. Endor is the closest town my father could have made it to in so little time. It's also known as Shunem, and they're notorious for harboring necromancers, men who have been cast out of Israel for practicing the dark arts the Philistines love to exploit. I try to push the idea from my mind as it takes shape, but I already know it's no use. I've always been able to see my father's thoughts and guess his plans ahead of him.

Suddenly weak, I grip the back of my chair while Saul continues to rant. "You dare to criticize me for doing what I must when the Philistines are at our throats? I am the king of Israel! I need a plan, I need resources, I need strategy to defeat these monsters, and what do my people do? They abandon me! The priests give me nothing. Our kinsmen have crossed the Jordan to hide. They all want to escape and run to David to be rid of me. Even you."

The terror in his eyes eats at me until I have to look away. He knows I've never abandoned him, even when I could have. But what good is truth to a man who won't believe it? Still, this is the first time in years I've seen fear overtaking his rage, overpowering it.

He drags a shaking hand through his hair and down his face. I see his sweat glimmering in the lamplight. "I went to Endor," his voice rattles. "There's a…woman there who knows how to… talk to the dead. She agreed to help me speak with Samuel about the coming battle, what we're up against."

Twenty-Two

"Speak. With. Samuel." I repeat it woodenly, and then the words start burning. A thousand protests spring to my mind and into my mouth, but all I can do is choke on them.

Everything he's ever done—the sacrifice, the hasty vow, the arrogant monuments, and overblown taxes, and broken promises—all of it seems like a single drop of water compared to the avalanche of this insurrection. We've been warned about this since the days of Moses. To consult with the darkness is to turn your back on the light. It's open defiance. It's the same as choosing other gods.

My head spins, thinking of the words written on Samuel's last message to Saul. What should have been his last. "Disobedience is like the sin of divination. To obey is greater than sacrifice."

And my father had brought him back from the grave just to hear God's judgment again? Worse than before? Never. Never in my life had I expected this. I stare at Saul, trying to wrap my head around it while everything in me clenches back.

You went to a witch?! You banished all the sorcerers and mediums from the land years ago, at the command of the Lord, and now you consult with the darkness? The same people who've uttered curses against us for Philistia? You turn from the God of Israel when we need Him the most?

But I can't speak. My thoughts are a tangle of torment while my father rushes to cover the silence with stinging excuses.

"I had to find out what was going to happen with this battle. I had to find out what to do. Abner sent spies a week ago to search the woman out. She agreed to cast the spell for me and bring Samuel forth. Though, to be honest, I didn't believe she would until she did. She changed. It was like her eyes disappeared, and the ground all around her became a tempest."

I flinch, my whole body revolted by the story. Saul's exhale is broken, and he rubs his face again like there's an image he can't dig out of his eyes.

"She didn't know who I was until it was over, and then she promised not to tell anyone."

The horror finally works its way through me, escaping in a deep moan. On my knees now, I press my fists into the ground, trying to make it stop spinning. Trying to pull myself out of this horrible pit where darkness is allowed to feast on me. I might as well be in a Philistine dungeon, defiled by their torture. But it's worse because my father has walked into the cage willingly. And closed the door on me as well.

My father. My king. How can he be a man who hunts other men, burns the homes of priests, and turns his back on Yahweh to consult with the dead? Does he know he's cursed our armies by his actions? Does he care?

Our eyes touch, and for the first time I see pain break through the tempest of his anger. He shouts, "Don't look at me like that, Jonathan! Samuel was the only one who could tell me what to do, give me any hope."

"Hope? *Hope!*" I finally surge off the ground and across the room. His eyes bulge in surprise, but I stop just shy of his face. "Do you even hear what you're saying? There is no hope this way!" I clutch at the air between us, yearning to grab the invisible cloud that blinds him and rip it to shreds. But it's too late. He's never listened.

My shout slants into a scream. "Why do you think Yahweh commanded us to root out witchcraft, to destroy idol worship? There is no hope in the dark, outside of God's ways. The God of our fathers has always been faithful to His people. All He asks is our faithfulness in return. He rewards those who stand with Him, who trust His heart, and do His will! You've seen it! Why do you fight against Him? Why not stand with Him and His anointed?"

"I am His anointed!" Saul roars, slapping his chest. "He chose me as king over Israel *first*. If you're talking of David, it should interest you to know that Samuel's favorite has failed us. And it hasn't done you any good to side with him," he rasps, his eyes swimming. "You'll die with the rest of us tomorrow."

His voice fails abruptly, shaken by sudden hoarseness. He takes two steps and crashes to the floor in a torrent of sobs. "There is no hope this time. God has turned against us. It was clear enough from Samuel's words. By the time David returns, we'll all be dead."

The words bounce off my ears, and fear splits open a chasm deep inside me. Unbidden, the battlefield stretches before my eyes, strewn with the bodies of men I know, and coldness chews through my limbs. There's always been a chance I wouldn't return. But it's the first time I've ever pictured death as a certainty, and it's revolting.

It's galling to feel courage draining away, fleeing along with every hope I've held to. Everything is dropping out from under me. Every assurance that's carried me through the loss and strain of the previous years. Any expectation that we'd make it through another battle on God's undeserved mercy, any hope that I'd see David return to Israel as king.

I picture my five-year-old son adrift in a land overtaken by Philistines, and the pain makes me double over, nearly joining my father on the floor. My mind races, grasping at any conceivable option. Go find David. Take my son to Egypt or Moab. Beg some sort of agreement with the king of Philistia. None of them are viable plans. Not anymore.

My father weeps on the floor, mumbling over and over, "God has forsaken us."

The more he says it, the more the dark pushes at the doors of my spirit, trying to break in. *How could Yahweh do this? How could He abandon you now? When you've torn your life apart choosing His will over the will of the king?*

But God doesn't willingly forsake men. Men turn from Him. The truth is a blade in my chest, and no amount of bitterness will remove it. I close my eyes and fold my hands into fists again, shaken to the depths of my being.

What can I do, Adonai? You are my King. I've walked before you with a loyal heart. I only wanted to serve. I wanted to see Israel prosper under your anointed one. Can I expect any mercy? Any hope for my son?

The grief turns sharp inside, like fangs ready to tear me apart. Then suddenly, the strangest peace seeps into my mind, starting small and then spreading through me like a bubbling brook, softening the edges—the way David's music used to.

My lips move in a voiceless whisper, "He is a faithful God, keeping His covenant of love to a thousand generations of those who love Him and keep His commands."

The promise from the Law of Moses settles me. But now I understand the panic I'd felt back home listening to Mephi recite those words to Naamah. Watching my son handle the truth I didn't think he was ready to comprehend. I had been feeling the cords of my control being severed. Though I had never expected to face this so soon, Yahweh was asking for me to trust Him again. With my child.

I swallow, recognizing the truth I hadn't been ready to accept before.

My son will have his own story, his own journey. He will be given the same chance as all men—to submit to God or reject Him. I can only pray he gives himself to the one King who is worthy. Adonai Himself. David will rule the people of God, and Yahweh will keep every promise He's made to him. Together, they will drive our enemies from this land and raise Israel up from whatever ashes Philistia will try to bury her in. I can be grateful for that at least.

My chest tightens. I'll never see David again. I'll never see him crowned or stand beside him as I'd planned. But I know

Twenty-Two

he will remember our friendship. God will honor the covenant between us. Samuel had told me whatever I did with David would come back to me. And if that's the only mercy I can expect, it's enough for me.

I breathe deeply, set the table back on its legs, and reach for my bow, fresh resolve tightening the parts of me that are flagging, ready to break. Checking for arrows, I slip my quiver over my arm and slide my battle axe into the sheath on my back.

My father looks up from his hands. "Where are you going?" His tone is panicked, but I barely turn around, lifting the tent door.

"To say goodbye."

* * * * *

No one follows me to the edge of our camp. They all heard me shouting, but they're understandably afraid to approach me with questions. The news will spread soon enough, though I'm sure Abner will conceal the worst from those who will need their strength to fight. I don't see the general anywhere, but it's just as well. I don't think I can face his efforts to steady me, if he has any left. Saul has broken me permanently this time.

Once I clear the guards at the perimeter, I break into a run, nearly sprinting into the growing darkness. The forest feels welcoming and sinister at the same time, absorbing my torment while waiting for me to break open. I'm winded long before I run out of strength, breathless around the reality that's too sharp to take in.

Mephi's voice dances in my head like the chattering of a little bird, and my courage caves in on itself like a dying ember. I love him more than life. Am I really going to die and leave him in a land infested with Philistines? What kind of father lets that happen? I picture men using this—disgruntled haters of the king trying to tear into Mephi, and I can't see through the anger pushing into my vision. *How can I do this, Yahweh?*

It was one thing to charge into battle at fourteen years old when I knew God was with me. It's another when I have a son. And I know we'll lose. I pound my fists against my head. I want to drop to my knees. I want to rage and weep. But no amount of grief or anger will save me or my son.

Every cord that's ever bound me to my father is being yanked and pulled by the force of my desire to live, to not abandon the people I love. All the rage I couldn't show before his face is scorching me, kicking down the doors of every memory to destroy the deepest hopes I'd held for him.

Twenty-Two

How could he go to a witch, after all the chances he's had to humble himself and ask for Yahweh's mercy? How could he endanger Israel and destroy his family with open rebellion? Did he think of Mephi? Did he think of me? Light-headed, I spin around, consumed with the urge to break something.

Saul has taken everything from me. He casually banished Ezra on the day I lost my daughter. With my wife breathing her last in Gibeah, he dragged me after David to risk my life at his side. He's taken his anger at himself out on me over and over, accusing me, beating me down. He's the reason I was kept from Naamah. He's the reason I'm going to die and never see my son grow up.

There's nothing around me to attack except trees. I send an arrow into one, spearing the trunk. But the familiar hiss of wood cutting the air isn't enough. And my hands are trembling too much to hold the bow steady. Flinging it aside, I reach back and pull my battle axe. I shout while I swing the heavy blade, thudding it into the bark until my hands start to throb.

I only stop when I remember I'll need to fight tomorrow. I'll need my strength. But what am I fighting for? Why even march on Gilboa if I'll end up spilling my blood over it? Watching my army spill theirs?

Anger spent, I feel grief springing up in its place, and I drop into it, facedown in pine-needled dampness. All I can think of is Mephi and the way he'd wailed when I'd said goodbye. The shuddering shield on Naamah's face had barely waited for me to be out of sight the next morning before dropping. Ziba's tightly contained dislike when he'd accepted my money haunts me. Can he be trusted? Will he follow my instructions for his sister's sake, or will he look for a chance to harm my son?

The maddening uncertainty is enough to make me want to seize my mule and ride back to Gibeah. Take my son and Naamah and go find David myself. But my brother is still with the Philistines, probably waiting for a chance to turn on them and help us. The thought brings stubborn hope back into view. My friend's return might not be soon enough to save me. But he'll come back for Israel. And I know he will help my son.

The soft breathing of the forest strokes my ears, and for a moment, it feels like any other night, camped under the stars on my way to a battle we'll win. I try to remember how I would sleep at the door of my tent every night so that I could hear David singing to Yahweh over the fire. How I'd be soothed by the peaceful exultation folded into each note of the lyre. David's songs always matched what lived inside me without voice.

Twenty-Two

Sitting up on my knees, I allow myself full breaths, savoring the rise and fall of my own chest. Trying to rest in the mercy of now.

In His kindness, Yahweh had enabled me to reach out to David instead of setting myself against him. He had bound us together in a friendship that had strengthened and built us both, carrying us along in His plan. And now, our covenant will save my son and lift Israel into the era of victory we've dreamed about since the judges ruled. I had seen it on David from the moment we met, and now that vision is all I have to cling to.

I rub my face, realizing it's wet with tears. But I don't try to steel myself. The time will come for that tomorrow. For now, I let everything flow. I stretch out on the ground, sobbing, and lay everything down at Yahweh's feet. As I did the first time I faced death in Aijalon over my father's rash vow.

Impossibly, what pours out over me in response feels like the sweetest relief. Lifted burdens. Fullness in place of what I gave up. If I follow Yahweh to the end, He may yet show mercy. He is mercy itself. Anguish still groans beneath the surface, but the shred of hope I feel when I speak His Name is enough to silence the torment. For tonight, it's enough.

Lifting my head, I sit back on my heels and let the night air cool the tears on my face.

Your will be done, Adonai. Make my brother a king who pleases you. Raise up your people as you promised. Set your protection before my son like a mighty shield, whatever happens. And strengthen me to defend Israel one last time.

TWENTY-THREE

David

"This is David's fault."

My ears burn, and my inner wound opens wider, threatening to pull me apart. I'm utterly spent, sick with the grief that won't stop pounding me like the fists of a storm on the mountains. Except this one won't break. It won't change. I blink, and I breathe, and I try to get up, but it's still true.

Our families have been taken by the worst of our enemies. A people so despicable in their violence that Yahweh ordered them exterminated. Which Saul failed to do. And now the chains of slavery and the flames of pagan altars await our wives and children. And it's my fault. I left them in the path of destruction to pursue something I hadn't even cleared with my Shepherd.

In light of all this, my covert exploits for Israel seem like a child's game. Just a fool's errand designed to taunt Achish and stay out of Saul's reach. I can almost see Samuel's disappointment.

Jonathan would never have let this happen. He would have given himself up first before letting them take his wife and child.

It's like an evil dream. All the shame I've carried, the fear that I was somehow destined to fail everyone who relies on me—now it's all been transferred from my mind to the mouths of my men. And I can't get away from the accusations, even from the upper caves carved into the hillside above Ziklag's ruins. Their voices carry, rage pushing through the hoarseness.

And they're right. All of them.

"He's had countless opportunities to kill Saul and end our misery. Instead, he compounds it by putting our families in harm's way, and now look where we are!"

"Why do we stay? Why do we listen? We should have known that serving Achish, even in pretense, would only bring trouble."

"Do you have any idea what those monsters will do to our children?"

"All of our wives will be defiled by sunset. There's no way to answer that crime except with blood."

"We should stone him."

Twenty-Three

The air pulls from my lungs, every inch of me focused on the silence edging the words. I'm not even sure who said them, but so many are muttering agreement. Too many. The rushing in my ears nearly drowns out the gentler words that follow.

"More bloodshed isn't the answer. I've lost family too, but we have to keep our heads. David was anointed by God. He is our only hope for a new kingdom. He's also our best hope of getting our families back. Give him time. He'll come up with something."

Abiathar's voice is the only one not writhing with rage, but it still feels like a blow. How can any of them still trust me? I would almost welcome retaliation. This is worse than what happened in Nob, because our families are alive and in torment. Amalekite slavery is just prolonged death, and every day I remain alive, I know I will see the face of every woman and child accusing me.

Ahinoam, who's probably terrified. Noble Uriah, who had stayed behind with Bathsheba. Abiathar's son, named Ahimelech after his father. The woman Ezra's learned to care for. Abigail.

I haven't eaten anything, but the empty cavern of my stomach groans with nausea anyway. I lean too far over the back ridge, barely hanging onto a protruding tree branch. The rocky valley swims, its depth spinning until I can't decide how far down it is. In all my years dodging death, I've never felt it come this close.

With my next breath, I let myself think it. I could let go. I could join my wives in death and atone for all the blood I've shed because of my anointing. But it wouldn't even come close. Even if my men killed me, it wouldn't bring our families back.

Resolve that's not mine grips my body, and I manage to back away from the cliff, collapsing at a safe distance. There's not an ounce of strength left in my body, and pain chews my limbs from a full night of sobbing. Even with all the agony burning me alive, listening to my men suffer is worse.

Yahweh. Yahweh!

I'm afraid to say His Name. Afraid to ask for help. But He's my Shepherd. And I have nowhere else to go.

My cry finally makes it past my throat. "Adonai, you promised goodness would follow me. You promised mercy. My whole life. You promised that my enemies would be scattered and that I would give praise to your Name with my victories. *You promised!* Where is all that now?"

Despair wants to choke me. I feel its whispers at the back of my neck, making me see the edge of the cliff again. Inviting the old wolves to rip into the wounds Yahweh has closed over time. But my mind fights back. My memory fights back with the praises from the pastures, echoing promises until I start to repeat them. Conviction starts to yank inner cords, stitching my heart back together.

In answer to each face appearing behind my eyes.

"You have kept count of my tossings. My tears are in your book."

My tears, and theirs.

A sob mangles the words, but my groanings feel more purposeful now. Like a drink offering poured out. My tears have been my food day and night as people mock me continually, sowing doubt and discord, demanding to know why God has forsaken me. Trying to make me believe it. But whenever I pour out my soul in song to Yahweh, I remember.

I remember how I used to go with the throngs in Gibeah, in Judah, in the Negeb, and lead them in procession to the house of God with glad shouts and songs of praise, a multitude keeping festival. Once again, my soul is cast down within me, flattened and drained of hope.

But what do I do? What have I done? Every time I was overcome with joy or gripped with pain. Every time I understood what was happening, and every time I didn't. Jonathan's awe gleams in front of me like a hand stretched out to lift me up.

Every time you're in trouble, you sing.

But it's more than that. I lift my head. "I remember you, Adonai."

I get up, looking straight into the mire of the foggy sunset. In every moment of my life, my God has been there. When I'd stumbled through the woods around Gath with chain marks around my neck, when I'd sat forgotten in the pastures night after night, when I'd waited for wisdom before a hundred different battles.

"It was always you, Yahweh. My strength always returned when I remembered you."

The words unlock the floodgates, and praise pours out of me, each refrain anointing my mind's shadows with light. It's like finding my way in the dark. Trusting the way I've traveled over and over again even though I can't see the path and don't know the future.

"You have delivered my soul from death, my eyes from tears, my feet from falling. I will not die, but I will live. I will see the goodness of the Lord in the land of the living, and I will proclaim it to all who doubt. I waited patiently for Adonai, and He heard my cry. He drew me up from the pit of destruction, from the miry bog. He set my feet upon a rock, safe and secure. He put a new song in my mouth. A hymn of praise to my God. Many will see and fear and put their hope in the Lord!"

How many times have I seen that vision already? Yahweh's vision. Israel gathered as one, worshipping in the strength of the Lord? I cup my hands as though my praises are filling them up. I press them into my chest, anointing myself with them.

"Why are you cast down, O my soul? Why do you writhe within me? Hope in God; for I shall again praise Him, my salvation and my God."

My eyes open, releasing fresh tears down my cheeks. The pain still lives. But I'm awash in the single drop of hope that's touched me. And it's enough to lift the weight. I drop to my knees, overcome. I'd once thought that Jonathan had been the one to lift my face whenever I was downcast. But even when it was him, it was Yahweh all along.

The silence breathes, lifting my chest in gentle rhythm. The peace enveloping me is different from the innocence of the pastures. It's still a garment of safety, holding back my enemies. But it's also invitational, drawing me onwards.

"I'm ready, Adonai," I say aloud. "Command me."

I swear I see His smile in the sunrise. Then there's a pause, like a hand on my back. I turn and see Joab standing several feet off. Watching me in silence.

Leaning into my hands and knees, I stand up, pushing past the aches. The trembling hasn't left my core, but fresh strength has been stroked awake. I walk to the edge of the plateau, stopping a few feet from my nephew.

"Joab, this is my fault…" I begin.

"Oh, you see that? Good, because I didn't want to be the one to break that to you." His face wears an expressionless mask that I've never seen and don't want to interpret.

"Joab—" Crossing the distance, I grab the front of his breastplate, and his face jerks, holding pain back. "It's my fault, but Yahweh is our deliverer. He has never left me alone, and even in the midst of my failures, His faithfulness is my shield and buckler. He still delights in those who follow Him. He will not abandon us."

Joab swallows, folding his arms. It's the first time he's ever pulled away from me since learning of my anointing. The bold spark in his eyes is buried too deep for me to find. He lifts one finger free. "Tell me one thing. Why? Why is He with you?"

I would laugh if my body didn't hurt so much. He has no idea how long I've wrestled with the same question. But the answer is so simple.

"Because He chose to be. Because I need Him. Because He's faithful to His promises."

All this time, I've cringed as my responsibility doubled and tripled. I've waited for Yahweh to turn away from me in disgust at my first mistake. And yet through each misstep and failure, I've found Him waiting on the edge of my self-loathing, ready to reveal the next step. Eager to build a king out of the unruly shepherd He somehow loved. As He does now.

I've always taken comfort in His power, but the depth of His kindness is still amazing me. He's the one we need to seek right now. He's the one who should be leading us.

"So," I snag a breath. "Tell Zadok to build an altar, and have Abiathar bring the *ephod*. If Yahweh gives us the strength, we will pursue those vultures and get our families back."

"As you wish, my lord," Joab murmurs.

The flint striking fire in his eyes is all I need to see.

* * * * *

Facing my men over the altar is the hardest thing I've ever done. I can feel their anger brooding like a tempest on a ridgeline, but my renewed hope is the slender cord holding it back. I watch the priests without blinking, feeling my next breath bound up in Yahweh's answer. When Abiathar delivers it, I nearly break down again. I drop to my knees, listening to the incredible kindness and redemption behind the words.

"Go after the Amalekite band; you will defeat them."

I repeat it to myself while my men weep in worship. Our God has not forsaken us. I can only pray our wives and children hold onto that same hope and stay strong until we chase them down.

In spite of our exhaustion, my commanders and I move quickly. Organizing the fighting men into groups, we gather the armor and weapons we've amassed from Gath, and I lay out instructions for the men who will stay behind to guard the baggage we can't carry.

My spies skirt the area looking for clues and discover an abandoned servant the Amalekites left behind. Sick and starving, the young man is barely able to talk, so I hand him over to my servants for nourishment. He's been lying in the open countryside for days. Once he's eaten and had water, he will be a valuable guide to take us down to his master's band.

We're almost ready to leave when Ezra joins me in the rubble of my house. In the time he's been with my men, he's never approached me alone, never spoken to me directly. The hair that's usually pulled back with a strand of twine is now falling over his face, obscuring emotion. He drops briefly to one knee, getting to his feet again before I can speak.

"My lord, I can't stay here," he announces. "God is with you, and I pray He gives you victory over this band, but I must go to Gilboa. The Philistines are amassing their greatest army against my king, and I have to be there to defend him." His face creases, and in one look, I can see everything he's lost, everything it's cost him to be here. "The prince was your dearest friend."

"Is," I remind him. I won't talk about Jonathan in past tense.

Ezra lifts his head all the way, looking directly into my eyes. "But he was my friend before he was yours. I am grateful to you, but you know the oath of loyalty I have to him. You are honor-bound to go after your family, and I know you will bring them all back safely. But let me go in your stead and fight at Jonathan's side. As you would."

His urgency tugs at my chest. There's nothing I can say to stop him. Nothing I'd want to say. He's right. I would go with him if it weren't for the Amalekites. Setting aside the axe I was sharpening, I place my hands on his shoulders, remembering everything I owe to this man. Before I commanded him, he shared his battle knowledge and his best friend with me without a hint of jealousy or contempt. Without a second thought.

And I know he did it for Jonathan's sake.

"Go, and may the Lord go with you," I tell him, pulling him into a tight embrace before he can edge away.

Relief clears his eyes, and for the first time, he looks the way I remember. The burden gone from his face, he clasps my hand and leaves the house. Retrieving my axe, I watch Ezra covertly as he walks over to the women, draws one aside, and embraces her, kissing her hand before calling a servant to bring his mule.

Twenty-Three

In a few moments, he's riding off toward the Judean hills. He'll skirt the mountains and hit the road that snakes north to Jezreel.

"You know he isn't coming back," Joab mutters from behind me. He's leaning against what's left of my wall, retying the cords that will bind his quiver to his shoulder.

Startled and offended, I jump down his throat. "I have never had a reason to doubt Ezra's integrity. Not now, not before. His loyalty and his skill in battle are unmatched. I've seen both firsthand. He will fight valiantly, and then he will return, if not right away, as soon as he can. There still may be many obstacles in between myself and the throne, Joab. Ezra's first loyalty was always to Saul and Jonathan."

Joab listens to my outburst without looking at me. Finished bundling his arrows, he walks away, leaving me to feel the rest of the icy blade that entered my side when he'd first spoken up. Standing there in silence, I feel it twist, taking my breath.

I'd rejected Joab's statement because it had nothing to do with Ezra's loyalty, nothing to do with him deciding to stay with Saul from now on.

Joab was implying that they'd lose. And die.

* * * * *

We ride south into the open space of wilderness that makes it ridiculously easy to track travelers. The rocky brush of Ziklag quickly gives way to open plains, and I smile grimly when the landscape opens up completely, giving us a clear view of the Amalekite's camp spreading over the valley. Thanks to the abandoned servant who's now guiding us, we've been able to reach the raiders much faster.

Trembling rage shudders through my limbs, and I rein everything in before flinging myself over the ridge. No tension. Just zeal. It's always the way.

Our battle cry shakes the ground, and my men pour into the camp on all sides, overwhelming even the sentries who don't have time to shoot. They must not have thought we'd pursue them, because there's hardly anyone standing guard. No battle formations. Just a rogue band of thieves. And they've entangled with me for the last time.

It's the first time in years that I've had a personal stake in any one battle, and it turns my practiced fighting movements savage. Jumping over bodies, we pounce on the tents, freeing everyone we can find, even captives taken from other camps. Unlike Saul in his failed campaign, we kill everyone, fueled by the pursuit of rescue. Once the cries of the wounded and dying shift into the joyous screams of our families, my heart nearly splits with relief.

Two little boys I recognize duck under my arm, throwing themselves headlong into their weeping father. Uriah rides past me with Eliam's daughter clinging to his back. Women scream and cry all around me.

"Abigail! Ahinoam!" I'm nearly hoarse with shouting into every tent. Until I hear my own name over the wails.

"David! David!"

I whirl around, but Abigail is already flinging herself at me. Breathless, I'm kissing her and holding her face in front of mine to make sure it's real. Ahinoam quakes in my arms, and I realize that she and Abigail still haven't let go of each other. Their wrists are marked from ropes, and their clothes are dusty and torn, but they're alive.

Unable to speak, I'm just gasping, shaking, crying. Still raging at what could have happened. But thankfulness is stronger, breaking through it all.

"Adonai, thank you!" I shout in between moaning, "I'm sorry. I'm so sorry."

Abigail's hand holds my jaw still. "David…David, we're all right. They didn't touch me. They didn't touch either of us."

Ahinoam's watery voice wavers against my arm. "He would have—the man who took us to his tent. But he had a heavy axe in the corner of the tent, and Abigail…." Her words fall apart, and she buries them in my chest, leaving me to imagine the rest. The thought of Abigail taking charge to protect them both is terrifying and beautiful.

The unshaken courage in Abigail's eyes is the most inspiring thing I've ever seen on a woman. I touch her chin, wanting to gaze at her and crush her in my arms at the same time. "You're the bravest woman I've ever met. You've been praying, haven't you?"

She closes her eyes, covering my hand with hers, and a tear slips over our joined knuckles.

"Every moment. And here you are." She wraps her arms around Ahinoam and me, pressing her head into my chest. Where my broken heart is beating whole again.

"Let's go home," I say. The words are sweet on my tongue, so I say them again.

Abigail's head comes up. "Home?"

"To Ziklag?" Ahinoam asks. "There's not much left."

I shake my head, fresh certainty gleaming in my smile. "I mean home. To Israel."

TWENTY-FOUR

Jonathan

I lift my father's armor into place, tightening the straps across his shoulders, fitting the greaves around his legs and over his hands. I sweep his scarlet robe around his back and fasten the cords underneath the metal edge at his collar. There's some comfort in the act, even if bitterness runs beneath the surface.

Helping him with his armor used to excite me as a boy, though he hasn't let me do it since his coronation, always calling for his armorbearers instead. But today, I arrived ahead of Gera, already waiting at the king's side by the time he awoke. After watching me for a few moments from his bedroll, Saul had stood up in silence, letting me help him without a word.

We don't have much time.

The hours since my father's return from Endor have smeared into a dismal blur that perfectly matches the threatening gray sky over our camp. We've been sleepwalking through battle preparations, hardly talking, barely resting. I can't see much except the images in my head. Mephi. Naamah. The grim masks of resignation on my brothers' faces tell me their families are on their minds too.

They know about the battle, that it's not likely to be won. My father had told them in a council meeting, leaving out the words of Samuel that he'd stolen from the darkness. I had pulled Ishvi and Malchi aside later to tell them that we might not make it, that something had changed, but they looked at me like I'd gone insane.

The strange thing is, I know I haven't. Even with the edge of my life only hours away, my mind feels clear, my resolve firmly planted in a steadfastness beyond my own strength. Amidst the chaos of war and the cacophony of politics, I've learned to steady myself on what I know to be true. I know David is the path forward for Israel, and because I know that, I'm at peace. Staring at that reality keeps me sane.

Since I returned from the forest, I feel more alert and awake. I've slept. Eaten. I've been able to strategize among the commanders without giving in to despair. My heart feels lighter, so I'm ready to deal with the boulder of fear that's stuck underneath it. And it's not because I'm made of stone. I know Yahweh has built me up for this moment. He's been doing it since I was a boy, fighting men twice my age and skill. Adonai has stretched my abilities further than I could have taken them. He's has always given me what I needed.

I'd felt the assurance the moment I awoke. But now that I'm alone with Saul in his tent, I can't deny the hint of panic fraying my nerves.

This is the last chance I'll have to deal with my father.

I reach behind him and lift his sword, holding it out for him to take. He slides it into his scabbard, letting me absorb what he has to say before looking up.

"You've fought beside me for years," he says in a dull voice. "You know the limits of my strength. If you see me wounded beyond recovery, I want you to finish the job. Gera might not do it if I asked."

His eyes glimmer into mine, broken blood vessels turning his gaze jagged.

"Do you understand?" he rasps. "I want *you* to end my life, Jonathan. Not some heathen. If they capture me, you know what they'll do. I will not end my days bleeding out on some pagan god's altar. Do you hear me? I won't do it! Promise me you'll do as I say." He hooks the edge of my collar, his fingers shaking.

The thought pins my throat shut. I know I can't possibly answer. Instead, I gently cover his hand with mine and remove it from my arm. My fingers are nearly numb with the piercing cold working its way through me.

I tighten the knot of his robe, trying twice before releasing the words. "I've given instructions to the commanders to hold their units in position and not deviate. Ishvi's thousands will charge first while Malchi's will wait in reserve. Mine will protect you. I've left a substantial unit with Ish-Bosheth in Gibeah to defend the city."

Not that he'll be able to hold onto it once David returns. But I've done what I could. I can only hope David stops the Philistines before they start pushing into our cities. They're already dangerously close to the Jordan. Many of our kinsmen have preemptively left the area, fleeing east to hide on the outskirts of our territory.

Saul tilts his head, and his eyes change, seeing me. "What of your son?"

"I've given Naamah instructions." The edge of grief is back, sliding up into my heart.

"Naamah?" Saul frowns, confused.

I swallow, remembering I haven't told him about her coming to work for me. "Michal discharged her some time ago. She's been my son's nurse since then."

My father's heightened breathing tells me I don't need to remind him what else she was. His tolerance drops out of sight, agitation surfacing. "I never could lose that family. Ever since Amalek."

Jerking away from me, he fiddles with the cords on his robe, retying them himself while aggravation fans the flames. "You were so valiant then, always ready to fight my battles. Putting yourself in harm's way first. Assuring me of your loyalty. You brought Agag to me yourself, remember? So that I could kill him."

And you didn't.

But I don't need to remind him. He's still not looking up, speaking to random objects around the tent while his tension seethes through the old wounded pride rattling in his throat.

"You ran from me after Amalek. Remember that? It took losing half the blood in your body to bring you back to me. And then I had to find you with her. The sister of a man who had the gall to blame me for their parents' death."

He pushes a cheerless smirk through his provocation. "It's the way of things, I suppose. I was rarely praised for my victories but always responsible for my defeats. I'll wager that's all you can think of now. How I've failed."

I've done this for years, letting him talk through his anger without comment. Waiting for the right time to speak. I used to ask questions, argue, try to force the truth through whatever cloud was blocking his vision. But I'd been a boy then. And my efforts always resulted in scars I couldn't get rid of, even after they healed. So, I keep my arms at my sides and wait.

Saul finally lifts his head, but his eyes still edge away from my direct gaze. "You were full of opinions back then. With every battle, you always had some word of wisdom to impart. In our moment of greatest need, where has it gone?"

He flings his arms, but his wildness is flagging. He's dancing on the edge of despair, and my heart trembles to see it twisting through his expression. I never wanted to see my father break. Never in a hundred years.

His eyes stop on my face at last. "I'm surprised you're even here. I thought the threat of death would be enough to send you crawling back to your friend, at least to save your son."

Twenty-Four

I close my eyes, inhaling. He's always done this. Since the loss of Yahweh's favor, he's tried to imagine me leaving him. Fought for it, even. His outrage would howl over my attempts to convince him I wasn't going anywhere. And I had to take it. On my back. In my heart. I had to watch him hurt me, determined to isolate himself. Everyone else told me to run, to fight, to let him destroy himself. But I'd stayed. Isn't my loyalty obvious enough now that I'm here facing death with him?

I blink hard, struggling to see straight. In a matter of hours, we'll be separated by a violence that's been long in coming. The Philistines will show no mercy, and Yahweh's protection will not cover us. This is our last moment like this. Father and son. And Saul's harshness is stealing even that from us.

Not this time.

Picking up Saul's knife from the table, I shift my focus, willing myself to see my father as he was when I was a boy. Before the anointing was received and lost. Before the crown filled his gaze and stole his heart, turning him against anyone who stood in the way. Desperation tears through, shredding the memories. It's too hard. The effort is stealing the strength I desperately need.

All I can see is struggle, conflict. Torment. The drive to prove something. After the humiliation of failing Yahweh, Saul's pride had broken forth against me, assuming that I was a threat, someone to bend to his will. Someone to use to display his authority to others.

Incensed by my silence, my father heaves an exaggerated sigh and snatches the dagger from me, bending to conceal it in his leg greave. He still thinks I despise him.

Turning my back, I stare at my own weapons on the table, gathering resolve. I finger one of my arrowheads before sliding it into my quiver. Absently, without planning what to say, I start to speak.

"Do you remember when you taught me to shoot? Not with the small bow Saba Ahimaaz made me, but later, after that raid on Benjamin's fields. You told me it would be different for me, that I wouldn't have to stand by while Philistines took what I'd worked for. You told me I could fight back. Become someone my brothers would follow."

My smile pulls stubbornly. "You called me Gideon, a mighty man of valor. We would go out to the fields, and you would drill me so that I could be an example to our kinsmen. You said I would be the first one they would look to besides you, and I had to be able to best any of them."

Twenty-Four

I fall silent for a moment, remembering how passionately I gave myself to it back then, willingly flinging myself into intense training battles against my uncles and my cousins at my father's command. They all marveled at the power and concentrated rage I possessed so young. Abba paraded me like a sharpened weapon, one he'd created.

What they didn't realize was that I was militant for one reason—I couldn't lose. It wasn't an option. Not after seeing the shame in Abba's eyes when he looked at the fields the raiders had torched. The work of generations, gone in a few hours. I knew that even if Israel never had a king, I would fight. I would be someone Yahweh could use to help our people. The desire consumed me.

I pull another arrow, resting it against my palms. "I hated my aim because you hated it. I measured everything I did against what you could do, and I always fell short. When I did well, I just wanted to do more. I would tell myself you just wanted me to be better, stronger. The anger wasn't you."

I pause, letting it all work its way through me. My whole life filling the tent around us.

"I'd respected you before, but after you were anointed, I could hardly contain myself. I was overjoyed that Yahweh had seen greatness in you. All I wanted was to fight beside you, to help you win victories with the Lord for Israel. I fought so hard when Achish's men tried to take me. Because I knew what losing me would do to you, and I couldn't let them…"

My wrist aches, and I realize I'm clenching the arrow. I set it down and turn to face my father, continuing, "When the darkness came, I was ready to fight anything in order to remove it from you, but it wasn't something I could do. While you fought to hold onto the throne, I grieved that I couldn't help you see the truth. I couldn't make you believe what I wanted you to believe. All I could do was stay."

The memories drop from my eyes, letting me see my father again. The instant that happens, he snaps to attention, hiding whatever was creeping into his face. His chest rumbles with an attempt to clear his throat. He crosses his arms over his chest, shutting me out.

"I was there. I know all this. Why are you repeating it now? When it's all come to nothing." His voice tightens. "You're going to die, and the blame will be on my head forever."

Pain stabs my eyes, but I step closer, speaking through the burn. "I'm telling you because there's something you don't know. About all of it."

Twenty-Four

He doesn't blink an eye. "And what is that?"

"I never stopped loving you." The words cut my throat open, but I've longed to say them for years.

Saul face wears a terror I've never seen. Healthy emotion being prodded awake after living trapped for decades. He breathes, shifts his weight, unfolds his arms. Tries to turn away.

"How—" His eyes fill, and he pauses to toughen up. "How can you be so accepting of this? You were meant to be king. That's all I wanted for you. That's why I...did everything. And Samuel took that from us. Yahweh—"

"Stop." I don't want to hear another word uttered against our God. Not when His faithful presence has guided me all this time. Not when He's here now, holding me steady. "I wasn't anointed to rule, Abba. Only to defend Israel. And I've done that. My work is complete. Other hands will take it from here."

For an instant, I'm afraid I shouldn't have come so close to mentioning David, but my father just scoffs quietly. "If that shepherd really cared about Israel, he would have come home when I told him to. He would have come back to help us."

"My lord—" Abba's servant Gera pushes into the tent, bending at the waist while gesturing outside.

"What? Speak up!" Annoyed to be caught in a moment of sentiment, my father is extra harsh.

Eyes wide, Gera merely holds open the side of the tent for Abner to enter, leading an armed, bearded man I don't recognize. For a moment. But when he drops to one knee, his face lights up in my mind, and his name explodes from my lungs. "Ezra!"

I step forward, but my father seizes my wrist.

Ezra meets my gaze once, then lowers his eyes again. "My king, I have returned to fight beside you against the Philistines. I was commanded from Gibeah, but not from my duty to your household."

My breath burns in my chest, waiting for release. My father stiffens, but much of his fight is gone. Too much.

"You came from David?" Saul demands.

Ezra's fists clench around his knee. "Yes, my lord. But in his service, I never raised my hand against any of our people. He allowed me to come back to you, promising to return as soon as he can."

"Where is he now?"

Twenty-Four

"Beyond Ziklag. Dealing with a band of Amalekites who took our families."

He lifts his eyes then, and I wonder if he's found a woman amongst David's company. Dismay winds through me. That's what has delayed David? An Amalekite raid? I wish for the thousandth time that we'd destroyed them all.

Saul lifts a hand. "Get up, Ezra. You will follow us into battle, though you may have cause to regret it. You can help my son with his armor. He's been too busy talking."

The faintest glimmer of humor in my father's eyes is encouragement enough for me, and before he stalks from the tent, he touches me briefly on the side of my face. As soon as he's gone, I heave Ezra off the ground, crushing him against my chest. He clings to me, talking into my shoulder.

"What are we up against? Have the spies counted regiments? How—"

"Don't." There's so little time, but the gratitude raging inside me is more powerful than anything I've felt in ages. Pulling back, I grip the sides of his face. "You came back."

Ezra smirks, reaching for my armor. "I would've come sooner if I thought you'd be marching into battle without your sword. Put these on. Let's go."

491

I fumble with my weapons, completely unwound. I can't quite laugh, but the thought that Ezra will be beside me has renewed my strength, along with the news he brought. "He's coming?" I ask, wanting to hear him repeat it. "David's coming?"

Ezra's mouth lifts in a small smile. "Yes. David's coming." He pauses by the tent door, watching me. "What's wrong?"

I just shake my head, breathing deeply as Abner's war horn pierces the air. I don't want our last discussion to be consumed with death. David's coming. Israel has a chance. That's all I need to know.

The desperate hope pounds under my breastplate while we join the others at the center of camp and march into the weak sunlight. Clouds drop over the face of the sun, and the hillside groans with the coming storm. Or is it the Philistines? Either way, everyone's heart is turning to stone. I can see it in the ashen pallor of the faces behind the Israelite armor.

The chilly morning air carries a sting through the valley. I pull in a long breath of it anyway, willing the memory back. The same clouds of defeat had gathered over Elah. But the terror had scattered like a fleeing winter chill when David carried the warmth of Yahweh's presence into the valley.

Twenty-Four

My body aches from the conflict I feel everywhere, urgency wrestling with hope. But it's always worth fighting that battle. Every tug of weakness always shifts my attention, locking my focus onto the One who carries the standard of Israel. Yahweh has chosen a new king in His mercy, not merely out of judgment. He will make sure our nation continues, no matter what.

Mephi's face smiles behind my eyes. As much as it hurts, I know he will continue as well. That blessing is all the reward I could want or need.

Ezra grips my shoulder, right below my old arrow wound. "By many or by few," he says. Right before the first arrows of ambush enter the air.

There's no challenge this time, no official call to arms. Philistines swarm the hillside from all directions, flinging restraint to the wind, and our plans for an orderly attack fall to pieces in seconds. Their ranks swollen with mercenaries and fresh recruits from Ekron, the enemy outnumbers us for the first time in years. And I can see it in the tattered movements of our forces. We weren't ready.

Offense abandoned, we shift into defending ourselves. Defending the king. Malchi's reserves join us sooner than I thought we'd need them. My father is battling fear more than any other enemy, fighting in tight circles, hardly advancing. Keeping close to me and my brothers. Until Ishvi is cut down. Then Malchi a few moments later.

Seeing them fall freezes the blood in my veins for half a second before their attackers are after me. My father is weeping as he fights, and when our eyes meet, I nearly double over. Knowing it would happen hasn't shielded us at all. My brothers are dead, and I can't even get to them. I can't mourn them or help them.

Shock and grief tear me open, leaving me vulnerable, but I can't stop. I drag desperate prayers through my teeth, letting pain bleed into my movements while I charge the battalion on the north side of Gilboa. I glare through the sting in my eyes.

The Glory of Israel does not change His mind. But He is faithful. He's faithful...

I duck just in time to feel the air sing around an axe aimed at my head. My elbow slams into the Philistine's jaw, and I trip over his body, colliding with Ezra. Not yet.

"Sorry, my lord," Ezra mumbles.

Sorry? For half a second, I remember the two of us as boys, practically crawling up the hill on our hands and knees to fight the Philistines at Michmash. Then, I blink.

Twenty-Four

A new shadow coats Ezra's face, covering what I recognize of him. He breathes once, then sags against me. My arm goes around him to catch his full weight, and his blood fills my hands, streaking down from the axe wound in his chest. He's already gone. I can feel it in the slump of his body, the emptiness in his eyes. The rage firing my veins shoves grief aside for the moment.

My friend slips to the ground, and I leap over him, swinging my sword in the direction of three men lunging at me. They're after more blood, and I can't stop, can't grieve. But something wild has been loosed, the anguish that started when I saw Ishvi and Malchi struck down. A piece of me had torn away and stayed with them, closing my brothers' eyes so they didn't have to die looking.

Now the rest of me is downfield, holding Ezra's forehead against mine. I should be there. Helping him somehow. Lending him my strength for his final moments. But it's too late. He's gone.

The pain poisons my fury, fueling and weakening my fight all at once. He's my brother too, like David, but I didn't tell him half as often. I haven't thanked him for what he did. Doeg was my mission, but Ezra had taken it himself, along with the consequences. He'd borne exile and danger and risked the king's anger—all for me. He should be alive right now. He should be back with David. He should raise a family serving the king who will take Israel forward.

But he's here. Dead. Because of me.

It's like a limb has been torn from my body. Something inside me won't fight the same. I'm staggering into Philistines, slicing randomly, accidentally. I dig a sword into a belly, cut a throat, smash my shield into someone's head. But one of them will retaliate. One of them will reach me.

Even anticipating it, the blow is staggering. A deep, heavy thrust to my gut, on the left side. I feel my ribcage move, and the edge of the sword keeps going, cutting up too high before it yanks free. I take it with little pain, but when I try to lift my arm, everything stops. Fire and ice slam into each other in my body while blood pools around my feet. My sight breathes and bends, unsteady as I wait for a follow-up blow. But nothing comes.

The pain drops, and a raging quiet consumes my senses. Things that should have sound are clashing and ringing noiselessly all around me. I can't hear, think, or breathe. I've gone down on my knees, and someone's holding my arms, but I can't feel it. A face is close to mine, eyes blazing, mouth open screaming, but it means nothing.

Nothing.

Then my ears erupt, and breath cuts through my lungs, and the pain that hits me pulls every bit of heat from my body. I still

Twenty-Four

don't feel the fingers biting my shoulders. It's my father. Holding me up. Screaming.

"Don't do this, Jonathan! Don't do it! Don't leave me!"

I finally figure out how to find his eyes, and they're bloody, all the white consumed by red and tears. He holds my chin, and I know the blood staining his fingers is mine. "Fight, my son. *Fight!*"

My heart bleeds. I can't decide if I'm actually speaking the exhale in my head.

I—have. Yahweh's calling.

My father sees it. Knows it like I do. He weeps against my forehead, every bit of courage shredded from his face.

"Jonathan, please kill me! If they take me, you know what they'll do!"

He shoves what feels like the hilt of a sword under my fingers, but I'll never do that. Never.

I push the handle back up against his chest, the motion digging pain through my eyes. There's no way I can talk, but he could always read my mind. I fasten my eyes on his, my fingers touching his face.

Yahweh is your salvation. Your Yeshu-hah. Call on Him.

I can see him drowning, trying to see, trying to believe. There's a stronger hand on me now, gripping my left shoulder, and my soul pulls after it. I'm not even here now. But then my father's eyes shift over my head, and terror pours into them.

Every movement is agony. Relying on my mind to propel my muscles, I shove Abba's blade deep into the ground and lean all my weight into it so I can stand. And turn. The advancing Philistine is blurry, but I can feel the grim smile glowering on my face to meet the hatred I know is on his. He'll have to get through me to reach my father.

Then somehow, I hear my own voice riding a borrowed breath. "You're too late. David's coming."

The man's snarl is muted by the spear going through me into the ground.

"We'll kill him too."

Not a chance.

The spear was too late. Unnecessary. Everything in me was already pulling away. I'm spinning in circles, unable to tell if I'm standing or not.

Twenty-Four

I see sky. I see the stream outside Gibeah, bubbling laughter pulling life through the dry grass.

I see the valley at Elah anointed with sunlight, and David dancing while Goliath's head rolls.

Stand with him, Yahweh. Keep him close to you. May he become everything, attain everything you ever wanted! Save Israel! Keep her as the apple of your eye. Save Mephi…

The words run like water outside of my mind. My fingers find my shoulder before everything becomes dark. And this time, there's a hand that grips mine back. Soothing warmth washes every inch of me, and I let go.

TWENTY-FIVE

David

The weight from my dream rides my shoulders as we cross into Ziklag.

Answering the threat to our families and restoring them unharmed to a place of safety has awakened the fight inside me. It's time to leave the pagan cities behind for good and be what we are in the open. Israelite warriors. Servants of the Most High God.

Now that I can think about it, the battle in Gilboa is consuming my senses. The flames stir so hot, I can almost feel the sting through my skin. I can't ignore such blatant threats to my people any more than I could let the Amalekites take my family. Achish's dark mockery has me convinced.

My dream in the forest wasn't merely a command to break with the Philistines. Nor was it just a revision of the old battle in Aijalon. It was a prophecy—the threat they've been holding over Israel for years. And I have to answer it.

But it could be a while before we can ride back into battle.

Ziklag isn't exactly home anymore, but everyone is trying to settle in, make sense of what happened. Abigail's courage has shielded her, but as soon as we'd ridden a mile outside the Amalekite camp, my wife had melted against my back and sobbed. Ahinoam is plagued by nightmares. The children I'm used to seeing full of confident innocence are now huddled in corners, staring down trauma, while their mothers pick through our charred belongings.

The raid has destroyed their sense of security as surely as it torched Ziklag's walls.

Fortunately, the spoils we took from Amalek mean we have plenty of supplies. More than enough to live on while we plan our next move.

Upon our return, I'd gathered my men to weigh our options, and everyone had agreed it was better to stay put for a while, let the women recover, and then regroup for battle once we'd decided whom to take and how to involve ourselves. Defying Achish so publicly will be no easy task, and once it's done, he'll retaliate. We'll need a more defensible position than the shell of Ziklag. A place with a fortress where our families can stay while we deal with the Philistines. We have to be ready to defend the nation, especially if Saul…

Twenty-Five

I will it from my mind, refusing my own premonitions, and turn my attention to the arguments breaking out between my men over the spoils.

"They were too exhausted to follow us, and now they want a share in the spoils?" Ethan fumes. "Just let them take their wives and children and go."

I wince at his fury. It disturbs me that men who've fought together for years are so quick to divide one another. Our life of wandering has made many of them defensive, eager to look out for themselves at any cost. But we cannot live clenching our fists and expect an abundant future.

Rather than deal directly with the troublemakers, I assemble my entire company and make it an ordinance. "Everything we came home with is from the Lord. He preserved us and gave us victory over the raiders. No one should return from battle and refuse to share with his brothers who stayed with the baggage. We will all share alike."

The discussion gives me an idea, but it'll take another day or so to work it out with Asa and my swiftest riders.

"I'd like to send a portion of the spoils to all the elders of Judah who supported us in the days of our exile," I tell them.

"Many of them allowed us to roam their land without trouble, and now that we have the means to thank them, we should."

My commanders agree to organize the distribution to elders from Bethel to Hebron and every town in between. Every place that gave us sanctuary, concealing our movements during our time with Achish. With each new plan, fresh anticipation flickers through the smoke, like those last moments of dark before dawn. It's good to feel hope surfacing, however bruised.

I can see it in the faces of my men and our families. Our exile is ending. We'll be home soon. But what will we find there? My heart races, eager and hesitant at once.

Since Achish's men are focused elsewhere, my spies have been able to move freely with little trouble, but I know the Philistines have made it past Gilboa by now. I could still try to cut them off before they cross the Jordan. I could send half my men there, half to Gibeah. Saul's son Bosheth isn't very experienced with battle. I doubt he'll refuse my help at a time like this.

"My lord!" Uriah's running, sword in hand. When he reaches me, he aims his weapon toward Ziklag's crumbling gate. "An Amalekite!"

Twenty-Five

I jump to attention, my own weapon held ready. But the man being led by my guards is obviously a straggler, covered in dust from the road, barely resisting.

"He says he's a hired fighter," Abishai tells me, shoving the man.

I look down at him. "You've come from the battle at Gilboa." When I realize it, dread fills my chest like a cloud.

"Yes, my lord."

I don't recognize him. He's panting, exaggerated emotion drawn into each breath. The dark points of an Amalekite brand climb his forearm, but his clothes are torn and his armor is mismatched and unkempt, probably stolen. He's a rogue soldier with no more personal interest in this than a common mercenary. Not to mention his kinsmen just got finished terrorizing our families.

Nothing in me wants to hear any of this from him, but I can't avoid it. "Well?"

His forced emotion heightens, and he gestures between us dramatically. "The battle was lost, my lord. Israel is under siege, and Gibeah will be under Philistine control in a matter of days. Many have fled to the wilderness beyond the Jordan. King Saul and his son Jonathan are both dead, along with the other princes and their armorbearers."

If he'd come up to me and sliced open my side, I couldn't have been more outraged. Marching into my camp and tossing their names at me like an afterthought!

Saul. Ishvi. Malchi. Ezra. Jonathan—

Each one hits my chest like a hot coal, and the sting enrages me. I advance on the Amalekite, my fists clenched against his stammering. "Tell me how you know this!"

Heaven help him if he's lying.

But once I see what's in his hands, I stop moving. Completely. Cramps seize my limbs like chains. Even the breath in my chest turns to ice. Saul's crown is unmistakable, and seeing it hanging from this man's arm unwinds my control. "Where did you get that?"

I don't recognize my own voice. It's almost a growl, hollow and clenched.

"From Saul himself, my lord." His attention keeps bobbing from my hands to my face, trying to judge how the news is affecting me. "The battle was fierce around him, and he was

Twenty-Five

badly wounded, and he saw me on the hill. I was fighting as a hired soldier, and he called to me, and said, 'What country are you from?' and..."

"And?!" I grit my teeth, rearing over him, and he spits out the ending.

"...and he begged me to come up and end his life. So, I did him that mercy, my lord, to prevent him from being captured and tortured. Jonathan was already dead; these are his armbands."

I jerk away as though he's laid a snake at my feet. He keeps talking, but his words are meaningless, drowned in the tumult overtaking my senses, assaulting my mind with a flood of images I hate and can't hide from. All I can see is Saul on his knees over Jonathan's body, reduced to begging an enemy to finish him. A powerful churning climbs my stomach, and I turn and stagger away, darkness rushing in over my eyes.

Grabbing for something to lean on, my fingers lock around someone's wrists.

"David..."

It's Joab's voice, but I can't answer him through the inferno taking over my chest.

"What's happened?"

I just shake my head, staring at Joab's breastplate. There's no way this is true. The man is lying. He's a lying Amalekite. They're the murderous ravagers who'd stolen my family. Why was he even on Gilboa? Why should I trust anything he has to say?

But the more I try to run from it, the more it chases me down. Jonathan's face blinks in my mind, and my breath halts again. He's gone. It's why I dreamed that night outside Gath. Why I felt the sudden urge to leave Achish. Too late…

The mounting grief is so monstrous that I jerk away from it.

Not yet.

I force my gaze up to Joab's, then carefully angle my eyes down to his sword. He lifts his chin, shifting his attention to the man behind us. I turn my head and speak to the messenger without moving. My feet are digging into the earth, trying to ground my body. "Repeat what you just said. Where are you from?"

"I am an Amalekite, my lord…a stranger to your land…"

As he drones on, I can feel the rage surging inside me, and I drink it in, chest heaving. Battle anger is familiar territory, and it's welcome for the moment. At least it's something to feel other than...

A sudden cry leaps up out of me, and I haul it back, choking. Grief is pushing into my face, but I set my jaw, aiming everything into the Amalekite's eyes. He doesn't deserve to see me break. "How were you not afraid to strike the Lord's anointed?" I rasp through a throat that's rapidly closing.

His expression freezes, but I wasn't expecting an answer. I won't ever hear his voice again. I hate him for telling me. I hate the image of him taking anything from my king. Or my brother. Joab barely lifts a finger before Uriah stabs the man through his heart, pulling his sword free in one swift motion. The Amalekite crumples to the ground, choking on death while I seethe over him.

"Your blood be on your own head for striking God's anointed."

Whether his story is true or not, he had no right to touch either of them. *No right.*

Something about seeing his body lying there unleashes the wail that's been building from my feet. Crossing the space between us in two steps, I swing my own sword and bring it down on him also, over and over. But it doesn't matter how many times I do it. The agony is still alive, tearing through my throat.

It should have been that Philistine under my sword. Like the first one in Aijalon who'd died at my hands before he could strike my brother. But this time, I wasn't there.

My wrist gives out, and I drop my sword next to the Amalekite's body. *I wasn't there.*

I'm on the ground now, screaming into the dust, but the pain just intensifies with every breath, and it won't stop being true.

He's gone. Jonathan is gone.

*****

I'm doubled over in the darkness with my head on my knees. I can feel myself breathing, but each lift of my chest is knotted with fresh pain.

In the murky blackness, I could imagine it's just another cave. That I'm still on the run from Saul, with Jonathan's friendship reaching out to me in ways his father could never comprehend. But the truth is more jagged than the walls over my head.

Only a hundred miles to the north, the blood of Saul's warriors soaks the ground. So many of the men who used to fight beside me are dead on the hills, their honor destroyed, their homes decimated. Destruction has finally overtaken the king who outran it for years, chasing me.

I knew I would never rejoice at Saul's death, but I had always pictured him dying in his bed, an old man. Not out on a hill with a Philistine spear in him. I had hoped that we might reconcile one day, and it gnaws at me to realize that we won't.

And then I remember Jonathan lies beside him.

I reel with it, raging at the way my brother has been taken from me. Cut out of my life like a torn garment. I had wanted him beside me all the way. Until now, I never realized how strong my hope had been. I had kept it in the back of my mind alongside the treasured promise of my kingship. But now, I can barely touch it for the pain.

I shove my knuckles into my eyes, but I can't shut out the sight of Jonathan on the ground, stripped of his armor, blood pulling from his mouth. He's fought countless battles, and I never once doubted that he would return. But now he won't.

Every breath attacks me with something else. Something he said. Or did.

His hands adjusting my grip on Ezra's sword. His arms pulling me into the embrace that held me together right before I ran. His determination to refuse hatred when everyone in Saul's court wanted me dead.

In my dreams, he gives me a hand up, snaps my arm back into place in battle, laughs when I hand him Goliath's rubies.

They're in my hand again now, sent to me by the men of Jabesh-Gilead who'd stolen back Saul's armor from the pagan temple of Ashtoreth. They've promised to do more, but it's a bitter comfort since my brother won't be returning with them.

"You are chosen of the Lord. You will be the next king of Israel. Don't doubt it again."

Those were his last words to me. The last time I'll ever talk to him. Unable to sleep, unwilling to stay awake, I sit up and let the pain seethe around me. My only comfort is that Yahweh has never been afraid of my tossings. I cup my hands around my mouth, moaning into them.

I didn't think it would be like this, Adonai. Back when I was anointed, I had so much hope. The best of everything was ahead. I wanted it because you gave it to me. Why did it have to lead here?

Twenty-Five

I had known the call of Yahweh meant surrendering to the fire. Trusting there would be life in the ashes, maybe even silver from the crucible. But this!

My heart is battle weary, badly mended. Like it won't heal. My mind aches, burdened by everything I've lost. Stretched out on the ground, I whisper into the thin silence that hangs around me.

"Did you really want a broken king?"

The sacrificial lamb from my old vision is the only answer I get. It flickers in my mind, silent yet full of words. Even without understanding it fully, I'd known that the lamb told a much longer story about the redemption of our pain and the gruesome cost to it. But somehow, there was life in his wounds. And Yahweh wanted me to know.

The thought awakens gratitude in the center of me. The smallest light cutting the blackness. Somehow, even in the deepest pits of anguish, Adonai has always drawn me close. Into a plan that is so much bigger than the steps in front of me.

Rolling onto my hands and knees, I rummage among my belongings until I find the songs scrawled on parchments. Offerings of my days, like I'd told Jonathan. Without meaning to, without really wanting to, I start to write. And just like every other time, it's the right thing to do. Everything that's wandering around in my head finally finds a home on paper. Everything I should have said to Jonathan but didn't.

It's more than a tribute. It's a lament. A way to give voice to what Israel feels but can't express. To help her honor the legacy of her first king and prince. With these words, Achish will be under no illusions. He'll know that I loved Saul and his sons, and I never intended to fight against them. I glare through my tears, clenching my fists against passion. Gath and Ekron will learn to think twice before celebrating this. I'm coming for them.

Just as soon as I can stand up without dizziness taking over.

It pushes back over me every time I think of Saul's headless corpse hanging from the gates of Beth-Shan beside his son's body. I had retreated to the caves to hide from the grisly messages that kept coming after the battle, but the images are carved into my mind like an evil brand.

I weave my anger into the song, praying that no rain would fall on the fields that had received their blood.

Asaph always seems to know when I'm writing something. Later that night, I fall asleep over the parchment and wake up to find my scribe standing over me, torch in hand, reading it.

Twenty-Five

I sit up on my knees and speak into the silence. "This one should be sent throughout the tribes. But first, I'll need you to arrange it."

Asaph nods without lifting his eyes from the paper. "We'll need a familiar tune Israel will recognize. 'The Bow' would be fitting," he says softly before leaving the cave without another word. I fold my fists into the floor.

"The bow of Jonathan never turned back.

"The sword of Saul never returned empty.

"In life and death, they were not divided."

The refrains soothe me while keeping my wounds open. Jonathan always said he would die at his father's side. Why did he have to be right?

I haven't been counting the days, so I don't know how long it's been since the news came. I can feel my mind trying to move on, but the effort is like clawing my way through boulders up a hillside. Something weighs me down. Holds me back.

Abiathar's concern reaches out to me in the dark.

"Have you eaten?"

I don't answer. He knows I haven't.

He moves closer, folding his arms. "Would it be easier to say it out loud?"

I wince. It's waiting right at the door of my spirit, so it doesn't need any coaxing. "Jonathan deserved to be king."

The sharpness of the words cuts the silence, tearing into what's trying to heal. Abiathar stays quiet far too long, and I start shaking again until his hand grips my arm.

"The kingship was never meant to be bargained over between men," he whispers. "It was never based on deserving. It's the choice of Yahweh. Jonathan knew that."

I rub my temples, knowing the ache won't leave. "Why would Yahweh want me to be king when I let my own brother die?" Somehow, the things I really want to say come to the surface easier with Abiathar.

There's little light to show me his face, but I can hear grief pulling at his voice. He kneels in front of me. "David, you would have helped them. We were too late."

"Yes. We had to rescue our families who were captured because I joined Achish and left them unprotected." Now that it's clear, it's unbearable. Regret is adding bitter poison to my grief, and I'm so weary of tasting it.

But Abiathar has lost men too. His father and brothers are dead. And right when he could have hated me, he'd chosen mercy instead. As he does now.

He grabs my shoulders, fierceness burrowing into me through his fingers.

"Listen to me. Jonathan knew he might not return. There was always a chance. But he willingly gave himself to the battles of the Lord because he trusted the One who went before him. He trusted Yahweh's plans for Israel. If your friend could die holding onto that assurance, then you can live with it. Yahweh's faithfulness is bigger than any giant we might face. As we've seen."

He lets that pulse in my veins a few times before letting me go. "The men don't say it, but they respected Jonathan. They knew what it cost him to align himself with you. They didn't know him as you did, but they honor him now."

I nod, thinking of the men of Jabesh-Gilead who'd promised to sneak back to Beth-Shan to remove the bodies and bury them properly. About the thousands who mourn them now, preparing to send my lament to the corners of Israel so that every city might hear it.

Abiathar's presence feels fatherly, even though he's no older than I am. Even though I'm spent of tears, I press my hands against my face and release everything again, trusting the shoulders of my God to bear these burdens so they don't kill me.

Take them, Yahweh. Please take them. I'm not strong enough.

I'm not strong enough. I know it more now than I did when I was a shepherd boy who'd never killed anyone. I'm not strong enough to carry Israel into the dreams of Yahweh, dealing with the bloodshed that will come against us, the rifts that will intensify.

The nation is broken and in need of rebuilding. Crimes will have to be answered for. Wars will be waged, taking more men from their families. And Yahweh's presence deserves a temple that I am completely unfit to build.

But once again, my Shepherd hasn't left me alone.

Abiathar's voice breaks. "The Lord your God is mighty to save. He has trained your hands for war and your fingers for battle. Didn't Samuel tell you that?"

"Yes." My certainty sounds muffled. I say it stronger. "Yes."

Abiathar touches the tear-stained parchment beside me. "He trained Jonathan too. Believe me, David. Jonathan would not have faced death if he didn't know our God could be trusted. Yahweh never left him. And He hasn't left you."

He pushes his cloak back, bending beneath the low rock shelf. I can sense it before he says anything else. Everyone is ready to move on. "The commanders have their thousands ready," he murmurs. "They've been telling the people to prepare."

"For what?"

"Wherever Yahweh sends you. They're ready to follow you, David. They've all seen how God has shown you the steadfast love He promised with the anointing. They're not afraid to go where He leads."

My chest moves, the doors of my heart forced aside to let hope back in. It's painful, but the ache isn't unwelcome.

Abiathar breathes deeply. "By the way, Talia had the baby this morning. A son."

I cringe, ashamed of the way the news bounces off of me without stirring much emotion. "Abiathar, that's—I'm glad. I'm sorry. I've been…"

I look away, feeling tugged toward the mouth of the pit again, but my friend's hand on my shoulder pulls me back from the edge. "I know." He pauses. "I named him Jonathan."

The name shatters something inside me, but relief sweeps in behind the break. I look into Abiathar's smile and allow my face to mirror his. I'm amazed that it can.

"He believed even when I didn't," I whisper, awe slipping in around the words. "His faith kept mine breathing." I stare into the pain for a moment longer and then let my shoulders relax. "He knew this day would come."

Abiathar straightens. "It's time for you to come back to us."

I nod, hearing Jonathan's admonition all over again. *You don't need me, David. Lean on the One who anointed you.*

Grief rises and falls with my chest, but somehow, it hasn't touched the deeper foundation. The determination that Jonathan taught me. Grasping Abiathar's arm, I stand to my feet and feel my way toward the cavern's mouth. It's time.

After the cave's darkness, even the weak light of evening stabs my eyes. I catch my breath, taking in the sharp scent of pine from the forest. Smoke from the campfires. Sweet incense. On the lower path near our tents, several of my men approach me one by one. Each of them acknowledges me personally, murmuring gentle condolences.

Twenty-Five

With each hand clasped, each shoulder gripped, my throat thickens with the cloud rising in my chest. The one that burns and weeps at the same time. I am so grateful for each of these men. Every one of them has committed to serve at my side and build my kingdom, giving me wholehearted support I could not have commanded from them.

But Jonathan was different. He was the mightiest man I ever knew. I can say that because I know where he got his strength. That's what bound us so close. He was just another man holding tightly to the God I love. But that meant more than anything else I've received from anyone.

Who else in my life showed me utter trust in Yahweh's goodness, even when victory was hidden, invisible? When it would've been easier to turn away and choose bitterness? Who more than my brother?

I close my eyes, but the flood of tears is too quick, dropping off my chin like oil.

You were special, my friend. A breathing gift from God. I've never been loved by anyone the way I was loved by you.

Except…

I breathe deeply and sudden peace rushes in to replace the clenching of before. Warmth spreads over my wounds, and I lean into the silence, my lips parting in a smile as gratitude splits my pain.

Only Adonai's presence can do that.

From the pastures until now, Yahweh has been my Shepherd, feeding my faith with truth that I would need to lean on in the darkness. How often had I trembled with fear, afraid to fail Israel, fail Yahweh? Could anyone be trusted with the dreams of our God? It's taken years, but I understand better now.

When Yahweh called me a man after His heart, He was calling me higher, waking up something that was only beginning to live. It was never about my ability to stand alone. He knew I would run to Him in weakness and in strength. That's what He saw. That's why He chose me.

And Yahweh's grace always follows His choices. I've learned that much from our history as a nation. I've learned that from Jonathan.

I duck through the door of my tent, and Abigail stands to her feet, exhaling my name with relief. She hesitates only a moment, reading me before she nestles against my chest, clasping her arms behind my back.

"I'm so sorry, my love." She mumbles the words into my shoulder, her voice shaking. "Abiathar told you about his son? Jonathan?"

"Yes." I hold her tightly. "Yahweh is doing something new. Everywhere."

"He is. Look." Abigail pulls back from me and holds the canvas aside for me to see through the door. "Look at them, David. After everything that's happened, they're encamped here still. Hundreds of our people who have risked their lives to stand by your side and wait for the fulfillment of God's promise. It's beautiful, isn't it?"

My arm still around my wife, I look out over the camp. My men stand at a distance, leaving me to myself, but every one of them is watching me from the door of his tent, weapons in hand. Ready and waiting. In the clearing, a handful of boys are sparring with wooden swords, no doubt dreaming of following their fathers and serving in my armies one day. As Jonathan's child probably did. Or does.

My heart twists, and I pull Abigail closer, lifting my eyes over the hills.

Help me find him, Adonai. Help me find Jonathan's son and show him the steadfast love you showed me through his father. Help

My Rival, the King

me shepherd your people the way you dreamed I would. Teach me to reveal your heart to them.

Because that will be beautiful.

TWENTY-SIX

David

At the counsel of the Lord, we travel to Hebron where the elders of Judah are eager to crown me, even if the rest of Israel isn't ready. Once, I would have dreaded the idea of one tribe moving forward without the others. But after everything Yahweh has done, I have no more reason to hold back.

My men ride behind me, their families fanning out in triumphant procession around them. The children who have grown up in the shadow of exile have become passionate youths who will fight under Joab in the days to come. Many more battles await them. But for now, the confident strength lighting every countenance encourages me. They no longer need to hide.

In the weeks since Gilboa's battle left the northern towns vulnerable, Israelites have been streaming south, skirting the Philistines' path to meet us. Ittai hasn't shown himself yet, but after his promise to defect to me, I've ordered my men to look out for him and welcome him when he does come.

Prophets and priests who have prayed for me for years in secret have now joined me openly, giving me their support. And the elders of Judah have sent word from Hebron.

"We're already gathered, waiting for the king Yahweh chose a long time ago," the message said, and the words have been burning in my veins ever since.

Handing my mule off to a servant, I bend to cup water from the brook that runs through Hebron, collecting in the Pool of Gibeon. By this time tomorrow, I'll be kneeling before my tribe's elders to receive the crown that was promised to me years ago in Bethlehem. The crown that already weighs heavy.

"The men of Jabesh-Gilead brought Saul's crown back from the Ashtaroth temple," Asahel informs me on his way past the brook. "They said it's already yours."

I squeeze his shoulder, saying nothing in response.

I've already sent a message back to the men of Gilead, thanking them for honoring Saul and Jonathan with a decent burial, but I still don't want to picture their bodies reduced to ash, their bones resting under some tree in Jabesh. I'm not ready to. Fortunately, I haven't had much time to think about it.

Twenty-Six

Since emerging from the cave, I haven't had a moment alone. My commanders have doubled my guard, making sure I'm never without protection, and my nephews have kept their spies on the move ahead of us, scouting every step before I make it.

Asa moves away, joining the others making camp in the forest, but it isn't long before Joab's reflection joins mine in the water.

"My servants have set up a council tent. We need you in there now."

I straighten up, but Joab grabs the side of my breastplate. "Hold it."

His armorbearer steps forward carrying a heavy scarlet robe with purple dye around the collar and sleeves. Something on top of it catches the sunlight, and I'm shocked to see a gold medallion with the face of a lion gleaming in my direction.

It looks like the same one I wore in Gibeah after Goliath's death. When Jonathan first made me a prince. I reach out to touch it. "Where did you get this?"

"It's from the Gilead spies." Reaching up to my neck, Joab unties the cords of my old cloak. Jonathan's. "It's time you wore your own."

I let the men drape the new robe over my shoulders, and Joab hangs the medallion over my heart. I stare at it, then down at Jonathan's rolled-up cloak in my hands.

Joab grips my wrist. "Bury it with him at Jabesh. Later. And be the king he always knew you would be."

My nephew's flashed grin stirs my confidence, and for the first time in years, I let myself be grateful he's here. Without reservation.

But Joab's sentiment flees as soon as we enter the council tent. His spies have seen and heard enough on the road to give us a good indication of what the future will hold.

"Even with all the unrest, it won't be easy to draw the other tribes to our side," Abishai warns, leaning over a table spread with every map he's drawn. "We've already received word that Abner has taken Saul's youngest son and made him king up in Mahanaim."

Every man in the tent stiffens while Joab lists the tribes who have followed Bosheth. "Asher supports him. Benjamin, obviously. The men of Jezreel, and Ephraim, and Gilead are with him, but Abner has declared him king over all the tribes of Israel. Except Judah."

Twenty-Six

Joab lifts his hand, and one of his spies speaks up. "Even after the decimation at Gilboa, they still have the reserve units Jonathan left with Bosheth in Gibeah. They'll rule in hiding, most likely until we drive the Philistines out of their towns. After that, I'm certain they'll turn on us. Abner fully intends to keep the throne in Benjamin's hands."

I lift my chin, adamant. "We will not sacrifice the position Yahweh has given us. Once we reach Hebron, we will inquire of the Lord and concentrate on receiving His guidance to defeat the Philistines. When the roads are safe again, I'd like to bring the Ark of the Covenant down here. Once we have a permanent fortress."

Saul rarely sought the face of Yahweh during his reign, and the consequences were devastating. I'm determined to do things differently. Even if it means restraining my nephews.

I narrow my eyes at them. "We will not take Abner's life. Or the life of Ish-Bosheth. I am confident that when the time is right, Saul's remaining relatives will turn to us for refuge, and we can forge an alliance there."

Bosheth will be easier to bargain with than his father was. But I only needed to meet Saul's youngest son once to know that Abner will be making the real decisions. The general's loyalty to Saul and Jonathan will burn fiercer in the face of their loss, strengthening Bosheth's grip on the throne. But Abner has seen too much death in his time. Perhaps he'll be weary of it and join me in peace. I pray he does.

I could use his help if I'm going to find the relative who concerns me the most.

I plant my fists on the table, swept back to my latest dream. The vision struck me on our first night of travel and hasn't left me since. In the wilderness outside Gibeah, a little boy was pinned under rock while wolves circled nearby. His resemblance to Jonathan had been striking.

"There's something else," I announce, watching my men's attention tighten on me. "Jonathan lost his wife and one of his children, but I never heard if his first son survived." I hold the silence for a few moments, finding each pair of eyes in turn, though most of the men avert theirs. "Does anyone know?"

One of Abishai's commanders finally clears his throat. "It's not likely, my lord," he hedges. It's clear he doesn't think this should concern me. "The fortress palace in Gibeah has been taken. Everyone fled for the wilderness just beyond, but it was mostly women and children, a dozen or so palace servants and scribes. They didn't have time to grab provisions, and the

Twenty-Six

Philistines razed the countryside in a matter of days. It's very likely that they...didn't make it, my lord."

I face him, staring straight into the possibility. "I'd like to know. I made a covenant with him."

My pulse jumps in my throat. I'll never get over that. When I was at my most vulnerable, the crown prince of Israel made a covenant with me. He saved my life. He kept my courage burning and sharpened my faith. He lifted me up when I couldn't stand. The least I can do is show the same kindness to his son.

I wait for my voice to settle before raising it. "God is my witness, as Yahweh has kept His promises to me, I will keep mine to the people He sent into my life."

When I look up, softer glances meet mine.

"We'll try, my lord," Abishai promises. And I know he means it. A gentle rumble of agreement follows his declaration.

"Are you even sure this son exists?" Joab asks.

"He does. His name is Mephibosheth." I fold my arms, not ready to tell my men about the dream. "I don't know where he is, but Yahweh sees him. He wanted me to know."

Joab nods curtly. "Any idea where to start?"

Just like that, her face enters my mind. The only woman who could give Jonathan pause in a room full of admirers.

"There was a woman who used to attend Michal back in Gibeah," I begin. "She was the sister of one of Saul's servants, and I remember hearing that she ended up serving in Jonathan's house after his wife died. I'm certain if we find her, we'll find the boy."

* * * * *

Hebron overwhelms me.

From the ancient stone mile markers to the meadow by the pool of Gibeon, divisions of armed troops cover the hills until I can't see the ground. The landscape is fully armed, tens of thousands of shields and spears lifting in my direction. When I ride into the clearing ahead of my men, a collective shout shakes the ground.

Under the lion medallion, I feel my heart beating, the flame of battle reignited. These are mighty men of valor. Fear no longer rules Israel.

I ride through the tribal ranks, recognizing men of Issachar, Zebulun, Reuben, and Gad. The men of Judah number in the thousands, their multitudes arrayed for battle. The fierceness they carry has turned their brows to iron and toughened their hearts for war. They've longed for this day for years.

Many of the priestly tribe of Levi have gathered as well, united under their own standard beside their chief elder Jehoiada. Sons of Manasseh and Ephraim, the two half-tribes come forward to greet their brothers who'd joined me earlier back at Ziklag, trying to avoid the Gilboa battle.

But every man here expects to fight.

They shake their weapons in the air, striking swords against shields until the clash of iron and bronze mounts into a ringing melody of triumph.

I lift my hand in answer, unruly passion climbing my throat. I've felt their support from a distance over the years, but to see them gathered here as one is remarkable. Unforgettable. They've come here because they understand the times of Israel, and they are committed to what Yahweh will do, even if all they have is a glimpse.

I've learned to value such vision and the way it equips men for the work of God. I've learned the cost of it. And now, to be tasting the reward…

It's too much. My eyes mist over, feeling the heart of Yahweh overflowing toward this multitude as they break into a mighty chorus, flinging words of praise to the skies.

"We are yours, David! We are with you, son of Jesse!"

My stomach drops. How can any man carry the weight of a nation and her destiny, let alone Israel's?

"You chose her, Adonai," I whisper. "You chose her as you chose me." The reality of it sweeps me off my mount and onto my knees. Chest pounding, I lift my hands and watch them fill with sunlight as dawn pours into the valley like anointing oil. "You chose me!"

Zadok the priest steps forward and takes my shoulders, lifting me up. His bright smile warms me deeply. "From your father's pastures, Yahweh has been your help. He will not fail to enable you now that your flock has increased by eighty thousand."

The men close enough to hear him erupt with joyous laughter, and my kinsmen from Judah immediately surround me, drawing me to the clearing by the brook. Positioned on a rock, Zadok still has to lift his hands high before he's able to quiet the crowd. Flanked by twenty-two priests from his father's house, he looks down at me. His face is gentle, but his words carry enough strength to be heard across the valley.

"David ben Jesse, we have gathered here because the Lord our God has made His choice. We believe that Adonai has set you apart and will highly exalt your kingdom for Israel's sake. If you will continually honor Him as long as you live, we will stand with you and your sons after you, and we will see our nation exalted over those who hate her. As we have witnessed before."

I feel the tremor in my chest, my left hand tensing around the hilt of Goliath's sword. My sling is still wound tightly around my other wrist, a tested reminder of what Yahweh can use.

This very town was once Kiriath-Arba, populated by giants like Goliath during the time of Israel's slavery. And now, it's known as *Hebron*, the house of binding friendship. I can't think of a more fitting place for Yahweh's promise to find completion.

Zadok places his hands around my head, his voice lifted in blessing. "Peace to you, Melek Israel, and peace to your servants. For the Lord your God helps you!"

Deeply stirred, I sense the moment shifting, pulling back to Bethlehem and my first anointing. Once again, there's oil. Witnesses. The blessing of a prophet. The choice of Yahweh. And once again, it's more than I can contain. Because the true gift is Him. The *Ruach* rushes into me again, filling my chest like a cloud, warming my face with Adonai's smile.

And all I can do is receive.

I stare into the eyes of each priest, prophet, and brother, everything I've hoped for rolling through me like a tide. We're doing things differently. We won't jump into battle without direction. We won't keep the Ark of the Covenant locked away. We won't oppress our brothers, turning the tribes into factions of resentment.

I am king, but Adonai will lead the way. As He should.

The priest settles the crown onto my head, and the sons of Israel lift up a shout that speaks powerfully of the battle at Elah where Goliath fell. Stronger than I was back then, I draw the giant's sword, lift it high, and shout with them. On the fringes of the armed companies, the women dance and sing, banging tambourines, and tossing their veils into the air. It's every return from battle, every celebration magnified a hundred times.

It's still sinking in.

Saul is gone. I am king. And Yahweh is with me.

Flushed with pleasure, I yearn to dance, to fling myself into worship, but the weight of what remains holds me back. War is still imminent. The Philistines remain at large, and across the Jordan, our own brothers wait to challenge me for this crown.

Twenty-Six

Will these same ones who rejoice around me now have the courage to face what's coming? The promise is complete, but the work is just beginning.

For the hundredth time since his death, Jonathan's words drift into view.

Teach them better songs.

Back in Gibeah when the streets first echoed with praises I wasn't sure I could handle, Jonathan had reminded me where they belonged. Where I belonged.

He'd put hope in my hands like a weapon, making me acknowledge it. Always pointing me to the source of our strength. Yahweh had equipped Jonathan to do what many men wouldn't have. And He is with me. Just like He promised. So, the future of Israel really is brighter than the sun over our heads. A laugh shudders through me, the promise of healing spreading over every memory I have of my brother.

"I will remember our God, Jonathan. The world will know that He is with us."

I smile down at the wrinkled prince's cloak still tucked beneath my breastplate, stained ragged with my tears.

"And I'll make sure the world remembers you."

EPILOGUE

David, son of Jesse, King of Israel

Seven years later

I rode into Jerusalem today, ahead of the Ark of the Covenant.

It was the fulfillment of a dream so long in coming. To bring the symbol of Yahweh's presence back into view, carry it to my own fortress, and unite the tribes under my rule. But even that became a battle.

I wasn't prepared for the weight of having the Ark so close to me.

For weeks, I was kept awake by the hum of fire buzzing in the ground around it, the air bending and whirring between the carved cherubim on its lid. For the longest time, I couldn't turn my back on it for fear I would fall dead, like poor Uzzah—slain where he stood after touching the golden chest that houses God's glory. After the priest's servant died, I didn't want to approach the Ark. I couldn't imagine moving it again.

I'm king, just like Adonai promised, but after all that's happened, I feel unworthy. Afraid. I never thought it would be like this.

The weight of murder hangs heavy on me, and I feel the stain on my hands every time I think of my old dream. Who am I to build a house for Yahweh's Name? The land still wears scars, like a grieving father bereft of sons. Mistrust and betrayal lurk on every side. I am responsible for so many deaths—a man of blood already.

Yet Yahweh is still the God of Israel. And it is before Him that I was crowned the king of His people. I yearn for His blessing to rest upon us, for everyone to see what God does with a life surrendered to Him, a sword raised in victory before Him! He is my great reward.

I was stunned to hear it from His own mouth as I prayed before taking the city of Zion. Adonai's voice is like the warmest oil, healing every wound. Even the one Jonathan left.

If things had been different, my brother could have been here with me. We planned it. How he would pray over me beside the prophet of God and then place the crown on my head. Instead, he entered his rest long before I was able to come home.

Epilogue

Of course, his bow didn't turn back. He never did. His friendship was like no other. I still struggle when I think of what I've lost. But he helped me as far as he could, throwing everything he had into making me the king Yahweh saw. I know that if he could have, Jonathan would have been beside me all the way.

And he would have danced.

I tried to explain it to Michal, but all she could think of was her servant girls and every other woman who saw me dressed like a commoner on the day I should have worn kingly robes. But to me, it was fitting. God called me from the pastures, and I presented myself to Him as He chose me. A shepherd. A worshipper. Jonathan would have understood why.

He knew the glory of working with the Lord, experiencing victory in places he never would have gone by himself. He knew the awesome terror of facing Adonai, weighed down by his own failings and having our God reach out in merciful discipline instead of judgment. He taught me to run to Yahweh daily, and now I know God's plan is more infinite than I ever imagined. His presence is the only balm for our pain, the only cleansing for our sins.

Oh, how I love the Lord my Strength! He is worthy of every praise. No matter what snares of death confronted me, no matter what torrents of destruction assailed me, the God of Israel was my Rock and my Deliverer, my *Yeshu-hah*. I put my trust in Him, and He saved me from all my enemies. Just as He promised. To know that the Lord has rescued me because He delights in me—there is no greater joy.

In all my wanderings, God was teaching me strength, training my hands for war and my fingers for battle, supporting me on all sides until nothing could come against me. I began as a humble shepherd, and now foreigners from mighty kingdoms come cringing before me. Through His gentle guidance, Adonai has made me great. I will praise Him forever for the steadfast love He has shown to me.

The Lord has given me vengeance, exalting Israel among the peoples, placing His presence within her as an everlasting blessing. One that even the Ark cannot contain.

I wish Jonathan could see it.

Most likely, he already does.

Our God has done everything He promised, and more. He's so good. More than we ever imagined.

And that's why I danced.

www.ingramcontent.com/pod-product-compliance
Lightning Source LLC
Chambersburg PA
CBHW020916080526
44589CB00011B/619